Marcella Says...

Marcella Says...

ITALIAN COOKING WISDOM
FROM THE LEGENDARY TEACHER'S
MASTER CLASSES, WITH 120 OF
HER IRRESISTIBLE NEW RECIPES

Marcella Hazan

HarperCollins*Publishers*

HarperCollins books may be purchased for educational, business, or sales promotional use.
For information, please write: Special Markets Department, HarperCollins Publishers Inc.,
10 East 53rd Street, New York, NY 10022.

Excerpt from "Little Gidding," from T. S. Eliot, *Collected Poems, 1909–1962*,
appears with permission from Harcourt, Inc.

All photographs are courtesy of the author's collection, except for
pages 69 and 357, © 2004 by Matthew Septimus, taken at the French Culinary Institute,
and page 87, by Mariarosa Rockefeller.

FIRST EDITION

Edited by Susan Friedland
Designed by Joel Avirom and Jason Snyder
Design Assistant: Meghan Day Healey

Printed on acid-free paper

Library of Congress Cataloging-in-Publication Data

Hazan, Marcella.
Marcella Says . . . : Italian cooking wisdom from the legendary teacher's mast
with 120 of her irresistible new recipes / Marcella Hazan—1st ed.
p. cm.
ISBN 0-06-620967-6
1. Cookery, Italian. I. Title.

· TX723.H3428 2004
641.5945—dc22
2004042892

04 05 06 07 08 ❖/RRD 10 9 8 7 6 5 4 3 2 1

In remembrance of those to whom I owe my beginnings

Grace Chu, pioneer and paragon of Chinese cooking instruction,
in whose class I first saw how cooking could be taught

Craig Claiborne, the generous and warmhearted
New York Times food editor who brought my work to public notice

Contents

Introduction

We shall not cease from exploration

And the end of all our exploring

Will be to arrive where we started

And know the place for the first time.

—T. S. Eliot

About This Book

A long time ago I fell in love with a slim, elegant man who had an aristocratic profile, an elegantly trimmed goatee, and a twinkle in his eye. I was eight years old. He was my grandfather Riccardo. I used to snuggle up to him in his big old chair of cracked brown leather that, like him, had a thrilling grown-up smell of tobacco, and he would tell me a story. The stories were about the adventures of Fagiolino and Sandrone, a pair of ludicrously mismatched scamps. Fagiolino—the Italian word for string bean—was tall, very thin, wicked, and devilishly clever. Whenever his scrapes were about to land him in serious trouble, he always managed to slip out of the noose, sometimes by putting Sandrone's neck in it instead. Sandrone was short, fat, fatuous, greedy, and eternally gullible. The only one of these tales from seventy years ago whose plot I can remember has Fagiolino and Sandrone sitting on an embankment by the sea at sunset, a glittering sunset that spilled golden light over the water. Sandrone pokes Fagiolino in the ribs and says, "Look over there how pretty it is, the sea shining like gold!" "You goose," replies Fagiolino, "it isn't *like* gold, it really *is* gold, a phenomenon of nature that can happen only when the sun hits the water at a very unusual angle. It may never happen again in your lifetime so take that rowboat tied up at the dock and get over there really fast, before the sun moves, and scoop up as much gold as you can load into the boat. I'll stay here to distract anyone who might catch on to what we are doing." Sandrone falls for it, but eventually he has to row back to shore drenched and shivering, with nothing to show for his struggles but a boatful of seawater. "You are too fat and slow," said Fagiolino. "By the time you got there the sun was already slipping out of the sky and all the gold had dissolved."

My grandfather must have run through his whole repertory several times. Whenever I asked him to tell me a particular Fagiolino and Sandrone story he would say, "You've already heard that one." "*Non importa, nonno,* it doesn't matter," I'd tell him, "I want to hear it again." I think he enjoyed the retelling as much as I did the rehearing. A good story wants to be told and be heard again and again. It's forever, like diamonds. Or like the flavor of good home cooking.

At It Again?

I can just hear the voices out there saying, "What's this, Marcella? Another book? When you brought out *Essentials of Classic Italian Cooking,* more than ten years ago, you told us it was going to be your final cookbook, but a few years after that you gave us *Marcella Cucina,* upon whose publication you assured us that absolutely and positively there would be no more cookbooks. Yet, here we go again. What's going on?"

"What's going on?" you ask. For one thing, I haven't stopped cooking yet and, if you like, you could regard the work in this book simply as an update on what continues to take place in my kitchen. I see it, however, as a narrative, a collection of tales that needed telling. Cooking is ideal material for stories. The expression "cooking up a story" is not an accidental one. The gathering and preparation of food is a tale without end, the oldest one in the memory of our race, perhaps the first use to which language may have been put at that prehistoric campfire. In Italy, when people meet and enter into conversation, even strangers, what they eat and what they cook is likely to be their number one topic. Anytime I happen to overhear such exchanges, whether I am on a water bus in Venice or in a suburban train out of Rome or on the air shuttle to Sardinia, it's a nearly sure thing that sooner or later—and it's almost unfailingly sooner—the talk will be about food.

In each recipe there is a story, an adventure with a beginning, a middle and—I hope—a happy ending. The characters that animate those adventures are ingredients, whose actions are prefigured by their dispositions but piloted by the cook, a cook whose role as navigator is succeeded by that of narrator. And that is my justification for writing this book: I have some delicious new stories to tell you.

Stories from Class

My food career began with the classes I first gave in the small kitchen of a New York City apartment in the 1960s. Cookbooks came later, but teaching cooking was my first and fondest love. Each class I taught was for me the enactment of a cooking episode, a performance that I elaborated with comments, flashbacks, and tales of offstage happenings that complemented the action taking place before us. I had so much I wanted to say that each year the class sessions got longer and longer.

In developing the format for this book, I have tried to adopt some of the discursive quality of my classes. After reflection, I chose not to tinker with the traditional recipe groups that I have always used. These familiar categories are the ones that make the most sense to anyone who wants to pick up a cookbook to look for and make a recipe. What I have done instead is to suggest the conversational tone of a lesson through a device that one may think of as a voice from the wings or from the prompter's box.

When I demonstrate a recipe to a small class I alternate between two voices, the instructor's and the friendly experienced counselor's. The instructor says, "Slice up an onion very fine, pour oil in the skillet, put in the onion, sprinkle with salt, turn on the heat to medium low, and cover the pan. Cook until the onion becomes very soft." The friendly counselor takes you by the elbow and says, "For this dish you don't want the onions browning quickly, you want them to cook slowly and turn very soft to develop all the sweetness of which they are capable. Therefore you must sprinkle them liberally with salt to draw out their liquid in which they can stew." In the book, the steps in the recipes and the "Ahead-of-Time" and other technical notes represent the instructor's voice. The voice of the friendly counselor is embodied in small blocks of text that are captioned "Marcella Says" that break in at any moment when it seemed relevant to me, whether it may be in the list of ingredients or in the middle of a cooking step. Some may find it distracting, but I am hoping that it will succeed in bringing most readers close not just to a recipe but to the cook who is demonstrating it.

The dishes I taught in my classes were simply the nucleus of the lesson, the central plot of the story, as it were. From that central plot I would spin off other subplots that I felt were essential to grasping the sense of a story that was larger than the making of any single dish. For example, if I had been making a vegetable soup in which the individual vegetables are sautéed in separate and successive stages—a procedure that Italian cooks call *insaporire,* making tasty—I might have prefaced the making of a soup with a discussion of the critical importance of *insaporire,* of how the process leads to the deeply satisfying Italian flavor that gushes not only from vegetable soups, but from sauces, stews, and vegetable dishes. As another example, if I had been frying, say, zucchini, I might have opened a parenthesis in which I discussed the different methods of frying and of making a batter that Italian cooks employ. I have gathered these and many other topics here into a single long opening chapter titled At Master Class, the name by which the classes I gave at home in Venice were known. I invite the reader to think of this book as her or his personal master class. Drop in at any convenient time for as long or as brief a time as the desire to know or the need for a quick answer may dictate.

Simple, True Italian Cooking

One of the titles that I had originally been drawn to was "Simple, True Italian Cooking," but I was persuaded to replace it with something that gave stronger emphasis to the conversational, instructional approach of the book. Nonetheless, simple and true Italian cooking is what I hoped to put between these covers and I'd like to explain what I mean by it.

Simple doesn't mean easy. One of the most difficult dishes to do really well is that triumph of Roman cooking, *spaghettini aio e oio,* thin spaghetti sauced with garlic, olive oil, chili pepper, Italian parsley, and nothing else, no, not even cheese. Simple cooking has no unnecessary ingredients, just as a machine has no unnecessary parts or a house unnecessary supports or a dance unnecessary steps. I can describe simple cooking thus: Cooking that is stripped all the way down to those procedures and those ingredients indispensable in enunciating the sincere flavor intentions of a dish.

When I say "true" I am not thinking about *fresh, local, seasonal, heirloom, organic,* or any of the other current code words of earnest gastronomic discourse. I assume that a conscientious cook will use the best ingredients obtainable, but that best is certainly not the same everywhere. The best that I had at the Rialto market in Venice, where I spent most of my latter years, was of quite another kind than the best available to me from the Publix store in Longboat Key, the little island off the west coast of Florida, where my husband and I now live. If I have learned anything from having had to buy most of my food at a supermarket, it is that, when it comes to putting food on the table, the ingredients, however ordinary or wonderful they may be, are no worse or better than the intentions of the cook. It is those that really matter.

It is not my intention when I cook to provoke surprise at the family table, or to dazzle guests with my originality or creativity. I am never bored by a good old dish and I wouldn't shrink from making something that I first made fifty years ago and my mother, perhaps, fifty years before then. I don't cook "concepts." I use my head, but I cook from the heart, I cook for flavor. Flavor must be more revelatory than exploratory. It wants to be disclosed rather than imposed; it is neither stylish nor pedantic, nor is it exhibitionistic. Like truth, it needs no embellishment. It is not the idea of a thing, but the thing itself.

Flavor reaches into what may be our deepest source of pleasure. The happiness that food can arouse is an endlessly renewable resource and has the capacity to outlast every other drive that propels our lives. It fades away only when life itself begins to. The kind of flavor I am thinking of has no other agenda but to express the truth that has gone into the making of a dish. Fidelity to that truth leads to the cooking that I strive to practice in my kitchen and that I hope I have communicated in my classes.

For Instance

I know as well as anyone can how slippery these standards are to hold to. Although I have given it my best try, I can't claim to have batted 1.000. Yet, as I look back at three decades of writing cookbooks, and at the hundreds of recipes I produced hoping to illustrate the Italian way to cook, as I understand it, I am relieved to see how many of those dishes approach the mark. As an example of what I have aimed for, allow me to cite a few of them:

From my first two books, now gathered into *Essentials of Classic Italian Cooking:* the cannellini bean soup with garlic and parsley that my father used to make; the chick-pea and rosemary soup; *passatelli,* the soft egg-and-Parmesan drops in broth; the simplest-of-all tomato sauces, the one made with just tomatoes, butter, and a whole peeled onion; the caramelized onions sauce; the *tortelloni* with Swiss chard that for me surpass all the fashionable stuffed pastas that have followed; my father's fish soup; *gamberetti all'olio e limone,* the minimally seasoned sweet shrimp that Craig Claiborne said awakened him to the genius of Italian seafood cookery; the grilled shrimp that I marinate the way the fishermen of my hometown do, in olive oil, bread crumbs, garlic, and parsley; the baked bluefish with potatoes; the chicken pan-roasted with rosemary, garlic, and white wine and the one in which, aside from salt and pepper, a chicken and two lemons are the only ingredients; the lamb stew with juniper berries made totally without cooking fat; the pork loin braised in milk, an ageless Bolognese dish whose title encapsulates the list of ingredients; the Swiss chard stalks, severed and baked with butter and Parmesan; potatoes with tomatoes, onions, and bell pepper; the chocolate, coffee, and rum dessert called Diplomatico.

I am very fond of, and myself cook a lot from, my third book, *Marcella's Italian Kitchen,* whose mussels baked with potatoes and fresh tomatoes from the appetizers chapter became one of the most popular dishes I have ever taught. I keep returning to that volume for some of its barebones pasta sauces (the fettuccine with lemon, the bread crumbs, anchovy, and olive sauce, or the one with bell peppers), for the fresh-from-the-garden fragrance of the vividly red risotto with tomatoes and basil, for the puréed fava beans with sautéed rapini, the fish in red wine, for the boldly garlicky lamb with cannellini beans, for the strawberries in balsamic vinegar, and for the darkest of dark chocolate gelati.

My last book, *Marcella Cucina,* the most beautiful book that any publisher has given me, was photographed in the city and house I still pine for, in Venice, in my rooftop home. I was never happier cooking than I was there and happy are the flavors of the dishes that landed in *Marcella Cucina*'s pages: The baked tomatoes stuffed with salmon; the many bean soups with vegetables; the mussel soup with *borlotti* beans, and the clam soup with couscous; the *busara* lobster sauce for pasta; the shrimp baked with artichokes and mozzarella; the chicken with cherry tomatoes; the Roman vegetable casserole; and, presaging perhaps of our move to Florida, the moist and fragrant orange cake.

Fast Forward

The present book documents the cooking I have done in the midwestern enclave of a small metropolitan area in southwest Florida. We have excellent theater, first-rate music, a tender climate, white beaches, mesmerizing sunsets, and a crescent moon recumbent over the Gulf but, gastronomically speaking, it is not the most notable spot on the map. There have been mornings when I roamed my principal source of ingredients, the Publix supermarket on the island, asking myself what in the world I was going to make for lunch. If you come across what would seem to be a great number of recipes for Savoy cabbage it is not because, as my editor wondered, Publix had a sale on it. It was, on a number of occasions, the ingredient that held the most promise for me and I enjoyed letting it fulfill its promises in soups, with meat, in salads. Just as I was delighted to find the different salads I could make with Florida's terrific avocados. Ingredients are always making suggestions that I like to listen to.

As it has turned out, we have had many very tasty lunches and dinners, to which I hope the recipes that follow are witness. While our neighbors were playing golf or bridge, my husband and I would sit at our table overlooking the Gulf of Mexico at midday, enjoying meals brimming with flavor. A cook living within reach of a decent supermarket and with minimal recourse to mail order and online sources should be able to reproduce any of those dishes. The experience has confirmed what I have always believed about where to look for flavor: Look no farther than the heart of the cook. And it has proven to me once again that, if you are passionate enough to cook the pure and simple Italian way, you can eat well wherever you may be.

At Master Class

✎ WHEN I GRADUATED FROM THE UNIVERSITY OF FERRARA I expected the degrees I had taken in natural sciences and in biology to lead to a life of teaching science and mathematics in Italy's state schools. Careers can be unpredictable, however, and their beginnings fortuitous. A chapter or two later in the story, I found myself in New York City, married to a man whose father was a devotee of Pearl's, a smart uptown Chinese restaurant. Few, if any, among those patrons of Pearl's from the 1960s who are still around can have forgotten her deft interpretations of Chinese home cooking. I certainly never have. At that time I wasn't working and repeated exposure to Pearl's repertory prompted me to put some of my free time to good use by learning something about the cuisine. I signed up for a Chinese cooking class taught by Grace Chu, a woman whom I have never heard anyone call anything other than Madame Chu.

Madame Chu opened two new worlds to me. One was the world of Chinese cooking, for which I developed as much affection as I have for the cuisines of my own country. The other was the world of cooking classes. I had never imagined that cooking was something that could be taught in a class. Up to then, what I knew about cooking had come from dipping into the memories of the food I had grown up with at home.

To my lasting regret, that first Chinese cooking course was also my last. Madame Chu took a sabbatical in China and my classmates looked around for something else to cook until she came back. One of them asked me what I was cooking at home. I told her and she asked if I could teach her and the others how to do it. "I'll have to think about it," I said. When I put it to my husband he was all for it. "Why not," he said, "you like to teach, you like to cook, and you have plenty of spare time." In October 1969, I gave my first Italian cooking class to six of my former classmates in a cramped New York City apartment kitchen, and that was the beginning of the end of my spare time. There has been little of it since.

In a few years, the New York kitchen was replaced by one in Bologna. The municipal authorities had built a vast and magnificently equipped facility for me, hoping it would draw American visitors to Bologna. I felt I owed it to the city to accept as many people as the place I had been given would hold and soon the classes were thronged not just with Americans, but also with students from throughout the world. With time, it became clear that I had to lighten my teaching burden and give smaller classes. My husband, moreover, wanted to live in Venice, a city where I had spent many years of my youth. The high-ceilinged, stainless-steel and glass brick Bologna kitchen eventually gave way to one nudging the sixteenth-century roof beams of a Venetian palazzo, which became our home for nearly twenty years.

In Venice I came full-circle back to the size of my original New York classes, never taking more than six students. The relaxed home setting and the closer contact with students allowed me to expand on and examine more deeply than I had ever been able to before those topics that I thought were essential to a well-grounded understanding of the Italian way of cooking. The scope of the culinary matters that were broached and the intimacy of the teacher-student relationship led my husband and me to call them Master Classes. Out of those discussions comes this book's At Master Class, which I warmly invite you to join.

Insaporire ❧ *A Passkey to Flavor*

It's regrettable that among English cooking terms there is no neat equivalent for *insaporire,* the verb Italians have derived from their word for taste, *sapore.* A literal, if awkward, translation is "making tasty." A crucial step in the making of most Italian dishes, *insaporire* is what you do to draw out and develop the flavor of a single or several ingredients. A cook in Italy giving a recipe to a friend will use the term and never feel the need to describe it. Italian cooks already know what is meant by it because they practice it virtually every time they go the stove.

A Definition

Insaporire takes place as the consequence of a procedure on which Italians bestow another lovely, unique verb, *arrosolare.* The root of that word is *rosa,* Italian for rose, the flower and its hue. It means to cook something in hot fat until it acquires a warm hue, although not necessarily rosy. It works like this. You sauté onion and/or garlic in butter or oil over medium heat until it becomes colored the shade you want in that particular dish. (Have the patience to cook the onion long enough, it may need more minutes than you think; and have the watchfulness to keep the garlic from turning too dark. That may happen sooner than you can imagine.) This is *arrosolare.* Then you put in the ingredient that comes next, usually a vegetable or the first of several vegetables, you raise the heat, and stir turning the ingredient over to coat it well: When it opens up to and swells with the savors of the onion or garlic or both, that is *insaporire.*

Correct Use of Heat

It's exceedingly important that you use no less and no more heat than you need. You don't want to start the garlic or onion on the highest heat because it may burn. You do need very high heat, however, to force an entry into the vegetables whose flavor you wish to expand. In the absence of brisk heat, they may simply stew in the pan, soak up fat, and taste flat or "boiled" as Italians describe it. In a pasta sauce with vegetables, for example, *insaporire* at lively heat makes the difference between a sauce with fully developed flavor and a bland one. Nor can *insaporire* be replaced by turning up the spice or garlic. That is borrowed rather than true flavor.

It is particularly important to apply high heat to those vegetables that, like large zucchini, say, release a great deal of liquid. Only after you have evaporated all of the liquid can the vegetable begin to appear "rosy"—*arrosolato*—and thereby become savory, *insaporito*. *Insaporire* does not take long, but it does not forgive distraction. You must monitor the moment attentively, stirring the onion or garlic to make sure that high heat does not scorch it. Once the ingredient in question acquires a depth of color indicating that it has been *insaporito,* you can continue the cooking at medium or even low heat, depending on the recipe.

Applying Insaporire *Sequentially*

There are occasions when you need to *insaporire* more than one ingredient. In such instances you apply the method successively to each single ingredient, thus layering its flavor over that of the ingredient that preceded it. An excellent example is minestrone, the Italian vegetable soup. Begin by sautéing the onion, then add the celery. Turn it over a few times and after two or three minutes add the carrot. Repeat the action, then add the pepper, then the potatoes. The leaf vegetables—cabbage, Savoy cabbage, spinach, chard, escarole, whichever ones you are using— come last because they shed liquid that, if released sooner, would have made it impossible to sauté the other vegetables, preventing them from becoming *arrosolati* and, subsequently, *insaporiti*. Continue to cook, stirring and turning over the leaf vegetables from time to time, allowing them to spill liquid and wilt. When that liquid has evaporated, their color deepens. Only then do you add the soup's medium, broth or water, as it may be.

Blanching as a Prelude to Insaporire

If you have had spinach or chard or a similar green that was properly sautéed in garlic and olive oil, you have known the rich taste that *insaporire* can draw from a leaf vegetable. To achieve it, you first blanch the vegetable, cooking it in a small quantity of salted, boiling water until tender. Then you drain it and squeeze as much water out of it as you can. You sauté cloves of garlic in olive oil until they become colored a deep gold, then you slip in the blanched spinach or other green. I must have taught this dish in nearly every course I have given and almost always a student would ask, "Why not skip the blanching, Marcella, and drop the raw spinach directly into the pan where you have sautéed the garlic?" The first time I heard that suggestion it seemed a reasonable alternative and, since I never pass up a good shortcut, I tried it. Unfortunately it doesn't work. First of all, one pound of fresh spinach is an awkwardly large mass of greens to throw into a pan. You could be spraying hot oil all over the stove. Nor can you salt it until it has completely wilted. But, most important, it doesn't really taste *insaporito* because it sheds so much liquid that the base flavor of the garlic and oil is diluted before it can adequately coat the spinach.

How Insaporire *Develops Flavor in Meat Stews*

When you are making the most heartwarming of meat dishes, a stew, you do not start with sautéed garlic or onion. You invert the procedure. Brown the meat first in very hot fat. When it becomes deeply colored, remove it from the pan, lower the heat, and then put in the onion or garlic. Had they been added first, they would have been burned by the heat required to brown the meat. When the onion or garlic has become satisfactorily colored, return the meat to the pan and turn it over to coat it well. At this point add the vegetable or—in a sequence resembling the one followed for minestrone—the combination of vegetables that characterizes the specific stew. If you are using tomato, put it in only after the vegetables have become "rosy," *arrosolati,* otherwise the juices released by the tomato will cause the vegetables to steam rather than sauté. From here on, you cook over heat barely high enough for a gentle simmer until the meat is tender.

Risotto

The guiding principle of *insaporire* is to cause an ingredient to bond its flavor to that of another and thus expand both. The classic risotto technique is an excellent illustration of this. Every risotto rests on a flavor base that can be as simple as onion alone richly sautéed in butter or the onion plus meat or seafood or a medley of vegetables or any single vegetable. Occasionally, but far more rarely, the butter could be replaced by olive oil and garlic may be added to the onion. Whatever the composition of the base—the possible combinations defy counting—the procedure is analogous to the one I described above when I discussed the making of minestrone. Just as the vegetables in a minestrone must be deeply savory, *insaporiti,* before broth or water is added to create the soup, the flavor of a risotto's base must be fully coaxed out of its components before the rice is added.

And here you see how the making of a risotto is a vivid example of *insaporire.* You add the rice only when the flavor of the base is robustly developed. You turn and turn the grains to coat them, launching the process whereby the flavors of the base will eventually be fused with the rice. It is to achieve that objective that, rather than adding the liquid cooking medium to the rice all at once, you ladle it in a little at a time so that the starch enveloping the grain can loosen slowly and commingle with the base. Nor will you be tempted to prepare that base separately and add it at the finish. No matter how alluring the ingredients may be on their own, they must surrender their individual identity for the sake of a more expansive flavor identity, that of the risotto. In essence, that is what *insaporire* is about: The lowering of barriers that confine flavors, the release of flavor that takes place when ingredients intermingle and yield to each other.

Summing Up

When you grasp the significance of *insaporire* and apply its methods, you implement the fundamental aesthetic of Italian home cooking. It is cooking that shrinks from capturing attention with showy, borrowed flavors. It holds that flavor resides within those ingredients that define a dish, and that the object of cooking anything is to open the way for that flavor to emerge. It is an aesthetic that, in my experience of food, makes the cuisine of the Italian home one of the most convincing of all.

When Is It Done?

"How long do you cook it, Marcella?" I never kept count, but I have no doubt that this is the question that came up most often during my teaching career. As a young wife, when I was beginning to cook, I must have asked my mother that same question a hundred times. Her usual answer was likely to be, "Until it is done." I have been many times on the verge of giving the same answer to my students, not out of waggishness but because it is really the one true answer. The natural comeback question, of course, is, "Well then, when *is* it done?" And to that I shall try to provide some answers.

There are so many variables that affect cooking time: What kind of heat are you working with, gas or electric or induction or wood burning? Exactly how hot is the heat you are using? How precise are the controls of your stovetop? How large is your pot? What is it made of?

Aluminum and copper conduct heat at high speed, steel alloys are slower, and earthenware can be very lackadaisical. How much liquid did you put in it? How fresh, or young, or tender, or carefully trimmed are your ingredients? The most critical variable of all may be, how done is "done," according to you? The approximate cooking times that you'll find in most of my recipes are subject to the exercise of your own judgment and taste. My hope is that those judgments and that taste may be mindful of the flavors and textures of good Italian cooking, and it is within such a context that I offer the observations that follow.

When Are Vegetables Done?

It has become common usage in the last several years to privilege crunch over flavor and serve vegetables that are acutely underdone. The practice is fashionable, but it does the vegetables an injustice and shortchanges our palate. The reason we trouble to cook vegetables instead of tossing them on the plate in their pristine just-harvested state is that heat loosens a vegetable's fibers, opening up the tight green embrace within which its flavor-bearing molecules are locked. The grassy crunch of barely scalded asparagus is not too different from that of barely scalded green beans or barely scalded broccoli. Mix them up, taste them blindfolded, and you might have trouble saying which is which. It is only by adequate cooking that you will draw out their distinctive flavors.

If you are cooking asparagus, green beans, broccoletti, or leek, pick one up when you think it has cooked long enough and hold it by one end. If it droops slightly, it's done; if it is still stiff, put it back. If you are skeptical, make this test. Cook a few green beans. Retrieve some very early, when they are still crunchy, but continue cooking the rest. Retrieve a couple after another minute or two, when they are still very firm. Continue cooking, then drain the rest when they are tender, but not mushy. Taste them, compare, and decide for yourself which have the most flavor.

When you cook cauliflower, broccoli, fennel, or zucchini, test them with a fork. If it enters easily, the vegetable is done; if the fork meets firm resistance, try again later. Bear in mind that young, fresh zucchini may take only a few minutes, whereas a large cauliflower will take substantially longer. If you are going to gratiné the vegetable after you've blanched it, it ought to be slightly underdone because it will continue to cook in the oven. Cooking leaf vegetables is easy—they are done when they become completely limp.

Mushrooms are a special case. The untamed, bosky quality that draws you to their flavor emerges with very long, slow cooking after they have completely shed their vegetal water. Forget about crunchy, don't aim for chewy. Cook mushrooms slowly in olive oil for at least an hour, longer if you are making a large amount, until they are gelatinously soft. Hover over the pan, and when your nose picks up a scent reminiscent of a dark, leaf-strewn forest floor, the mushrooms are done.

BEANS, POTATOES, BEETS, AND OTHER ROOT VEGETABLES Beans and root vegetables cooked al dente are an aberration. They are done only when fully soft. If you are cooking dried beans, taste them after they have simmered about an hour. If they are yieldingly tender, they are done. Poke potatoes and root vegetables with a fork; if it enters easily, you can stop the cooking.

Pasta and Rice

Al dente means firm to the bite, but not undercooked. In the mouth, pasta should feel chewy, but not rigid. Bite a piece in half: The color of its cross section should be golden yellow throughout. If it has a white center, it is still not fully cooked. Rice is cooked when it is firm, but no longer chalky. Bear in mind that even after you've turned off the fire, the heat of the pasta or rice will continue to soften it. Therefore, stop the cooking when, in your opinion, the pasta or rice is still very slightly underdone.

About Chicken

In Italian cooking, chicken is done when it is cooked all the way through and comes easily off the bone. A fork poked into the meatiest part of the thigh should enter without resistance. To cook all of the chicken to a more or less even degree of tenderness you proceed knowing that the breast is much less juicy than the rest of the bird and becomes dry and tasteless when overcooked.

If you are roasting a whole bird in the oven, you start it breast up to crisp the skin, then you turn it to protect the breast from drying out. If you are grilling chicken, it is desirable to detach the breast. Start grilling the other parts and when they are just a few minutes short of being cooked, put the breast on the fire, skin down. If you wish to keep the breast on the chicken, brown it, skin side down, then turn it and baste it frequently. If you are poaching chicken, add the breast separately to the pot when the all other parts of the bird are close to being done.

In a chicken fricassee, which has other ingredients, you must first brown the cut-up bird, breast included, in very hot fat. After browning, remove the breast pieces from the pan before you add the other components of the fricassee. Return the breast pieces to the pan only when the other chicken pieces are a few minutes away from being done. Remember, the chicken is done when its flesh is so tender it falls easily off the bone.

Grilling Fish

Fish grilled in the Italian style is neither half raw nor overdone. The flesh near the bone or in the thickest part of a fillet should be flaky, moist, firm, and slightly dewy. It must not be dry, nor may it be gelatinous. Please do not emulate the currently prevalent restaurant style of serving salmon whose quavering center is flaming pink.

Grilling requires careful calibration of cooking time and intensity of heat. The best method is the one I learned from the fishermen of my hometown on the Adriatic, who first season a whole raw fish with salt and lemon juice, dampen it with olive oil, coat it with bread crumbs, and then cook it fast over strong heat. It may take under ten or twelve minutes for a whole fish or fillet, depending on its thickness, and considerably less than that for a thin fish steak, but don't just go by the clock. Check the fish early, probing its thickest part with the point of a sharp knife to see whether it is losing its raw translucency. When you have done it successfully a few times, you develop an instinctive feel for how long it takes.

About Crustaceans and Mollusks

Such shellfish as shrimp, crayfish, and lobster take very little time to cook; live clams and mussels require just enough heat to force them open and release their juices, whereas squid, octopus, and cuttlefish are tender when cooked very briefly or lengthily, but not in between.

CRUSTACEANS To boil shrimp or crayfish, I put salt and two to three tablespoons of vinegar in a pot of water, bring it to a boil, and drop in the shrimp with their shells on. They are done when they change color after the water has resumed boiling. If they are very small, they are cooked almost instantly. If they are of large size, they may take two or three minutes longer. I cook lobster the same way: a 1½-pound specimen in 10 to 12 minutes, longer for a larger one, but never longer than 20 minutes, regardless of size.

CLAMS AND MUSSELS Cook clams over high heat in a skillet or sauté pan with a little bit of water, which helps them snap open sooner. They do not all open at the same time, but once they do they must be taken out of the pan or the meat will become tough. Stand over the pan and use a slotted spoon to remove each clam as it opens. The clam juice is a rich source of flavor, but it needs to be filtered before you use it in a sauce or a risotto or a soup. Cook the juice down at a lively simmer to concentrate its flavor before you add the clam meat.

For mussels, you don't need any water in the pan because they open up quickly. Nor do you need to take them out one by one because their meat does not toughen as quickly as that of clams. If I am making a fish soup or a sauce with mussels in the shell, I drop them in at the last minute when the dish is nearly done.

SQUID, OCTOPUS, AND CUTTLEFISH The intrinsic tenderness of squid, octopus, and cuttlefish vanishes after the first few minutes of quick cooking, but returns after they have cooked slowly, for 45 minutes or more. If you are making fried calamari, all they need is a minute or two in very, very hot oil. When using squid or octopus for a seafood salad, drop them into rapidly boiling water and retrieve them after just a minute or two, when they lose their translucency and become opaquely white. If they are part of a stew, however, cook them along with the other ingredients of the dish over gentle heat for 45 minutes or more, depending on their size.

Frying ◈ Friggere

When I think of all the people I know who will cook anything as long as they don't have to fry it I think, sadly, of what they are missing. Of all the methods for preparing food through heat— grilling, baking, boiling, poaching, steaming, stewing, roasting, braising, sautéing, frying—frying is the only one that, when competently performed, respects the full integrity of the ingredient that it is cooking. Brillat-Savarin, the French philosopher of gastronomy, gave the best description of what frying does to food: "It surprises it," he said. It makes me think of those examples of candid photography in which the subject is taken unawares, exposing personality traits or emotional states with unequivocal clarity. Every other method transmutes food, delivering it to us in an altered state. Frying strips away only the rawness and by its quick, deep heat encapsulates the ingredient with all its intrinsic qualities—the juiciness, the taste, the texture—intact.

When, after I was married, I began to cook, the first thing I learned to do and do well was frying. At the beginning, I fried partly out of instinct and partly out of the recollections I had of my mother and grandmother frying. Within a short time, I found in that instinct and in those memories the principles and simple methods of frying correctly that I have followed to this day.

The Right Pan and Other Equipment

✦ My favorite pan was a 16-inch thin-gauge rolled iron skillet with sloping sides that I used with gratifying results for the better part of the last thirty years. When I moved to Florida I left it behind in Venice because the electric stovetop I was obliged to install in my condominium kitchen could not accommodate it. If you have a large enough gas burner and can find such a pan I strongly recommend it because it fries a variety of foods quickly, evenly, and crisply. You can nonetheless fry quite well on any one of the good-quality frying pans that are available. Make sure it is a *frying* pan with sloping sides, and not a sauté pan with straight sides. Get a 12-inch pan because when you are frying you can never have too much room.

✦ I have never used a deep fryer and so I cannot say anything about it except that it has never tempted me. Nor can I say anything about thermometers because I have managed so far to get by very nicely without one. I judge the oil's heat by holding my hand just above—please not *in*—the pan, palm down. It's a safe, immediate, and direct way to judge the intensity of the heat that the oil emanates. If I have reason to believe that the oil is hot, I test it by slipping a drop of batter or a small piece of whatever I am frying into it. Or I dip just the corner of a large piece that I am going to fry. If the oil is hot enough, it will instantly sizzle.

✦ A couple of flat metal spatulas will be useful when you must turn something over and a few broad slotted spoons are necessary to remove food from the pan without scooping up fat. When I remove fried food from the pan, I drain it on a cooling rack placed over a tray lined with paper towels or foil to collect the drippings. I rarely blot it directly on absorbent paper because it can make the food soggy, while the rack keeps it perfectly crisp.

The Frying Fat

✦ *Vegetable Oil* A neutral-tasting vegetable oil such as corn oil is what I use most of the time. It adds no flavors of its own, is easy to control, and does the job cleanly and efficiently. I do not use peanut oil because it is not flavorless.

✦ *Butter* On those occasions that I use butter, as for example in making a Milanese-style veal cutlet, I combine it with 1 or 2 tablespoons of neutral-tasting vegetable oil. The vegetable oil lifts the fat's burning point to a higher level and diminishes, although it doesn't eliminate, the chance that the butter will burn. Moreover, it does not affect the butter's flavor.

✦ *Olive Oil* Olive oil can impart deep flavor to fried foods and that is the reason I rarely use it. When I am frying, I want my ingredient's flavors to spring lightly forth unburdened by the inescapable presence, whatever its merits may be, of olive oil.

✦ *Lard* I no longer put it in my recipes, but for flavor and crispness nothing equals lard as a frying medium. Potatoes fried in lard are the most devastatingly good fries you can eat. Lard's burning point is on the low side, so you have to monitor it carefully to keep it from overheating and developing a disagreeable burned fat odor.

✦ *The Amount of Fat* Liquid or liquefied fat must rise no less than 1 inch up the sides of the pan.

Coatings and Batters

✦ *No Coating at All* On those occasions when I want softness rather than crispness I will fry a sliced or diced vegetable, such as eggplant or zucchini, just as it is, with no flour or other coating.

✦ *Flour Alone* I use flour when I am seeking a drier surface with more texture than what I would get if I used no coating at all. If I am frying vegetables that are naturally moist when cut, such as, for example, sliced or julienned zucchini, I drop them in a bowl of flour, turn them over, then I shake them in a pasta colander to remove the excess flour. If the cut surface is dry—eggplant slices that haven't been steeped in salt are an example—I sprinkle water over it to moisten it so that the flour will adhere.

Marcella Says: **When frying foods coated with flour, you must be prepared to fry immediately. The fat should already be hot. If you leave a flour coating waiting for even a minute it will become soggy and the purpose of frying will be defeated.**

✦ *Breading* Before I apply a breaded coating, I pat dry the piece of meat or vegetable that I am preparing to fry. I dip it into beaten egg, and then I hold it up over the bowl, allowing all the excess egg to flow back into the bowl. I don't add any salt to the egg because salt draws moisture and may keep the coating from achieving crispness.

Marcella Says: **Make sure you have coated the piece with bread crumbs on both sides before you press on it with your hand, otherwise the egg will come away on your palm.**

I then turn the piece I am coating in bread crumbs, dragging it over the crumbs on both sides. When I have breaded both sides, and only then, I pat it down in the crumbs with the palm of my hand, turning it two or three times. If you apply the breading firmly and in the sequence I have described, it will keep for two to three hours until you are ready to start frying.

NOTE: If you are breading very moist food whose surfaces cannot be blotted dry, as for example sliced tomatoes, dredge it first in flour, shake off the excess, then dip it in beaten egg, followed by bread crumbs, as described above.

✦ *Pastella Batter* For a crust that is crackling crisp and airy there is no other batter that can equal *pastella*. It is made with flour and water and no other ingredient. I don't even add salt because it would draw moisture from the ingredient to be fried. The proportions are 1 cup plus 2 tablespoons of flour to 1 cup water. Use *pastella* batter for any vegetable that can be fried. An excellent example is Belgian Endive Fried in Pastella Batter on page 339. You can mix the ingredients for the batter either by hand or in the food processor.

HAND METHOD

1 Pour 1 cup of lukewarm water into a bowl.

2 Gradually sift flour into the bowl with one hand, while with the other you beat with a whisk or, just as effectively, with what we used before we owned whisks, two dinner forks held together by their handles, the prongs separated.

3 Stop adding flour as soon as a clean dry spoon dipped in the batter comes out veiled by a fine coating.

FOOD PROCESSOR METHOD

1 Put 1 cup plus 2 tablespoons flour in the food processor bowl fitted with the steel blade.

2 Turn on the machine and while it is running slowly pour the 1 cup lukewarm water in a very thin stream through the feed tube.

Pastella batter makes it easy to check if the temperature of the oil is hot enough for frying. Let a drop of the batter fall into the oil you have heated: If it floats immediately up to the surface, the oil is ready for frying.

Marcella's Way to Fry

Once I start frying, I focus on maintaining the fat at as constant a temperature as possible. Therefore I put only a few pieces of food into the oil at a time. If I were to fill the pan, the temperature of the oil would drop. I pay attention to where in the pan I have placed the first pieces so that later those will be the first ones I shall turn over. I never turn them over more than once. When the first pieces are done well on both sides, I remove them, transferring them to a cooling rack, and replace them with uncooked pieces. At this point, those that were left in the pan will probably be ready to be turned. Frying in sequential batches, as I have just described, is what keeps fat at a steady and correct frying temperature. Never fill the pan at one time nor ever empty it completely before you have finished. In the first instance, the fat's temperature drops, and the food in the pan absorbs too much fat and becomes disagreeably greasy. In the second instance, if you empty the pan all at once while you still have food left to fry, the fat's temperature rises abruptly and may scorch the pieces you put in next.

As soon as one batch is done, I put it on a cooling rack and salt it immediately. As I have already pointed out earlier in this section, a cooling rack is to be preferred to blotting on paper because the air circulates, drying the surface of the food without letting it become soggy. Add salt while the food is very hot because it will be difficult to salt adequately once it cools. The taste and texture of fried food declines precipitously if it is reheated or kept warm. It must be served at once, while fresh and crisp and piping hot.

Pasta: A Short Tour of the National Dish

I am not sure that for a country whose cuisines have such a deep-seated regional bias it is correct to speak of any Italian dish as a national one, but if one had to be chosen pasta would no doubt get the votes. A plate of linguine, or fusilli, or fettuccine, or tortellini, or whatever on any day the chef may fancy, is now an inseparable part of fashionable Italian cooking. In Italy itself, however, there are zones where, historically speaking, it is only recently that pasta has become standard fare at home and in restaurants. Consider that just two or three generations ago, a visitor who traveled solely in major areas of the north and center of the country—in parts of Lombardy, in the Veneto, and in Tuscany—might rarely have seen pasta on a menu, if at all. How the making of pasta in Italy was ignored in certain places while it was putting down strong roots in others, and how in its chosen sites the craft developed in separate directions is one of the more intriguing food stories.

The North

If there had been any substance to the myth of Marco Polo bringing back pasta from China when he returned to Venice, today the Venetian kitchen would be the source of Italy's most accomplished homemade pasta. The very opposite is true. There may be some cooks in Venice who make pasta at home, but I have never met or heard of any.

What Venetians have become particularly successful at is adopting factory-made formats from central or southern Italy, such as *spaghettini* or penne as partners for the exemplary products of their sea. On the other hand, that other latecomer to the Venetian table, the gummy gratinéed fettuccine that, on a few regrettable occasions, I have sampled in restaurants, is among the clumsiest dishes of its kind I have known. There is a single pasta dish that Venice can legitimately claim as its own, and it is an exceedingly sapid one. It is *bigoli con salsa,* spaghetti-like strands made of whole-wheat flour that are tossed with a sauce of salt-cured sardines and a lot of onions.

Along with the Veneto region, the other lands of the northeast once under Venice's rule, now known as Friuli-Venezia Giulia and the Trentino, were far more hospitable to risotto, polenta, gnocchi and other dumplings, and soups than they were to pasta. Even today, those are the dishes they do best, because they come from the heart, and it would be thoughtless to pass them up in favor of yet another generic plate of pasta. Moving westward on our tour we come to Lombardy, a region where nothing can seriously compete with risotto for the affections of its natives. There are a few pockets of resistance, however. In Valtellina, a district on the border with Switzerland, there is some enthusiasm for *pizzoccheri,* a noodle made partly from buckwheat flour, that is cooked with potatoes and Swiss chard and sauced with garlic, butter, and a local soft cheese. Bergamo and Brescia also like to offer, as an occasional alternative to rice and polenta, their own pasta, *casonsei,* a kind of ravioli with an idiosyncratic filling of spinach, almond macaroons, raisins, cheese, and salami.

A major challenge to the domination of rice in Lombardy comes from the food-mad city of Mantua, where rice and polenta share honors with such a sumptuous variety of homemade egg pasta that you might wonder whether you are still in a region ruled by Milan or have inadvertently slipped into the one governed by Bologna, Emilia-Romagna. Mantua is indeed administratively a part of Lombardy, but its gluttonous heart beats to the gastronomic rhythms of its neighbor from across the river. It is no coincidence that the only area outside of Emilia-Romagna where Parmigiano-Reggiano cheese can legitimately be produced is in the province of Mantua.

As a native of Emilia-Romagna, I know that when judging its pasta my objectivity may be suspect. Yet I am not alone in believing that in that celestial realm of *pasta all'uovo fatta in casa*— homemade egg pasta—Bologna is the orb around which circle the luxuriant pasta planets of Modena, Parma, Reggio, Ferrara, and my very own Romagna. The basic golden-yellow dough of Emilia-Romagna is composed solely of whole eggs with sunset-red yolks and gossamer flour— not semolina or durum wheat flour—from Emilia's Po River plain. In that dough there is no salt, no olive oil, no water. Women, preferably with warm plump palms and the leverage provided by substantial haunches, lean into it and roll it out by hand to transparent thinness using a narrow yard-long wood dowel. All the classic formats—*tagliatelle, pappardelle, tagliolini, garganelli* (hand-rolled penne), *lasagne, maltagliati* (soup noodles for *pasta e fagioli*), *strichetti* (bowties)—are cut from that dough. For the more pliant dough that is needed for such stuffed pasta as *tortelli, tortelloni, tortellini,* and *cappelletti,* milk is added, and spinach, of course, is used to make green pasta. Girls of my generation were taught the craft of hand-rolling dough even before they became teenagers, and they became so adept at it that they could produce enough pasta for lunch in the same time or less than it takes a cook today to make a salad. Lunch in Emilia-Romagna, preceded by little or no breakfast and followed by the lightest of suppers, is the one important meal of the day and can well be defined as the moment when you sit down to a plate of freshly made pasta. I had a cousin who began lunch with *tagliatelle* and meat sauce every day of his seventy-five adult years.

Emilia-Romagna may well be the True Church of egg pasta, but there are other persuasions that have their believers. Piedmont, in the northwest, like the Veneto in the northeast, is worshipful of rice and polenta, but it also has great reverence for the only pasta native to its territory, *tajarin,* a narrow noodle made from dough kneaded with a large proportion of egg yolks. Some local cooks like to inflate the proportion, allowing it to reach as many as thirty or more yolks per kilo of flour. West of Piedmont, facing the sea, the region known as Liguria has a unique tradition of pastas that are paired with the fragrant sauces of the Italian Riviera, abounding in herbs, nuts, and soft young cheeses. Liguria's dough reverses the Piedmontese emphasis on eggs, using few eggs and adding water. On occasion, the water could altogether replace the eggs. This practice may not be related to the Genoese reputation for stinginess, but on the other hand it may. The most celebrated of Ligurian pastas are the narrow noodles called *trenette,* made to be served with pesto, fine green beans, and sliced boiled potatoes. Also notable are the stuffed pastas—ravioli and *pansoti*—filled with wild greens and fresh sour cheeses. The sauce for *pansoti* is that lovely creamy concoction made of walnuts. A uniquely Ligurian shape is *trofie,* tiny hand-turned corkscrews of pasta that are sauced with pesto.

The Center

A substantial change comes over the pasta landscape of Italy when we leave the north for the central regions of Tuscany, Umbria, Abruzzi, and Lazio. In this part of the country, only the Marches, immediately south of my native Romagna, has a pasta tradition that leads back to the one of its northern neighbors. Here, in fact, you can order *cappelletti,* pasta "hats" very similar to those of Romagna, stuffed with minced meats, or *tortelli* filled, as *tortelloni* are in my town, with greens and ricotta, or *taglierini* comparable to Bologna's *tagliolini.* They make lasagne in the Marches, but they call it *vincisgrassi,* a meatier, more heavily loaded version than Bologna's.

Today, some of the finest producers of spaghetti and other boxed, dry, semolina pasta are in Tuscany, but when I first began to spend time there in the 1950s, visiting my husband-to-be who lived near Florence, I came upon Tuscans who hadn't had any experience of twirling spaghetti on a fork. Any place that makes soups as glorious as those of Tuscany need not apologize for catching up with pasta so late in its day. Even now I'd be loath to order pasta in a Tuscan trattoria when a *ribollita,* or any soup with beans or with *cavolo nero*—kale—is on the menu. I would also pass up *pici,* a gummy, hand-rolled pasta cylinder shaped like very thick spaghetti. I'd make an exception in hunting season for *pappardelle sulla lepre,* broad egg noodles served with hare cooked in olive oil with red wine and tomato concentrate. That creation stands in solitary splendor as Tuscany's finest native contribution to the national pasta treasury.

Umbria, Italy's navel or, as it prefers to be known, the country's green heart, is more celebrated for its lentils than for its pasta. Its one indigenous homemade pasta is *stringozzi,* also called *ceriole,* a short, thick strip of dough made of flour and water that housewives shape by twisting it along a knitting needle-like tool. It goes deliciously with Umbria's marvelous sausages, of which there are none better. These days, *stringozzi* are more likely to be store-bought than homemade, and spaghetti is probably even more common than they on the Umbrian table. Common, however, may not be the word to apply on those occasions when the spaghetti is blanketed with a sauce of grated black truffles, another of the region's specialties.

Abruzzi, a region of magnificent mountain parklands on the Adriatic side of central Italy, embraces the two great pasta traditions: homemade pasta made with eggs and dried factory-extruded macaroni pasta made of hard semolina flour and water. Nowhere in Italy will you find the industrial craft of making spaghetti, penne, and all the full range of dried pasta shapes exercised at a more accomplished artisanal level than in Abruzzi. (Please see page 34 for the names of the best producers along with a description of the qualities that high-quality macaroni pasta must possess and are the ones that you should be looking for.) Abruzzi cannot match Emilia-Romagna's broad range in homemade egg pasta, but it does have a notable format of its own— *maccheroni alla chitarra*—for whose making a guitarlike tool was developed. The *maccheroni* are a narrow noodle square in cross section and the "guitar" is a sturdy rectangular wooden frame on both of whose sides steel strings have been fitted. On one side the strings are farther apart than on the other so that one has a choice of making the noodles broad or thin. A sheet of compact egg dough usually made with hard semolina flour is rolled firmly against the taut, sharp strings and when these are plucked the cut *maccheroni* fall free. They are served with a variety of sauces in which there may be more or less tomato and more or less chili pepper. I particularly like it with a meat sauce made with lamb.

The cooking of Lazio is really the cooking of Rome, the region's capital, where both homemade and factory-made pasta are represented. Rome's homemade egg pasta repertory consists essentially of one format, *fettuccine.* These are slightly narrower than Bologna's *tagliatelle* and the dough is not as fine because many Roman cooks add water and salt. Butter, cream, and cheese make the most widely known sauce for fettuccine, the version on which a restaurateur called Alfredo bestowed his name. The sauce that Romans would recognize as their own, however, is a dark one that contains the juices from a meat roast, chicken giblets, dried mushrooms, tomatoes, and pork fat. Another homemade noodle that you will find here is *tonnarelli,* which is none other than Abruzzi's *maccheroni alla chitarra* under another name. Another dish appropriated from Abruzzi is *bucatini all'amatriciana.* That spicy sauce made with pork jowl, tomatoes, chili pepper, and a dense shower of grated Pecorino originated in Amatrice, an ancient Abruzzese town that through modern redistricting fell inside Lazio's administrative grasp. Let no one mistake, however, the authentic Roman accent of such earthy classics as *spaghettini aglio, olio, e peperoncino*—thin spaghetti with garlic, olive oil, and chili pepper—and *spaghetti alla carbonara,* that palate-gripping sauce of sautéed pork jowl, lots of black pepper, and beaten egg.

The South

In the south of Italy and on the islands of Sicily and Sardinia pasta may sometimes be made at home—and then with dough that is kneaded partly or wholly from hard golden semolina flour and water—but it is factory-made, dried, extruded pasta of excellent quality that wins the day.

Campania, the region that has given us Vesuvius, Pompeii, Naples, Capri, and the Amalfi Coast, has given us something else for which we may be even more grateful. It was at the dawn of the nineteenth century that the first efficient, large-scale commercial production of dried pasta—spaghetti and all its siblings—was successfully established in some of the outlying districts of Naples, thus making available to the world the kindest and most conveniently packaged gift that has ever been put into a cook's hands. The Neapolitan genius for marrying a vibrant, light-handed sauce to factory pasta is unmatched elsewhere, a heaven-sent talent grossly caricatured by the cooking of most so-called Neapolitan restaurants abroad. There would seem to be hardly any incentive for the cooks of Campania to try their luck with homemade egg pasta, but they do. Their most ambitious effort is the Neapolitan *lasagna*. (It's *lasagna* in Naples, *lasagne* in Bologna.) It is filled with a sauce made from several different cuts of pork, onions, tomato concentrate, and wine, and layered with meatballs, sausages, mozzarella, and ricotta. They make it for carnival, and not unreasonably, wait a whole year until the following carnival to make it again.

Elsewhere in the south, pasta made at home has had to yield to the popularity and convenience of the store-bought kind. The women who still make it are more likely to do so to mark the festive nature of special occasions, rather than depending on it as everyday fare. Homemade in the south is practically synonymous with handmade, and in the handmade pasta of the southern Italian home kitchen we can recognize the prototypes of what eventually became *penne, fusilli, bucatini,* all the classic shapes of factory-made macaroni.

In Sicily and in other southern regions, patient housewives make small hollow pasta tubes from a dough of hard semolina flour and water by flattening the dough, cutting it into small rectangles, curling the rectangles around a knitting needle, then slipping them off and setting them aside to dry. Sardinia's favorite pasta, *malloreddus,* is now produced commercially, but I have seen it done by hand. A very compact dough of semolina flour, water, and a pinch of saffron is broken off into small lumps that are then rolled against a ridged tool or on the steel mesh of a strainer to form finely etched, tapered shell-like shapes. The couscous-like granular pasta known as *cuscusu* in Sicily and as *fregula* in Sardinia is commonly available there at a baker's shop or at the grocer's, but some women continue to make it at home. They spread a mixture of coarse and fine semolina flour over a work surface, sprinkle it with saffron-accented water, and run the fingers over it until it lumps into so many tiny pellets.

Apulia's *orecchiette* crown the peak of the handmade pasta pyramid. *Orecchiette* start as *cavatieddi,* another Apulian specialty, and *cavatieddi* start as small cylinders of firm dough made from semolina flour and water that are shaped on a board with the curving, dragging motion of a knife blade. To make *orecchiette,* you press your thumb into a *cavatieddi* and slide it against a wooden board, molding it into a miniature bowl whose convex side is roughened by the board's slightly textured surface. *Orecchiette* take a long time to cook, twenty minutes or more, and even then it is a notably chewy mouthful. The ancestral sauce consists of the braising juices released by stuffed meat rolls cooked at length with homemade tomato concentrate. The rolls themselves are served separately, later, as the meat course. My heart, however, goes out to another sauce. It is made with *cime di rapa,* known in American markets as broccoletti or rapini. These are blanched, chopped, and sautéed in olive oil with garlic, anchovies, and chili pepper. You toss the *orecchiette* with the sautéed rapini, then add a fine drizzling of raw olive oil and a liberal grating of Pecorino cheese.

I hope never to become so feeble that I am unable to respond to the potent call of this dish, or so blasé that I'd be indifferent to the teasing bitterness of a soft, spicy, deep-green rapini sauce pooling in the hollows of sinewy, coarse-textured, golden pasta. If I had to point to one dish as a model of qualities that I treasure in Italian cooking—frugal ingredients, simple execution, forthright flavor—there might be scores to choose from but none would come closer to the mark than *orecchiette con le cime di rapa.*

Inside Boxed Macaroni Pasta: Everything You Had Never Suspected You Really Needed to Know

"What is there to know about a package of spaghetti?" you ask. *"A lot,"* I say. *"Why does it matter?"* *"Because taste matters."* It may seem hard to believe that there are significant differences between the spaghetti or penne or rigatoni in one box and those in another, yet the differences are there for anyone to taste. One pasta brand can vary from another in color, in texture, in firmness, in fragrance, in receptivity to sauce, in intrinsic flavor.

Let us start with a definition. Macaroni, to use the word for boxed pasta derived from its equivalent in Italian, is made from a mixture of semolina—hard wheat flour—and water that is kneaded into dough, pressed through dies perforated to produce various shapes, hollow or solid, short or long, concave or flat, and then dried. Those steps in the basic production process never change. What changes with each producer is how they are performed. And it is precisely how the steps are performed, how the dough is kneaded, what the dies are made of, how long and at what temperature the soft, newly formed macaroni is dried, that determines the tasting qualities of the pasta you will drop into your pot.

The Making of Good Pasta

Good macaroni pasta is made slowly. It is kneaded slowly with cold water to produce compact, sinewy dough; it is extruded through slow coarse bronze dies, developing a grainy surface that feels lively in the mouth and grabs greedily at sauce; it is dried at a low, slow temperature that won't burn up the rich but fragile fragrance of fine semolina. However, if you are a large-scale industrial producer aiming to put your spaghetti on every supermarket shelf, you don't want to know about slow kneading, slow bronze dies, or slow drying temperature. You knead dough in one fast step with lukewarm water; you extrude with smooth Teflon-coated dies through which the dough flows with the speed of a mountain stream rushing downhill; and your drying chambers are quick-working high-temperature ovens. On the old slow road to high-quality macaroni, the costs are greater and the production is smaller, but happily for the good home cook, there are a number of pasta artisans in Italy who travel on it still.

Names Worth Knowing

It has been two centuries since the first successful commercial productions of pasta were launched in the Neapolitan hinterlands and for much of that time we looked to Naples for quality pasta. I remember the splendid macaroni of Carmine Russo, Amato, and Voiello. Voiello has fallen into the hands of Barilla, and it has been a long time since I have come across the other two. Today we look elsewhere, principally to Abruzzi.

The pioneers in the making of premium macaroni in Abruzzi were the De Cecco brothers who set up their plant at the foot of Mount Maiella in the town of Fara San Martino, where they utilized the pristine cold water of the spring that spills down the mountain's slope. The exceptional qualities that have been attributed to this water have made of Fara S. Martino one of the celebrated centers of artisanal pasta production in Italy. Other well-known producers who knead their dough with water from that spring are Del Verde and Giuseppe Cocco. I could not ask for better pasta than Cocco's. When I visited the plant, Mr. Cocco was eager to point out that the impeccably looking works, although recently constructed, were modeled not on the most advanced machinery available, but on a facility designed fifty years earlier. The kneading at Cocco is broken up into four separate steps that approximate the rhythm of hand kneading, and the pasta, depending on the format, may dry for as long as two days.

Good water, bronze dies, slow drying is what all pasta artisans have in common. Because they are artisans, however, their approach is strongly individualistic. Carlo Latini, while he makes pasta in Abruzzi, grows the wheat for it in his native Marches. He has revived strains that other farmers had abandoned because they were low yielding, but whose exceptional aroma and flavor he prizes more than mere productivity. Latini pasta has the most distinctive flavor of any, but it needs special vigilance in the cooking. It must be drained while it still appears to be undercooked because it softens rapidly in its own heat in the serving bowl.

Giancarlo Zaccagni, a warm and immensely engaging man, attributes the excellent quality of the pasta that bears his name to an antique machine that he rescued from a junk heap and rebuilt himself, using an unorthodox assortment of parts that include ball bearings from a Ferrari racing car. Zaccagni's contraption slowly kneads and extrudes pasta whose mouth feel, when cooked, is the closest in buoyancy to that of handmade pasta.

It is surprising to find macaroni of unsurpassed quality in Tuscany, a region whose contributions to pasta are of such late date. The macaroni that the Martelli family from the small Tuscan town of Lari puts into a bright yellow package have some of the longest drying times in the industry. The semolina they use is responsible for the immensely satisfying toothy quality of this pasta. The flour comes from a mill in North America that processes hard wheat with remarkable body. Martelli's spaghetti and penne exhibit all the muscle of that flour because of the unhurried kneading of the dough. When Dino Martelli showed me his mechanical kneader he said it came with three speeds, but he couldn't guess how fast it might go because they had never used any of the settings but the first and slowest one.

Other producers whose pasta I like are, in Abruzzi, Rustichella d'Abruzzo and the Due Pastori brand from Nonna Luisa. An admirable entry in the quality pasta competition comes from Benedetto Cavalieri, whose plant is at the heel end of the Italian boot, in Apulia, the region whose broad plain yields some of Italy's best hard wheat.

Matching a Pasta Shape to Sauce

Macaroni, unlike egg pasta, enjoys successful couplings with both butter-based and olive oil-based sauces, but not all shapes work equally well with all sauces. Long, thin strands—spaghettini and linguine—ought to be your first and possibly only choice to carry sauces that are cooked in olive oil and served without cheese, especially those with seafood and with vegetables. The sturdier strands—spaghetti, *bucatini*, and long-style fusilli—take cheese well, whether the sauce is made with oil or butter. For all the sauces that have butter and some meat—sausages, ham, pancetta, or meat sauce with beef or veal—and are tossed with grated Parmesan cheese, choose short macaroni such as penne, fusilli, *conchiglie*, or rigatoni. For baked pasta, rigatoni are strongly recommended because theirs are the thickest walls, hence they maintain some firmness through the two stages of cooking—boiling first, then baking—to which they are subjected.

Other Useful Points to Keep in Mind:

✦ Start cooking the pasta when everything else is done. Cooked pasta must not wait. Never stop the cooking before it is done. Cook from beginning to end without interruption.

✦ When boiling pasta, the more water you use the better it will taste. Macaroni cooked in insufficient water has a gummy consistency because its excess loose starch was not dissolved. Calculate at least 4 quarts per pound.

✦ Cook at a very lively boil.

✦ Add salt only when the water comes to a boil and wait for the boiling to resume before dropping in the pasta. Use noniodized sea salt, preferably coarse, or kosher salt. Add 2 tablespoons for 4 quarts of water. Never put olive oil in the water.

✦ When you drop the pasta in the pot, stir it immediately, or it will stick. Stir at first continuously for half a minute. Long pasta, such as spaghetti or spaghettini, rises and separates while it cooks, assuming you are cooking with ample water, and does not need to be stirred again. Short macaroni collects at the bottom and sticks to itself and to the pan unless you stir it periodically until done. Always keep the water boiling briskly.

✦ Do not be guided solely by the cooking times on the box. Taste for doneness. Drain the pasta when very slightly underdone, because it will continue to soften while you toss it.

✦ Do not serve pasta with a pool of sauce resting on top, no matter how pretty it may look. Toss the macaroni with sauce immediately after draining it. Toss conscientiously to distribute the sauce evenly and to coat all the pasta. It is only with thorough tossing that you achieve a satisfactory fusion of pasta and sauce. No other step is more important.

✦ If the sauce was made with olive oil, drizzle a little raw oil over the pasta when tossing it. If the sauce was made with butter, add a pat of butter, letting it melt in the pasta while you toss. If the dish calls for grated cheese, add it while tossing the pasta. Bring extra cheese to the table as an option, not as a required addition.

✦ Pasta must not sit and wait. Serve it immediately, and tuck in promptly, preferably deferring the launch of an extended conversation until you have had a hot forkful or two. The serving bowl in which you toss the pasta and the plates for the table should be warmed before you use them.

Why and How You Should Be Making Your Own Egg Pasta
∾ Pasta all'Uovo Fatta in Casa

When, in my 80th year, I started taking driving lessons, I thought how much harder it is to learn to drive a car than it is to make pasta at home. You can teach yourself to make pasta, and it's even possible to get the hang of it on the very first try. It may seem unarguable that if one had to choose it's the car that is indispensable, not the pasta. As it happens, my experience would demonstrate the reverse. Until I moved to Florida, I had always lived without a car. For twenty years I lived in Venice, where there is not a car to be seen, and I never felt the lack of it. But if I had had to go without *pasta all'uovo*—homemade egg pasta—my family and I would have been deprived of one of the greatest pleasures that life has given us.

Can there be a market that does not offer some form of egg pasta, either dried or so-called "fresh"? I doubt it. Is there any point, one might wonder, in mixing flour and eggs at home, when you can cook something out of a package picked so effortlessly off the shelf? My answer, as you may guess, is yes, there is a point, a considerable point. Commercially made egg pasta is produced as though it were spaghetti or penne, squashed at high pressure through shape-forming dies, and heat dried. The flour the plant uses is semolina, the same hard wheat flour with which they make macaroni. Factory methods and factory ingredients are essential to the quality of macaroni, but macaroni and homemade egg pasta are two distinct products, gloriously equal in their goodness, but conspicuously different in how they express it. What one responds to in homemade pasta is its lightness, its buttery texture, its suave entry into the mouth, a deeply satisfying cohesion of pasta and sauce, and a buoyant, palate-caressing richness of taste. The only egg pasta that delivers such sensations is one that you make at home, using low-gluten white flour for your dough and thinning it with gradually applied low pressure. Take into account, moreover, that when you make your own pasta you can produce noodle shapes that are usually unavailable commercially, such as *tonnarelli, pappardelle,* and *maltagliati*—the finest cut of all for *pasta e fagioli.* You can make the only lasagne that are worth doing. You can fill your homemade *tortelli* and ravioli with stuffings whose quality and freshness no store-bought version can equal.

My model for egg pasta made at home is Bologna's *pasta all'uovo.* It is made from whole eggs and the low-gluten flour that Italy classifies as "00." No olive oil, or salt, or water is ever added. In the cooking school I had in Bologna the class on homemade pasta was spread over two days, giving each student a chance to roll out pasta dough entirely by hand, using the traditional long, narrow hardwood pin. Some of the students continued working on it at home, sending me photographs that documented their proficiency. Infrequently though it may have happened, I ranked it as one of the most gratifying achievements of my teaching career. There is no doubt that rolling it by hand, when executed skillfully, produces the finest of all egg pastas, but because it can be a daunting craft to master it would be a pity if it discouraged anyone from making pasta altogether. You can make very good pasta very easily with commonly available tools. The method I have developed while working alone at home on the recipes for this book is of a comforting simplicity. If I can learn to drive, anyone can make excellent egg pasta, following the procedure I am about to describe.

The Equipment

You need a food processor for kneading the dough and a pasta machine. A pasta machine has a set of adjustable rollers through which you will thin the dough and a pair of noodle cutters. It may be hand-cranked or electric. I tested the recipes in this book with the roller and cutters that KitchenAid has had made in Italy for its standing mixer. These solidly constructed attachments profit from the mixer's powerful and steady motor. Do not waste money, time, and materials on any of those lamentable contraptions into which you dump flour and eggs and from which you extrude wholly unsuitable strands of a gummy substance that ought not to be called pasta.

The Layout

You should have available a fair amount of counter space on which to work the pasta and lay it out to dry. We do not hang pasta to dry it, but spread it flat on cloth towels. If you do not have enough counter space for this, you can lay the towels on the dining table. Unless one of the counters is made of butcher block, it would be helpful for you to get a wood pasta board to work dough and cut pasta. (Please see the Appendix for a suggested source.)

The Ingredients

Whole eggs, preferably extra-large, and unbleached all-purpose flour. I use King Arthur. So-called "pasta" flours are not suitable for homemade egg pasta because they are too high in gluten.

Making the Dough

We measure homemade pasta by the number of eggs we use, hence we would speak of a pasta of two eggs or more. A two-egg pasta can serve three or four persons. I recommend that you start at that level and move to larger amounts only when you have become quite comfortable with handling dough.

✦ Pour 1 heaping cup of unbleached all-purpose white flour into the bowl of the food processor fitted with the metal blade. Break 2 eggs into the bowl and run the machine until the flour and eggs mass together.

✦ Open the bowl and poke two fingers into the mass. It will probably feel rather sticky. In this case, add ½ tablespoon of flour, cover the bowl, and process again. Open the bowl, test the mass again, and if it proves to still be sticky, add another ½ tablespoon of flour and run the blade again. Follow this procedure, repeating it, until the dough is no longer sticky and feels springy to the touch.

✦ Remove the ball of dough from the processor bowl, place it in the center of a wooden work board, and mold it with your hands into an evenly rounded shape. Press the heel of your palm against the dough ball, curl your fingertips inward, and push the dough away from you, pressing it and stretching it against the board. Let the ball come back toward you, then push it away from you again with the heel of your palm. When it lengthens into an oblong shape, fold it back on itself, turn it halfway around, and stretch it once more against the board. Always push it away with the heel of your palm. Perform the kneading operation for 1 minute, trying to give the dough ball at least one full turn. This is a brief but essential step in which the warmth of your hand and of the wooden board helps the dough achieve the compact, firmly fleshed consistency that is one of the distinguishing features of good pasta. When done, wrap the ball in foil or plastic film and let it rest at room temperature for at least 15 minutes or up to 1 hour.

Rolling Out the Dough for Flat Noodle Pasta

IF YOU ARE MAKING FETTUCCINE, TONNARELLI,
PAPPARDELLE, TAGLIATELLE, MALTAGLIATI, OR LASAGNE

◆ Spread several clean dry cloth kitchen towels flat over work counters or over a table if necessary, but not over the work board itself.

◆ Mount the cylindrical rollers onto the machine and set them at their largest opening, which on most models is #1.

◆ Unwrap the ball of dough, mold it with your hands into a thick salami shape, and cut it into several equal pieces—six if you are making two-egg pasta.

◆ Flatten one of the pieces of dough, pummeling it with the flat of your hand. Insert the narrower end between the rollers and run it through. Fold one end of the stretched out strip toward the middle, then fold it again. Run it through the rollers again, then repeat the whole operation once more, thus giving the dough its final kneading. Place that first pasta strip perfectly flat on the towel whose edge is nearest to you. It should lie perpendicular to the counter and alongside it, parallel to it, you place all the strips that follow.

◆ Take up another piece of dough and repeat the exact same procedure. When done, lay this second strip alongside the preceding one, taking care that they do not touch or they will stick to one another. Roll out the remaining pieces of dough, one by one, in the same manner.

◆ Close down the rollers by just one notch. Pick up the first pasta strip you laid down, insert the narrow end between the rollers, run it through and return it to its place on the towel. Make sure it is lying flat with no folds or bumps. Repeat the operation with all the pasta strips, taking them up one by one in the same order in which you had laid them down originally.

◆ Close down the rollers one more notch and repeat the procedure you have just gone through. Continue thinning the pasta strips, always in the same order, closing down the rollers by just one notch each time. As the strips get thinner, they get longer, so you will have to let them hang over the edge of the counter. Always make sure that they are lying perfectly flat and that they are not touching each other. If they are getting to be so long that they are unwieldy, cut them in half. Stop when the pasta is as thin as you want it. Ideally, it should be thin enough that you can distinguish the pattern of a dish towel or a newspaper headline through it. (When making *tonnarelli,* refer to the thickness guideline given further on.)

Before you can cut the dough into noodles, you must let the pasta dry for 15 minutes or more, until it begins to feel leathery yet pliant. The time is wholly dependent on the humidity, heat, and ventilation in your kitchen. Turn the strips over from time to time so that both sides become exposed to the air. Don't let the pasta become too dry because it will crack and split as you cut it. Don't try to cut it when it is still too soft because the still-moist noodles would stick to each other.

Machine-cut Noodle Formats

FETTUCCINE Mount the broader of the two sets of cutting rollers that come with the pasta machine, and run each pasta strip through them. Unfold the fettuccine and spread them out on the towels you have laid out as described on page 39 in the Layout paragraph.

TONNARELLI *Tonnarelli* is the name used in Rome for *maccheroni alla chitarra,* the pasta from Abruzzi. When cut on the steel strings of the pasta "guitar," as described on page 31, the noodle is square in section, as thick as it is broad. It is a marvelously versatile noodle that combines the finesse of egg pasta with the firmer, toothier bite of macaroni. It is easily made on the machine, but you must be careful to roll out the pasta so that it is not too thin. Its thickness must be equal to the width of the space of the grooves in the narrower of the two cutting rollers, which is the one you will use for making *tonnarelli.* After cutting each strip, unfold and spread out the noodles on the towels.

Hand-cut Noodle Formats

PAPPARDELLE *Pappardelle* is a broad Bolognese noodle, ¾ to 1 inch wide with rippled edges. It is cut by hand with a fluted pastry wheel. Lay a pasta strip out on the wooden board and cut it lengthwise into ribbons, working parallel to the strip's edges. Spread the freshly cut noodles out to dry on a tray lined with a clean, dry, cloth dish towel. Pappardelle noodles give a substantial and satisfying fillip to rich sauces made in the Bolognese style.

TAGLIATELLE   This is another Bolognese cut, a straight noodle slightly broader than fettuccine. There is no cutter for it, so you must do it by hand. When a pasta strip dries to the pliant consistency of soft leather, fold it lengthwise into a loose, broad, flat roll. Cut the roll crosswise at ¼-inch-wide intervals. Unfold the cut roll, separate the long ribbons of *tagliatelle* pasta and spread them out to dry on tray lined with a clean, dry, cloth dish towel. *Tagliatelle* is the classic cut to serve with a Bolognese meat sauce.

> *Marcella Says:* **Italians cut pasta with a broad, straight-edged knife. The straight edge gives you a clean, straight cut. A Chinese cleaver will work as well, but if you don't have one, you can substitute a sharp 8-inch chef's knife.**

MALTAGLIATI   This short, irregularly lozenge-shaped noodle, whose name translates to "badly cut," is the most luscious one to use with *pasta e fagioli,* surpassing any of the more common macaroni formats. To make *maltagliati,* fold a pasta strip lengthwise into a loose, broad flat roll, as you would for *tagliatelle.* Cut off one corner, then cut the other corner so that the strip comes to a point. Then cut off the point, cutting straight across the strip. Continue thus until you have done the whole strip. Unfold and spread out the noodles. One pasta strip makes a lot of *maltagliati,* and you may not want to use more than two.

Drying Freshly Cut Noodles

The simplest of all the pasta steps is drying fresh noodles, but you must do it with care to avoid messing up all the work you have done to that point. When pasta is fresh and moist, it is very sticky. To keep your noodles from becoming an inextricable mess, do not pile them up, but spread them out loosely on one or more cloth-lined trays, letting air circulate around them. You can use them immediately while they are still soft, and their cooking time will be extremely brief. Contrary to what I have found many cooks believe, you don't need to cook flat, homemade pasta the same day you make it. Once dried, noodle pasta will keep for months. You may want to make more than one kind of noodle, cook some right away, and put the others aside for another time. To dry long noodles for keeping, gather several strands while they are soft and curl them into nests. Lay the nests on towels, making sure they do not overlap, and let them dry at room temperature for a full 24 hours. When absolutely dry, pack them in a large cardboard box. You can make several layers, interleaving each layer with paper towels. Do not refrigerate. Store in a dry cupboard. It will take longer to cook than when freshly made, but it will have exactly the same tasting qualities. If you made *maltagliati,* you may well want to keep a supply. You can't make nests with them, so spread them out on a tray and let them dry completely for 24 hours. When absolutely dry, you can collect them in a small tin or in a plastic bag with a zipper closure.

LASAGNE After rolling out the pasta strips you must cut them for lasagne while they are still soft.

✦ With your cleaver or chef's knife, cut the strips into rectangles about 9 to 11 inches long.

✦ Set a large bowl of cold water near the range, and lay some clean, dry cloth towels flat on the work counter.

✦ Pour 4 quarts of water into a large saucepan, bring to a rapid boil, add 1 tablespoon salt, and as the water returns to a boil, slip in 4 of the cut pasta strips. When the water returns to a boil, cook the pasta for just a few seconds, then retrieve the strips with a colander scoop or slotted spatula, and drop them into the bowl of cold water.

✦ Pick out the strips, one at a time, rinse them under cold running water, and rub them delicately, as though you were doing fine hand laundry. Squeeze each strip very gently in your hands, then spread it on one of the towels to dry.

✦ Repeat the procedure until you have cut, cooked, drained, and rinsed all of the pasta, 4 strips at a time, and laid it out on towels to dry. Pat the strips dry on top with another towel.

> *Marcella Says:* **This washing, wringing, and drying of pasta for lasagne is a necessary nuisance. Dipping the partly cooked pasta into cold water stops the cooking instantly, which is important because if lasagne pasta is not kept very firm at this stage, it will become horribly mushy later when it is baked. You rinse it to remove the gluey starch on its surface, otherwise, when you are ready to use the strips, they will have become stuck to the towels on which you laid them out and tear apart.**

From this point on, assemble the lasagne as the specific recipe directs. Lasagne is, admittedly, the lengthiest pasta to put together and, to my husband's regret, I don't do it that often myself.

Consider, however, that you can do it a day or two in advance, refrigerate it, and all you have left to do when you want to serve it is pop it in a hot oven. If you make it taking no shortcuts and conscientiously following the directions I have given, you will produce a dish of such unsurpassable and triumphant goodness that it will give you, as it does me, a giddy feeling of exhilaration.

Rolling Out the Dough for Stuffed Pasta

Whereas you cut noodles from partly dried pasta, you need very soft pasta to make ravioli or tortellini. To keep the pasta from drying out, you must work with just one piece of dough at a time, thinning it all the way through notch by notch as described in the above directions that refer to flat noodles, and stuffing it immediately, according to the specific recipe, while it is still very soft. Only when you have thinned and stuffed one pasta strip should you roll out another piece and repeat the stuffing procedure. While you are working with one piece of dough, keep the others that are waiting to be thinned tightly wrapped.

Saucing and Serving Homemade Egg Pasta

Meat, seafood, and vegetables are interchangeable and equally desirable elements in sauces for egg pasta, but what rarely changes is the fat in which they are cooked, and it is likely to be butter. Fat stops on the surface of hard macaroni pasta, but it seeps into the open pores of pasta made at home with eggs and soft flour. Egg pasta tends to feel lean and slithery when it has absorbed olive oil. When it swells with butter, egg pasta achieves the fluffy consistency for which it is deservedly prized.

As to the proper serving plate, bear in mind that the law of gravity does not make allowances for the delicacy of homemade egg pasta. If you pile it into a deep bowl, it will be squashed by its own weight. What you want is a shallow platter with a low rim so that the pasta can spread out. The platter ought to be hot and the individual plates should also have been warmed. Toss noodles by reaching under them with a spoon and fork and mixing them with sauce as you pull them up. Toss ravioli and other stuffed pasta turning them over gently to keep them from splitting. Always add a small pat of fresh butter to the hot pasta as you toss it. I am inclined to do so even if the sauce was cooked in olive oil. Add the freshly grated Parmesan cheese when you are tossing, before bringing the platter to the table, to allow the pasta's heat to melt it a little.

How to Cook a Pasta Sauce

There are, of course, pasta sauces that are never cooked at all, whose components may be mashed, blended, chopped, macerated, or simply tossed, anything to set off their seasoning powers without having to use heat. Pesto or *cacio e pepe,* sheep's milk cheese and cracked black pepper, are familiar examples of a raw sauce. A cooked sauce, on the other hand, is a concentration of flavors, a reduction that is achieved through evaporation by heat. The degree of reduction that is necessary may be minimal or substantial, the volume of evaporation can likewise vary and its rate may range from minutes to hours, depending on the kind of sauce you are making, and those considerations are what will determine what kind of a pan you use. No useful measure of evaporation and reduction is going to take place under cover; therefore, your choice will have to be either an open skillet or an uncovered saucepan.

When to Use a Saucepan

With its tall straight sides and a relatively small diameter, a saucepan lets you cook at a slow rate of evaporation. The example of two totally different sauces illustrates how it works. A *ragù,* the classic Bolognese meat sauce, for instance, is a complex assemblage of ingredients: Butter, onion, carrots, celery, ground beef, tomatoes, milk, wine, and nutmeg are the irreplaceable components to which one may sometimes add pancetta, ground pork, peas, or dried porcini mushrooms. For them to come to a full development and harmonious integration of their flavors will take some hours, a process that requires the slow evaporation of the milk, of the juices from the tomatoes, and of the wine. Another example is the sweetest, most elemental of tomato sauces, the one that you make by putting butter, a whole, peeled onion, and tomatoes all at the same time in a saucepan and cook at a slow simmer for an hour or so, depending on the compactness or wateriness of the tomatoes. The onion must cook long enough to transmit its sweetness to the tomatoes, while the liquid of these slowly simmers away until they are reduced to the density of sauce. A saucepan that will contain all the ingredients snugly is what you want in both these cases, a medium-size one for the *ragù,* a smaller one for the tomato sauce.

When to Use a Skillet

The broad, shallow surface of a skillet is what you need for rapid reduction. If you are making the sauce Neapolitans call *al filetto di pomodoro,* with sections or "fillets" of solidly ripe plum tomatoes, olive oil, garlic, and basil, you look for fast release and evaporation of the tomatoes' liquid to preserve their fruity consistency and fragrance. An analogous example is the sauce of peeled strips of bell peppers sautéed with olive oil and garlic. You want to cook them just long enough to concentrate their sweetness and coat them with the flavor of the garlicky oil, but you don't want to keep them so long on the fire that they turn to mush. If you are making a clam sauce, the clam juices must be quickly and completely reduced before you toss in the clam meat. For the elegant sauce of prosciutto and asparagus, the asparagus don't need much cooking because they have already been

blanched. You sauté the prosciutto over chopped onion, and after quickly cooking off any lingering moisture from the asparagus you sauté them briefly to coat them with prosciutto essence. One last example of rapid reduction and evaporation is an Alfredo-style cream sauce and its variations with gorgonzola or other cheeses. It doesn't become a sauce unless the cream is reduced and reduced fast.

To sum up, there are slow-cooked sauces and fast-cooked ones. For the former you need a saucepan, for the latter—of which happily there are so many—a skillet.

When is the Sauce Done?

You can sometimes tell just by eye, but on many occasions you must also taste. In sauces that have tomatoes you will find that when the thin watery juices of the tomatoes evaporate as they cook down, the butter or oil in the pan begins to run clear. Scoop up a little bit of the sauce with a large spoon and tilting the bowl of the spoon toward you, see if the fat that collects at the back and edge of the spoon looks clear. Or, use the spoon to wipe a patch of the pan's bottom clean: If the tomato is done, the spoon's trail will be followed by clear fat. It could happen too that the fat is running clear, but the other ingredients are not done. You must taste to know, and if you find that additional cooking is necessary, add a tablespoon or two of water and continue cooking until it has evaporated.

Tasting for Seasoning

If you taste the sauce alone, you might be misled because it could taste more salty or peppery than it actually is. To judge how it is going to taste later on pasta, taste it over a little piece of bread. It is rare these days for people to use too much salt. They are more likely to err in the other direction, but in the event that the sauce is on the salty side you can compensate by holding back on the cheese when tossing the pasta and by adding some fresh raw butter or olive oil, whichever was used to make the sauce. When making a sauce that will cook for a long time it is difficult to judge at the beginning to what extent the ingredients will cook down. It is prudent, therefore, to add salt toward the end, when you can see exactly how much sauce there is to season.

Broth, Homemade Convenience Food

One definition of convenience food is a desirable ready-made edible that supplies what you do not prepare yourself because you either lack the time or inclination for it or do not possess the tools for the task. I'd like to formulate a different category of convenience food: Something that you can produce in advance at home at any opportune time, expending little effort and employing no particular skill, something that you can store and use on subsequent occasions to enrich your cooking with a flavor of your own making. Homemade meat broth is in the very front rank of this category.

What Is Broth?

Broth is the water in which you have cooked one or more cuts of meat together with some vegetables, herbs, and spices. It is not a concentrate. It is not stock. There is no stock in Italian home cooking. Broth is subtler. It is light-bodied and fresh, gently rounding out the flavor of any dish in which it has a role. Because broth is made not with carcasses or baked bones, but with solid meat, there is an immense bonus to making broth the Italian way, and that is the succulent boiled meat itself. If you are using brisket, or pot roast, or shank, or short ribs, the long, slow cooking demanded by the broth rewards you with luxuriously tender meat whose fine, delicate flavor cannot be matched by any other cooking method.

Basic Italian Broth Updated

The small adjustments that, over time, I have brought to the broth I was making did not change anything fundamental about it. It became, I believe, a trifle richer and a little more fragrant, but I was careful not to overload it in order to keep intact its basic elegance and versatility. The ingredients listed below are the components of a broth that I believe is as tasty as it is lighthanded.

✦ *The vegetables:* carrot, celery, a small onion, one peeled potato, half or less of a bell pepper, a whole, small tomato

✦ *The herbs:* a few stems Italian flat-leaf parsley, two or three bay leaves

✦ *The spices:* Tellicherry whole black peppercorns, a tiny, tiny piece of nutmeg

✦ *The meats:* juicy cuts that are suitable for slow cooking with at least some pieces on the bone.

The principal meat is beef, but some veal will add finesse to the broth. Do not use either pork or lamb. If you want to put in some chicken, do not use the carcass, only meat on the bone. Unless it is a very special kind of chicken, I omit it because long cooking extracts too much pungency from factory birds.

A stockpot or other large saucepan as described below in the first step

4 to 5 pounds beef plus a few marrowbones

> *Marcella Says:* **You could use a single piece of pot roast or brisket as long as it has some bone attached, but it is preferable to have an assortment that combines a single piece of solid meat with some short ribs or shanks.**

Optional: About 2 pounds veal, with the bone in, such as the shank, breast, or shoulder.

Fresh cold water, following the directions below to determine the exact quantity

Sea salt, either coarse or fine

1 medium potato, washed and peeled

1 medium onion, peeled

1 medium carrot, peeled and cut in half lengthwise

1 celery stalk with leaves

½ bell pepper, red or yellow, stem, seeds, and pith removed

3 or 4 stems Italian flat-leaf parsley, without the leaves

A few whole Tellicherry black peppercorns

2 or 3 whole bay leaves, either fresh or dried

1 whole ripe tomato

A very small piece of nutmeg; any more than a fragment risks making the broth bitter

A large fine-mesh steel strainer

Several ice-cube trays

YIELD: *Boiled meats and broth, the quantities depending on the amount of meat and water used*

1   Your pot should be large enough to contain all the vegetables and meat, water to cover by 2 inches, and preferably be narrow and tall enough to keep the water level high. A 6-quart stockpot is appropriate.

    Put all the meat you are using in the pot and pour in enough water to cover it by about 2 inches. Lift the meat out and set it aside. Pour the water into measuring containers, note its volume, then pour it out because you want to start the cooking with fresh water. Rinse the pot clean of any blood or bits of meat and fat it may contain. Pour fresh cold water, the volume you made note of, into the pot.

> *Marcella Says:* **The quantity of water you use is critical: Too much and you'll end up with watery broth, too little and it will be insufficient to cook the meat well. The procedure described is admittedly peculiar, but it gives you exactly the amount of water you need.**

2   Rub some salt into all the surfaces of the meat.

3   Add salt to the pot and put in the potato, onion, carrot, celery, bell pepper, parsley stems, peppercorns, and bay leaves. Cover the pot, bring the water to a slow boil, and cook for 15 to 20 minutes.

4   Add all the meats and the marrowbones, cover the pot, and turn the heat up to high in order to return the water to a boil as rapidly as possible. When the water has begun to boil again, adjust the heat to cook at a steady, but very gentle simmer, keeping the pot covered. Do not let it boil fast. If you find that even at your burner's minimum setting the water boils too rapidly, set the cover slightly askew to release some of the steam's pressure.

5   After 1 hour, add the tomato and nutmeg. Turn the meat over, using tongs or a long-handled fork.

6   Cook, always at a gentle simmer, for 2 hours more. The meat should feel very tender when poked with a sharp fork.

Serving the Meats Hot

When they come steaming hot out of the broth, the meats taste their sweetest. You have a wide choice of serving options. The simplest dressing that you would find Italians using would be a little salt, juice just squeezed from a lemon, a fine olive oil, and some cracked pepper. There is no better foil for the tenderness and fine flavor of the meat. There are, however, many other sauces available. In this book, turn to page 320 for the Bell Peppers Sautéed with Anchovies and Black Olives. In my previous book, *Marcella Cucina,* there are two lovely ones that need no cooking, one made with bell peppers, garlic, anchovies, and capers, another with apples and basil. You'll find two classic ones, *salsa verde,* with capers, garlic, and heaps of parsley, and *peperonata,* a warm sauce with both bell and chili peppers and smothered onion, in my earlier volume, *Essentials of Classic Italian Cooking.* You can also accompany the meats with Italian mustard fruits (see page 108 for my version), or with such not necessarily Italian condiments as horseradish, chutney, or any variety of mustard.

If you'd like to serve the meat warm within a day or two after making it, refrigerate it covered in some of its broth. Reheat in that broth.

Serving the Meats Cold

If there are leftovers or if you want to serve all of the meat cold at another time, look up the Cold Boiled Beef Salad on page 260. It is amazingly good, as delicious a way of serving beef as any I have known.

Storing the Broth

✦ When the broth is done, remove the meat and either serve it while still warm as described above, or refrigerate it moist, using some of the broth to cover it if you intend to reheat it. Refrigerate it with no broth if you plan to use it as a cold dish.

✦ Discard as many of the vegetables as you can easily retrieve from the pot.

✦ Set a fine-mesh steel strainer over a large bowl and pour the broth through it.

✦ Cover the bowl with plastic film and refrigerate it for one day, or at most two.

✦ When you take it out of the refrigerator you will find that fat has congealed on top in the form of a solid yellow layer. Lift the fat out a piece at a time with a large, flat spatula, and discard it.

✦ Once you have removed the fat, use a ladle to spoon the broth into empty ice-cube trays. Spoon gently from the top. When you get close to the bottom, you will find a deposit of sediment. Spoon up as much of the broth as you can without dredging up sediment and discard what remains. Put the trays into the freezer.

✦ When the broth is frozen solid, unmold the cubes, put them in airtight plastic freezer bags, label them, and return them to the freezer. If you are keeping the cubes longer than 2 months, thaw, boil the broth again for 15 minutes, and refreeze it in the ice-cube trays.

Why You Made the Broth

You will have no problem finding wonderful uses for your frozen broth. It will elevate any dish of which it is a part. No other liquid medium can equal it when making a risotto, any kind of risotto except those with seafood. Use it for all your soups. If you want to be extravagant with it, use it instead of the two or three tablespoons of water that you sometimes add to a stew, a fricassee, or a sauce. When you freeze it there may seem to be a lot of it, but as you begin to use it you will wish that you had more.

Herbs, Garlic, Spices, Salt, and the Pursuit of Flavor

Flavor may be pursued down many tempting roads, but take heed, some of them might be dead ends. One of those is the prodigal use of herbs. I have come across such phrases as "I use a ton of herbs in my salad for complexity and zip" or, more romantically, "I came home from the market with an armful of herbs." I have spent most of my life in the markets of Italy, and I have never seen anyone leave with an armful of herbs. The single herb that an Italian cook will buy in quantity once or twice a week is a large bunch of flat-leaf parsley because a couple of tablespoons of chopped parsley go into so many dishes. But while on one day she or he will get a sprig or two of rosemary for the roast chicken, on another it could be a few bay leaves for the soup or for boiling chestnuts, or some sage

leaves for the beans or for a game bird, or a skinny bunch or two of basil from which a few leaves will be slated for a tomato salad or a sauce made with fresh tomatoes. Only when making pesto would one buy more basil. On less frequent occasions, strongly conditioned by local usage, one might pick up a little bit of thyme or marjoram, or oregano or wild fennel; more rarely—and for most Italian cooks it could be never—will a small amount of saffron, chives, borage, or tarragon be tucked into the shopping sack.

In any dish coming from the hands of a careful cook, the principal ingredient, or the combination of ingredients, expresses flavor that is intrinsic to it. If it didn't have a flavor of its own there would have been no reason to cook it in the first place. The seasonings—and aromatic herbs must be considered no more than seasonings—are chosen for the natural and congenial relationship they can form with the ingredients that they accompany. Herbs are there to support, to propitiate, to accent even, an expression of intrinsic flavor, not to strut in front of it and replace it.

Garlic

The unbalanced use of garlic is the single greatest cause of failure in would-be Italian cooking. I certainly don't shrink from using garlic, as you can see from leafing through my recipes. But I don't want my sauces, my clams, my potatoes, my chicken, my roast veal to taste of garlic; I want them to taste of themselves. Garlic is there because of its unique ability to spot that taste, to prompt a lively perception of it, but it must remain a shadowy background presence—it cannot take over the show. I use garlic in different ways, the whole clove or chopped, sliced, smashed, in every way except pressed. I seldom cook it any longer than it takes for it to become colored a very pale gold. On those occasions when I need it to be a nut-brown color, I use the whole cloves so that when they are done I can remove them from the pan before cooking anything else in it. Garlic is the most supportive ingredient you will ever use, but use it to advance flavors, not to club them senseless.

Spices

I don't have a spice rack in my kitchen, nor do I believe you will find many Italian kitchens that do. I do use some spices, but far fewer than are popularly presumed to be a requisite of accomplished cooking. My principal spice is black pepper, whole Tellicherry peppercorns in a grinder. I don't use white pepper or keep previously ground pepper because neither has the aroma of freshly ground black pepper.

I also use chili pepper, just enough to wake up the taste buds, but not so much that would anesthetize them. If I made a fetish of authenticity (what a slippery concept that is), I would use only the small red chili peppers—*peperoncini,* similar to cayenne peppers—that cooks in Italy are accustomed to employing. And, of course, I do use them, although only in the dried state because I have never seen them fresh here. The dried ones I have in my kitchen now are imported from Calabria. *Peperoncini* can be quite hot and because of their potential for mischief are sometimes called *diavolicchi,* little devils. But I am also grateful for jalapeños, which I couldn't get in Italy. They not only supply bite, which is not unkind when they are used in moderate quantity, but an entrancing aroma that is quite compatible with Italian flavors.

The only other spice I make use of is nutmeg that I grate into Bolognese meat sauce and some pasta fillings. I grate it fresh from the whole nut and the trick is not to exceed either in restraint or liberality. Too little nutmeg is insignificant, while too much produces a bitter taste. I grate a little of it at a time, I taste, and if necessary, I grate and taste some more until it is right.

Salt

If you are persuaded that even within the context of a balanced Italian meal the adequate use of salt could affect your life expectancy, you will not want to read any further. I am concerned here solely with the gastronomic importance of salt, and it is huge. Cooking that lacks salt lacks flavor. When it is used judiciously, it is not salt that you taste but the unbuttoned natural flavor that salt, and salt alone, can draw out of ingredients. If you have a really good tomato, split it in half, sprinkle a few grains of sea salt on one half and none on the other. Try both halves and ask yourself which of the two tastes most of tomato. If you are willing to waste a glass of red wine, you can have a demonstration of what a powerful propellant of aromas salt can be. Fill two wine glasses about one third of the way up, pouring from the same bottle. Mark one of the glasses. Turn away and have someone sprinkle a little salt into one of the glasses, making a note of which one it was. Swirl and sniff each glass. One of the two glasses will have a more conspicuous bouquet than the other, and it will be the one with the salt. Just smell it, don't drink it.

Putting a saltshaker on the table doesn't compensate for insipid cooking. Pasta needs to cook in water that has been liberally salted, beans have to be salted from the start, a beefsteak has to be generously rubbed with salt before you put it on the grill. Soups, vegetables, stews, fricassees, sauces, all these must be salted before they finish cooking so that they can release their flavor. Salt added at the table comes too late to promote a full release of that flavor.

To distract a palate up against the dumbness of a saltless or undersalted dish, cooks are dressing up their dishes with high-impact condiments, with herbs, with chilies, with garlic, with exotic fruits, with balsamic reductions, and confits of various natures. They are layering, they are crusting, they are resting them on beds of this or that. A palate regularly deprived of the flavor that ingredients owe to wisely administered salt risks atrophy. It may become incapable of recognizing food that is either insipid or cosmetically altered, ornamented and spiced up for what it is and, even more sadly, for what it is not.

Knowing Beans

You rarely see in a market the fresh shelling beans that one uses in Italian cooking, and even when you do their season lasts little longer than the life of a fruit fly. If you love beans, and how can one not, the usual choice is between beans that are precooked and canned and those that are dried. Few must be the cooks who have never used beans from a can and to my regret I am not among those few. Rather than struggle now against the tempting convenience of having precooked cannellini ready at arm's reach to drop into a soup or toss in a salad of tuna and onions, I no longer have any canned beans at all in my cupboard. (Except for canned chickpeas, as I explain further on.) I only keep dried ones, which compels me to plan ahead, six hours for soaking and about one hour for cooking. It's a small price to pay for enjoying the profound good taste of beans that have been carefully cooked in the savory style of the Italian home kitchen.

Buying and Storing Dried Beans

There is a notable difference in quality among dried beans, as there is among all naturally harvested products. When I lived in Venice, the dried *borlotti* beans I bought in the winter for soup were sold loose out of a barrel marked Lamon, the choicest district for mountain-grown *borlotti*. Because they came from the most recent harvest, their skin was taut and glossy and they were heavy in the hand, testifying to their youth. I can't expect to find freshly dried Lamon *borlotti* where I live now, on a barrier island off the west coast of Florida, but that doesn't mean that I must settle for mediocre supermarket beans. Nor should you. In many large and smaller cities in this country and in some suburban malls there are specialty food stores that stock good dried beans. If none of those places are easily accessible to you, you can shop for beans by mail through food catalogues or online. (See the Appendix for some of my sources.)

Store beans in a dry place, preferably in a tight-closing glass jar that keeps the humidity at bay and lets you see at a glance which beans you have and how many. Try not to stock more than a year's supply, not because they could spoil, they surely won't, but to make room on your shelf for the sweeter-tasting beans coming from the most recent harvest.

Which Beans to Get

There exist two categories of beans—or legumes, to use the broader and more accurate term—
Old World and New World. Among the varieties that originated in antiquity in the lands rimmed
by the Mediterranean, lentils, chickpeas, and favas still have an important place in the Italian
kitchen. We can exempt lentils and chickpeas from this discussion. There is no commonplace
alternative to dried lentils, which moreover do not need to be soaked before cooking. Chickpeas, on the other hand, are the one legume that you don't want to buy dried. It isn't solely
because cooking them thoroughly takes such a long time, and it assuredly does, but because the
canned ones, particularly those put out by Goya, can be so good.

You may not always find dried fava beans when you want them, but should you come
across them, get them even if you are not out looking for them. They deserve a place in your
larder, if only to make that devastatingly tasty dish from Apulia, *Purea di Fave con le Cime di Rapa.*
The recipe for it is on page 310. There is also an old dwarf version of the fava bean, called
cicerchie, that has recently been rescued from oblivion and is now available from dealers in Italian
foods. It has a more earthy and gutsy taste than the fava, and just like it, is delicious in soup,
with meat roasts and fricassees, and on its own as a vegetable.

Out of the scores of varieties that were first cultivated in the New World, two have put down
deep roots in Italy, cannellini and *borlotti.* White, creamy, thin-skinned cannellini are the beans that
Tuscany has made its own. They are grown throughout Tuscany and the other hilly regions of
central Italy, but a few sites have been identified that favor production of superior cannellini. The
most celebrated of these sites is Sorana wherefrom come, in despairingly small quantity, sweetly
nutty beans of extraordinary creaminess with skins so thin as to be imperceptible. I have seen at
least one book written in praise of the cannellini of Sorana, which may be one of the most coveted
and hardest to get agricultural products in Italy. If we can't have Sorana beans here however, we
needn't feel deprived because excellent cannellini as well as other beans are available from the
mountain farms of America's Northwest.

Borlotti are the beans beloved of northern Italy, of the Veneto in particular, but they are no
less dear to Lombardy and Piedmont. They are related to the cranberry bean and, like it, are
among the most beautiful of legumes. The pods have flamboyant streaks of flaming pink on a white
background, and the beans themselves, when still fresh, are gorgeously marbled in purple and

pink. Curiously, when cooked, they turn a modest dark brown. *Borlotti* are the most desirable beans to use in that Venetian specialty, *pasta e fagioli,* and they are excellent with pork sausages, in which Venice also excels. They are a fleshy, rib-sticking kind of bean with a rich distinctive chestnut taste. In addition to cranberry beans, another variety that *borlotti* are closely related to is called tongues of fire.

Occasionally in Italy you may come across giant white beans that are called *fagioli grandi di Spagna,* Spanish beans, comparable to the American butter bean. They are hardly as common as cannellini and *borlotti,* but they are quite delicious. They are succulent and mildly nutty, with the thinnest of skins.

With the exception of lentils, the following soaking and cooking directions apply to all the dried beans mentioned above.

Soaking and Salting

I always soak dried beans even if the instructions on the package say it is not necessary. Soaking cleans, tenderizes, and sweetens the bean.

✦ Decide how many beans you will need—after cooking, 1 cup will swell to approximately 3 cups. Bear in mind that it's not necessary to use all the cooked beans at once. You can refrigerate the excess for 4 to 5 days or freeze them for a longer period of time.

✦ Pour the dried beans into a mixing bowl. Add enough cold water to cover by 1½ to 2 inches. Add a pinch of salt and stir.

> *Marcella Says:* **When you are cooking in an established tradition some of the notions you go by consist of received wisdom that you do not think to question. I had always been told that you ought not to salt beans until they were cooked at least halfway, otherwise their skins could toughen and crack. It was advice that I followed and transmitted. Recently, however, I started salting my beans from the moment I soak them and not only have I discovered that it has no dire effect on their skins, but indeed it has a very beneficial effect on their taste.**

✦ Soak for 6 hours or even overnight. If possible, check on the beans after 2 or 3 hours. If they have absorbed so much water that they are no longer well covered, add more. If the water has become turbid, empty it out, put the beans in a colander, rinse them, put fresh cold water in the bowl with a pinch of salt, put the beans back in, and stir gently.

✦ After the beans have soaked at least 6 hours or if you are soaking them overnight, on the following morning, transfer them to a colander and rinse them under cold water. Now your beans are clean, fully reconstituted, and ready to be cooked.

AHEAD-OF-TIME NOTE: You can soak the beans 2 or 3 days in advance of cooking them. When you have finished soaking them, drain them, rinse them, pat them dry in a kitchen towel, then put them in a plastic bag with a zipper closure or another tightly closed container and store in the refrigerator.

Cooking

Slow cooking in a small quantity of lightly salted water is what causes beans to transcend their starchiness and reveal all their naturally luscious taste. To that water I add a tablespoon or two of olive oil because it is so companionable a flavor for the bean that to me it seems indispensable.

✦ Choose a saucepan that is neither too broad nor too narrow for the amount you are cooking. You don't want the beans to lie sparsely on the bottom or to pile up too thickly. Pour in enough water to cover the beans by about 1 inch, add a little bit of olive oil and a pinch of salt, stir gently, put the lid on the pan, and turn the heat on to medium.

✦ Don't stray far from the pan so you can see when the water starts to bubble. When it does, turn the heat down, regulating it so that the water simmers at a steady, but subdued pace. Leave the lid on the pan, but if you have difficulty in keeping the simmer from going too fast, adjust the lid so that it is very slightly askew, allowing some of the excess steam to escape. Stir the beans once or twice, gently using a wooden or plastic spoon to keep from bruising the skins.

✦ Once you have the beans going at a desirable pace, you no longer have to watch them (although you might want to check up on them once in a while). In the very unlikely event that the beans have soaked up every drop of liquid before they are cooked, add a little bit of water. It should not take much more than an hour to cook them, but there are variations among beans, some take less, others more. Taste them after 45 minutes. Beans are cooked when they are fully tender, their centers creamy, not mushy. If they are still al dente, firm to the bite, they are not ready; and because they are not yet completely cooked, they cannot fully release their flavor. In this case, continue cooking, always at a gentle simmer, tasting the beans for doneness every few minutes.

OPTIONAL SEASONINGS If you are going to add the cooked beans to a dish that has its own distinct flavor accents, such as a stew or a soup, for example, I would not add any seasoning to their water but salt and olive oil. If the beans are going to play an independent role, however, either as a side dish on their own (see the serving suggestion below), or in a seafood salad, or as an accompaniment to a piece of Pecorino or other hard cheese, they would benefit greatly if you enrich their cooking medium with a sprig of fresh sage leaves and 2 or 3 garlic cloves, peeled and lightly smashed.

A SERVING SUGGESTION To experience a full measure of the pleasure your home-cooked beans have to offer, set some aside to have alone, undistracted by other ingredients. Whether they are freshly made or reheated in their broth, spoon the beans while still lukewarm onto a small plate. Moisten them with a scant spoonful of their broth. Taste and correct for salt. Drizzle with fruity olive oil. Sprinkle with a few robust twists of the pepper mill. Accompany with crusty bread, using it to make sure that not a drop of their ambrosial juices is left behind on the plate.

Storing Cooked Beans

There are so many ways in which you can enjoy the beans that it is worth your while to make a substantial amount. What you cannot use the same day you can refrigerate for up to 5 days in a tightly sealed container, preferably glass. It's not prudent to store them in the refrigerator for much longer because they might ferment. In the freezer, however, you can keep cooked beans safely for up to 3 months. For the freezer, zippered plastic bags are the most practical containers. Whether refrigerating or freezing, store the beans in their broth.

The Taste-Altering Power of Dried Porcini Mushrooms

I have worked with dried porcini mushrooms a lot. I have used them in risotto, in soups, with seafood, in pasta sauces, with potatoes and other vegetables. One of the experiments I was most pleased with was when I discovered that by adding them to ordinary fresh cultivated mushrooms these could taste like the foraged wild kind. Wherever I have used dried porcini, I have found that in some mysterious way the intense flavor they contribute also bestowed on the other ingredients of the dish an enhanced ability of their own to stir the taste buds. It's my hunch, and perhaps someone, someday may do the research that would confirm it, that when they are dried, porcini expand our palate's ability to respond to flavor, somewhat like, but without the discomfiting side effects of, monosodium glutamate. Whether or not such a connection will be scientifically established may be of more interest to writers of magazine pieces than to cooks. All that matters to us is to know how to use dried porcini so that we can experience the potent way in which they can alter our ability to perceive flavor.

About Porcini, the Fresh and the Dried

Porcini is the Italian name for *Boletus edulis,* the most sought-after member of the bolete family of wild mushrooms. It cannot be cultivated, but it is found all over the world, including some wooded areas of the United States. That it has become popularly known by its Italian name is not just an accident of fashion. I have had *Boletus edulis* from many parts, from Asia, North Africa, France, Slovenia, but the most luscious by far are the ones that had been gathered in the fall, after a hot and humid summer, in northern Italy, particularly in certain zones thickly wooded with chestnut trees in Piedmont, Emilia-Romagna, and the Veneto. When grilled slowly over the embers of a wood fire or sautéed equally slowly in garlicky olive oil, the creamy, fragrant flesh of healthy fresh northern Italian porcini is one of the greatest treasures the vegetable world can bestow on us.

In their fresh state, Italian porcini have a dome-shaped cap that may vary in color from light to dark chestnut. The underside of the cap has no gills, but a spongy mass of tiny tubes. The stem is bulbous and possibly even tastier than the cap. Cut open an example of sound, young porcini and the flesh you expose will be a solid, creamy white. It is only from such choice mushrooms, gathered early in the season before they become too mature, musty, or wormy that the most desirable quality of dried porcini is produced.

Choosing and Keeping Dried Porcini

Dried porcini are not an alternative to the fresh. Their flesh has been shriveled and after cooking its consistency will be of little interest. What they are—and what they are meant to be used as—is a powerfully endowed flavor-enhancing substance in which the aroma of fresh porcini has been concentrated and made extraordinarily penetrating, somewhat in the way that the heady scent of perfume in a vial exceeds that of the flowers from which it was produced. The aroma of all fresh produce is fragile, and its moment of greatest intensity is short-lived. To enjoy the benefits that dried porcini can deliver you must work only with those that have been made by desiccating prime examples of the fresh. Take a close look at the slices inside the package that you are buying. They should consist of large, solid, creamy sections. Pass up those packets that appear to be stuffed with dark, withered, crumbly pieces. They will not have much to offer in the way of alluring aroma because the mushrooms they have been processed from had already lost most of theirs.

Dried porcini keep very well for a long time if properly stored. I keep mine in a used coffee tin or in a tightly capped glass jar on the bottom shelf of the refrigerator. They will maintain their fragrance stored that way for a year or longer. If you should be traveling in Italy late in October or November, when the choicest dried porcini become available in the stores, buy as many as you think you can use. They are all but weightless and will become a precious addition to your pantry.

Reconstituting Dried Porcini to Prepare Them for Cooking

✦ Drop the porcini into a bowl and cover by about 1½ to 2 inches with lukewarm water from the tap. Let them soak for 30 minutes or more.

✦ Retrieve the mushrooms with your hands, but do not discard the soaking water. That soak has become a porcini-scented liquor that you will want to use. Squeeze the reconstituted porcini with your hands, letting the liquid they release drop back into the bowl.

✦ Rinse the mushrooms thoroughly under cold water to clean them of any embedded soil. If they are nice large pieces, I will probably cut them up before cooking them to distribute their flavor more efficiently.

✦ Fold a paper towel or place a coffee filter in a strainer and set the strainer over a clean bowl. Pour the liquor of the porcini soak through the towel or filter to strain the dirt deposited by the mushrooms.

Use the filtered liquor as well as the mushrooms in any dish that calls for them, following the directions of the specific recipe. However you employ them, the porcini liquor must evaporate completely during the cooking and you'll find that the longer you cook the mushrooms the more effusive the release of their aroma will be.

On the Importance of Bread Crumbs

It is not insulting to bread to call it stale because freshness is merely the first of its many useful lives. In one of its subsequent appearances it may be in your soup plate, bracing up a minestrone or a bean soup, or you may run into it at dessert time, in the form of bread pudding, or there it might be, midway through the meal, softened up with milk and kneaded into the meatballs. But the most common form in which it circulates is that of crumbs.

A function of bread crumbs is to draw off moisture. When coated with crumbs, food fries or browns crisply because its surface is dry. A useful thing to know about bread crumbs is that they harbor a powerful attraction for olive oil. If pasta is sauced with olive oil and no Parmesan cheese is used, one might toss it with bread crumbs to pull the sauce together. Or, if one chooses to grill fish in the glorious Adriatic manner, marinating it first with salt, lemon juice, and olive oil, bread crumbs are the medium that transforms the marinade liquid into a protective and flavor-enhancing coating.

Breadcrumbs are a neutral agent. They must safeguard, but not interfere with the flavors of the foods they are asked to protect, hence they must never be loaded with other flavors of any kind. They ought not to be either powdery fine or coarse. They should be absolutely dry, better if lightly toasted. Good crumbs, therefore, may be described as dry, medium fine, and totally unflavored. There are no crumbs you can buy that satisfy these criteria so well as the ones you can make at home, and with a food processor the procedure is swift and effortless. If you buy bread for your table you can make crumbs for your kitchen. Here is how I do it:

◆ Start with very good plain white bread, free of seeds, herbs, raisins, or nuts.

◆ Collect the bread left over from the table in a large brown paper bag that you will store in any dry place. When the bag is full, spread the pieces of bread on a baking sheet, put it in the oven, turn the oven on to 200°, and let the bread dry at that temperature for an hour or more.

◆ Break up the bread into small pieces and put as many of them into the bowl of a food processor as will fit loosely packed. Turn on the processor fitted with the steel blade and run until the bread is ground to a fine, uniform consistency. Transfer the ground bread to a large bowl, and fill the processor bowl again with another batch of bread to be ground. Repeat until all the bread is ground and collected in the bowl.

◆ Choose a strainer whose mesh is neither too fine nor too large. Place it over a clean empty bowl. Spoon some of the ground bread into the strainer and sift it through into the bowl. Empty the strainer of any crumbs that won't go through, spoon some more of the ground bread into it, and repeat until you have sifted all the crumbs.

◆ Choose a large glass jar with a tightly fitting lid, fill it with the bread crumbs, close it, and stow it in the refrigerator. The crumbs will keep in excellent condition for many months.

Recycling Leftovers

However good it may have been the first time, my family has always been averse to eating the same dish twice. In that they are no different from other Italian families I know. The very word for leftovers in Italian—*i resti*—has an unpleasant connotation. I am careful about how much food I cook and put on the table, but when my calculations are off and there are leftovers I have to consider how I can transmute them into a different and unrecognizable form if I want to serve them again. Here are some of those solutions.

Recycling Stews and Fricassees into a Pasta Sauce or a Base for Risotto

✦ Detach all the meat from any bone to which it is attached, whether it is beef, lamb, pork, or chicken and grind it. If using the food processor, be careful not to overprocess it. You don't want a paste, but tiny bits of meat to which some consistency remains. You may also chop the meat with a chef's knife or cleaver, chopping it rather fine.

✦ If there are vegetables in the stew, chop them with the meat, but remove and discard any potatoes.

✦ If there is tomato in the stew, add one fourth as much again of cut-up raw tomatoes, either from a can or peeled, ripe, fresh plum tomatoes and some salt.

✦ Put the ground-up meats and vegetables in a skillet with 1 to 2 tablespoons of butter, if the stew had originally been made with butter, or with 1 or 2 tablespoons of olive oil if the stew was made with oil. Turn the heat on to medium and cook for about 15 minutes, stirring frequently. Freeze in a zippered plastic bag and, when the stew is no longer fresh in anyone's memory, thaw this ground-up version and use it as a pasta sauce or the flavor base for a risotto.

Recycling Vegetable Dishes

If I find myself with surplus gratinéed asparagus, or sautéed zucchini or mushrooms, or spinach or green beans sautéed with butter and Parmesan, boiled green beans, or with some *peperonata*—the pepper and onion sauce for boiled meats, or with a forkful or two of rapini sautéed with olive oil and garlic, or even with a dollop of tomato sauce, from any one of the above I can make a frittata. I chop the vegetables rather fine, mix them with eggs and Parmesan, and follow the frittata method described on page 104. I can choose to serve the frittata hot. Or I can let it come to room temperature, cut it into dice, and serve it with drinks.

When mashed potatoes are left over, I make really delicious croquettes with them, mixing the potatoes with an egg and some Parmesan, shaping the mix into little cigars about 2 inches long, rolling them in bread crumbs, then frying them in hot oil.

Grilled Meats

You can make tasty meatballs from grilled beef, veal, or pork or with a combination of the three. Grind the meat fine, add chopped onion, chopped parsley, 1 egg, some bread soaked in milk, shape the mixture into miniature meatballs, roll them in bread crumbs, and fry them in hot oil.

Cheese

You might find yourself left with various pieces of cheese that are too small to serve individually. They can make an exceptionally savory pasta sauce or risotto. Cut the cheeses into very small pieces, put them in a small saucepan, and pour in milk to a level just short of covering them. Over very low heat melt the cheeses, stirring frequently, then let the milk simmer slowly away until the mixture is thickly creamy. Taste to make sure that the flavor has not become too sharp. If it has, correct it by adding 1 tablespoon of sweet butter. Toss the sauce with hot pasta. Or make a simple risotto cooked with chopped onion sautéed in butter, then during the last minute or two of cooking swirl in the cheese mixture.

Fruit, the Refreshing Dessert

With such alluring creations as tiramisù, panna cotta, zabaglione, zuppa inglese, cannoli, and many other similarly tempting confections, you'd expect that most Italians would look forward to ending their meal with dessert. Yet few do and even those few do so infrequently. When the time to fold up the dinner napkin approaches, an Italian will favor refreshment over repletion and have fruit instead of dessert. It's a choice that is charged with expectations of the pleasures engendered by seasonal flavors. Late in the spring come the sweet, firm-fleshed *duroni* cherries followed by berries, either foraged or farmed. The first ripe days of summer bring peaches, plums, apricots, and melons while figs are at their most luscious at August's end and early in September, along with sugary table grapes. October is for persimmons, blood oranges are for Christmas, and apples and pears bridge the gaps until it's time for cherries to come around again.

The common practice is to bring fresh fruit to the table in a large bowl with a bowl of cold water on the side for any that ought to be rinsed. There are times you may not want or need to do more than this. But many fruits, even when of the supermarket kind and imperfectly ripened, hold untapped within them ravishing reserves of flavor that can be released with just a simple marinade.

Marinade Components for Fresh Fruit

Some of the components of my marinades are used singly, some must be conjoined, and some are always present:

✦ *Sugar* It is essential to every fresh fruit preparation. It macerates the fruit, making its juices flow, giving its flesh a more luscious feel, and enhancing the sensation of ripeness.

✦ *Citrus zest and freshly squeezed juice* It may be of orange—one of my favorites—tangerine, lemon, or grapefruit. A citrus marinade can be used alone, adding only sugar.

✦ *Wine* It is generally used just with sugar alone but occasionally, see the instance cited below, with mint. It should be white because you want neither the obscuring color of red wine nor the astringency of its tannin. It can be either dry or sweet, still or sparkling. Among Italian wines, one made from the muscat grapes grown in Cannelli, such as Moscato d'Asti or Asti Spumante, contributes its own peachy aroma to the fruit. The pear-redolent Arneis is another appealing choice. Because its fruitiness and freshness agree so well with fruit, Prosecco tops my list of dry sparkling wines. Victor and I also like the floweriness and vibrant acidity of Rieslings and the spiciness of Gewürztraminer. Intensely sweet late-harvest wines of any provenance add concentration to the marinade. Dry Marsala is an excellent match for ripe cantaloupe.

> *Marcella Says:* **You may well hesitate about spending too much for the wine, considering that many of its nuances will be submerged by the aromas of the fruit and of the other components of the marinade.**

✦ *Vinegar* Either red wine vinegar or balsamic vinegar can be used on red berries as described further on.

The quality of wine vinegar has rarely attracted adequate attention, yet it is no less important than the quality of the olive oil you use on a salad. Unfortunately nearly all the wine vinegars on the supermarket shelf are to vinegar what plonk is to wine. French wine vinegar made by the Orleans method makes an impeccable choice. Also look for vinegars produced by some of the Italian wine estates or for premium Spanish vinegars.

In a world of no compromises, when using balsamic vinegar, you would use only 25-year-old or older Balsamico Tradizionale from Modena or Reggio Emilia. The younger Tradizionale—silver or beige capsule—is an adequate alternative. If the only other choice available were the cheap supermarket balsamico, I would not even attempt to make the dish.

✦ *Mint* It is good with tropical fruit or with small berries, as described below.

✦ *Ground Black Pepper* With red berries and vinegar, see details below.

The Basic Marinating Procedure

✦ All fruit, unless otherwise indicated and with the obvious exception of berries and grapes, must be peeled and cut into ½-inch pieces. Strawberries, if small or medium in size, should be cut in two, if larger, into three or more pieces. Unpeeled fruit must be washed in cold water and gently but thoroughly drained.

✦ Put the fruit in a bowl and pour the sugar over it before adding any other ingredient. The amount of sugar depends, aside from one's taste, on the following considerations: If you are using an intensely sweet wine, or if the fruit is itself exceptionally sweet, somewhat less sugar is needed. If the fruit is tart, as some berries can be, compensate with an extra measure of sugar, just as you should if using lemon or grapefruit juice in the marinade.

✦ When pouring liquid over the fruit, there should be just enough to pool to a depth of about ¾ to 1 inch at the bottom of the bowl.

✦ When the fruit and marinade have been combined in a bowl, turn the fruit over several times, using particular gentleness with berries because they bruise easily.

✦ Refrigerate for a minimum of 1 hour, 2 or 3 would be even better.

✦ See specific instructions below for special ways to marinate berries.

A Brief Guide to Fruit and Marinade Combinations

This is not a definitive listing nor would one be either feasible or desirable. A great appeal of these preparations is the pleasure of discovery as you improvise and find new affinities between fruits and marinades. The couplings described below are those that have given me most pleasure and may serve either as examples to emulate or to enlarge upon. In the markets there are many more fruits available than can be listed here and you should feel encouraged to experiment with as many as seem promising.

Bananas, sliced into disks, with peeled orange sections Marinate in sugar and the zest and juice of any of the four citrus fruits listed OR dry or sweet wine.

Berries: raspberries, blackberries or mulberries, blueberries, red currants, fraises de bois or cut-up strawberries—an assortment of some or all of the above Use sugar, lemon zest and juice, fresh mint leaves, and, optionally, sparkling wine.

Fraises de bois Unlike any of the other preparations, this one is "shakered" and served immediately. Place the fraises in a bowl no larger than you can grasp very firmly with your two hands. Pour on sugar, a thimbleful of red wine vinegar, and a few grindings of black pepper. Place a small plate over the bowl to cover it, grasp the bowl, and rock it with a gentle back and forth cocktail shaker motion for 5 full minutes. The action will very lightly mash the berries, integrating their juices with the sugar, vinegar, and pepper. Serve at once.

Strawberries, cut up Toss gently with sugar, then refrigerate until ready to serve, but no less than 1 hour. When ready to serve, drizzle with a small amount of good balsamic vinegar, turn the strawberries over gently three or four times, and serve at once.

Grapes Either white seedless or black grapes with seeds (seedless pale red grapes are tasteless) may be used singly, but are more fascinating together. If using black grapes, halve them to pick out the seeds. Marinate with sugar, lemon zest, and orange juice. Refrigerate for a few hours, but not overnight because fermentation might begin.

Mango Peel, slice, and marinate as is with sugar and either dry or sweet wine.

Peeled orange sections with cut-up strawberries and raspberries Sprinkle with sugar and orange zest and juice.

Oranges, peeled down to the flesh and cut into disks less than ½ inch thick Spread the slices in a deep serving platter and sprinkle with sugar, and moisten with lemon zest and juice. Turn the slices over once or twice, then refrigerate for at least 4 hours, but overnight is better. Turn the slices over once or twice before serving.

Peaches, pears, apples peeled and cut into bite-size pieces; bananas sliced into disks; and an optional assortment of other fruits such as berries, citrus sections, grapes, melon Marinate with sugar and the zest and juice of 1 lemon or orange. Toss gently two or three times and refrigerate for 2 to 3 hours. If you have some Maraschino cherry liqueur, add some to the marinade. You may also use other fruit-based liqueurs such as tangerine, but skip any that are too emphatic in taste and that would blunt the delicate fragrances of the fresh fruit.

Cantaloupe melon, diced or cut with a melon baller Combine with sugar and dry Marsala wine.

Peaches peeled, pitted, and sliced, either alone or with raspberries Marinate in sugar and orange zest and juice, or dry or sweet wine.

Peaches and pineapple, cut into chunks Soak in sugar, sweet wine, and fresh mint.

Pineapple cut into chunks with bananas sliced into disks, or pineapple cut into chunks and raspberries Combine with sugar and the zest and juice of any of the four citrus fruits listed OR dry or sweet wine.

Artichokes to Zucchini:
The Why and How of Prepping Vegetables

Cooks in Italy use vegetables a lot because they love them, as well they might because nowhere else in the world are any cultivated that can taste so good. And they cut, slice, and peel them not to make them look pretty, but to encourage them to give the best of their taste in the cooking. Whether your greens have come straight from the garden or if they are somewhat short of perfection as they sometimes are in my supermarket, Italian prepping procedures will elicit their best possible performance. The vegetables will cook more efficiently, release sweeter, fuller flavor, and, because all their least tender parts have been removed, they will be pleasanter to eat. I wish I could make prepping more attractive to you by claiming it's a snap. The truth is that, when you cook as many fresh vegetables as Italians do, it can take more time than almost anything else you do in the kitchen. Take into account, however, that it's a task you can undertake at any convenient moment, often even a full day in advance of cooking.

Artichokes

A basic principle underlying the preparation of most vegetables is that, there being no point to cooking the inedible, you pare away whatever is too tough or too stringy or simply not enjoyable to eat. The most striking example is the artichoke. No other vegetable conceals so much tenderness under so tough an exterior. Its core is so buttery that it can be sliced and added raw to a salad—a delicious thing to do, by the way—whereas a large proportion of the surrounding layer of leaves will no more yield to any form of cooking than wood shavings might. In whatever manner you choose to cook an artichoke, whether in a stew or a soup or a pasta sauce or in a frittata, or as a baked, sautéed, fried or even raw vegetable, your full enjoyment of it depends on how ruthlessly you have pared away all but its most tender parts.

✦ To prevent the artichoke from turning black and staining your hands, keep a halved lemon by your side and use it from time to time to rub the vegetable while you work on it. Cutting off the artichoke's top with scissors or a knife won't do the job: To judge which part of a leaf is tough and which is tender you must use your hands. Grasp the tip of the outer leaves and bend them back, one at a time, pulling them toward the base of the artichoke. Break them off short of the base, at a point where they snap easily. As you snap off more leaves, the tender part that you are exposing begins to lengthen. Continue pulling the leaves off one by one until you reach a central cone of leaves that are green only at their very tip, and whose pale, almost colorless base is at least 1 inch long.

✦ The green tip of that central cone of leaves is tough, and you must eliminate it by slicing off at least an inch from the top with a sharp knife. Rub the cut areas of the artichoke with the lemon half, squeezing juice over them to keep them from discoloring.

✦ The central hollow of the artichoke is now visible and at its bottom you see a cluster of very small leaves whose prickly tips curve inward. Cut off all those little leaves and scrape away the fuzzy "choke" beneath them, being careful not to cut away any of the tender bottom. If, by chance, you have a small paring knife with a rounded point, this is a good place to use it.

✦ Take a fresh look at the outside of the artichoke and locate areas of dark green at the point where you snapped off the outer leaves. This is tough stuff and must be pared away. Detach, but do not discard the stem. Except for the stem, the artichoke is ready to cook now or to be cut into wedges or sliced up, as the recipe may require. If you are not cooking it immediately, drop it into a basin of cold water that has been acidulated with the juice of half a lemon.

✦ Turn the stem bottom end up and observe how, at its end, a layer of green encircles a whitish core. The green layer is tough; the white core, when cooked, soft and delicious. Pare away the green, all the way around, leaving the white intact. If it's very thick, cut it in half lengthwise. Add it to the basin with the lemony water and later cook it along with the rest of the artichoke.

BABY ARTICHOKES In recent years I have been working with miniature artichokes that come to my supermarket in two-pound sacks containing about 20 artichokes. I prefer them first of all because their flavor is more explicitly "artichokey" than that of their overgrown siblings, and second because the tenderness of their leaves makes them easier to clean. You clean them exactly as you would the large artichokes, except that there is no choke to remove. Because of their size, you will need more of them, a negligible drawback when compared to their virtues. There is one dish—the upended *carciofi alla romana* (in which the full stem is left attached to the artichoke)—for which baby artichokes would not be appropriate because their stems are small to begin with and many have been cropped.

Asparagus

From the point of view of design, the tips are the most distinctive feature of the asparagus stalk. From the point of view of taste, they are surpassed by the meatier portion of the stem to which they are attached. Unfortunately a substantial part of that juicy stem is often left on the plate because it has not been made fully edible. The moderate amount of time and effort that it takes to strip it of its thin but gristly cladding is generously compensated for by the full utilization of the fine flesh of this precious vegetable.

✦ Slice off 1 inch or more from the dry butt end of the asparagus stalk to expose the moister part of the stem.

✦ The tough green fibers that sheathe the juicy core of the stem must be pared away. Hold the spear with its tip pointing toward you. Starting at the butt end, use a sharp paring knife to make an incision about ¹⁄₁₆ inch deep, tapering off to nothing when you approach the base of the tip. Give the spear a quarter turn and repeat the procedure. Continue turning and paring until the stalk is fully skinned.

✦ Strip off any leaves sprouting below the tip.

✦ Soak the trimmed asparagus in cold water before following the specific requirements of the recipe you are using.

Broccoli

The sweetest part of this vegetable's flavor is packed into its fleshy stem. To get at it you must remove the fibrous and bitter rind that envelops it.

+ Detach the full length of the stem from the florets. Remove and discard any leaves.

+ Place the florets in a bowl of cold water to soak.

+ Using a sharp paring knife, working lengthwise along the stem, peel away all the stringy green rind until you expose a pale, moist core. If the stem is exceptionally thick, slice it into two long halves.

+ Wash the pared stems under cold running water. Empty the bowl where the florets had been soaking and rinse them in several changes of cold water. At this point you can proceed with the recipe you are using.

Celery

The common way to remove celery's filaments, or strings, is to snap the stalk backwards and pull down. If that is what you've been doing you will still have been swallowing some filaments. To strip them away almost completely, I peel away the first cluster of strings using a swivel-blade vegetable peeler. I then complete the job the old-fashioned way, bending the stalk backwards against its spine, and pulling down when it snaps. Now the celery is virtually free of strings and ready to use in a stew or in a vegetable dish. When I must chop celery fine for a sauce or for the flavor base of a risotto or soup, I don't do anything about pulling away any filaments, however, because they will have been cut too short to be noticed.

Garlic

How you prep garlic is subject to the degree of control that you want to exercise over its power, which in good Italian cooking is never allowed to go unbridled. There is just one recipe in this book, the Bottarga Pasta Sauce on page 150, where a clove of garlic is sautéed with its peel on, otherwise, the first step is always to peel the cloves. To release more scent in less time, chop the peeled cloves very fine. To hold that scent in check, use the whole clove, which gives you several options: You may cook it to the color of the palest cream or allow it to go to a nut brown. In the latter instance, you would in most cases remove it before cooking anything else in the pan. You could lightly smash the clove, which would give you a slower release of the aroma than chopped garlic, a good way to go if the garlic is going to cook in braising liquid. For some of my tomato sauces I slice the clove very, very fine and, after the briefest of sautés, let it simmer in the juices of the tomato. Slicing it thin and simmering it in juice do marvelous things to garlic's fragrance, transforming its brashness to charm. Farthest from it is the pungent pulp that comes from a garlic press, an ill-conceived gadget that has never found even an icy welcome in my kitchen. Nor do I force the garlic to exude juice by pressing it with the flat of the knife against a cutting board—as I have seen chefs do—for the simple reason that I have never discovered how to brown juice.

Green Beans

When I learned to speak English, they were always called string beans. Presumably the string has been bred out of them, but I still find vestiges of it. The only way I can be confident that I have eliminated it is to snap each bean back at both ends. Moreover, I prefer to detach the ends because even if the bean is fully cooked they remain tough.

Leeks

Any time I see someone lop off all the tops from a bunch of leeks, I think, What a pity, there is still so much good stuff there. I begin by removing the roots. Then I cut off all of the leek at the butt end, as far up as it is still white. Next I strip away the green outer leaves of the tops until I expose a pale, whitish-green area, which I detach and add to the previously cut bulb. I continue to strip away more of the dark tops until I expose another tender pale patch, which I add to the others. And I continue thus until only some dark green tops are left, which I discard.

Onions

TO USE THEM RAW We use raw onions in salads of all kinds, most often with mixed greens, but also with homecooked cannellini or *borlotti* beans or with very good-quality canned Sicilian or Spanish tuna packed in olive oil. The untempered pungency of raw onion can be overbearing for the milder ingredients with which it must consort so, whenever possible, I start out with a less aggressive variety, such as the Florida Sweet, which has become my favorite, or Vidalia, or Maui, or my least favorite, a Bermuda Red.

After eliminating the root end, I cut it into thin slices, cutting across the onion, that is perpendicular to the way it grows. When you cut across a whole onion thus you produce rings.

Unless I am making fried onion rings I am more comfortable cutting the onion first from top to bottom in half, laying the cut side down flat against a cutting board, and then slicing across it to make half rings.

I pull the rings apart and drop them into a bowl with enough cold water to cover amply. I plunge my hands into the bowl, grasp all the onion slices, and squeeze them firmly. The sharp juices I force out of them turns the water milky white. I replace it with fresh, cold water in which I let the onion soak for as much time as I have before I have to use it. An hour or more would be ideal, but less will do if I am rushed. During this time, I repeat the procedure, squeezing the onion and replenishing the water, two or three times. When I am ready to proceed, I drain the onion and squeeze it dry between paper towels. Even an ordinary white or yellow onion acquires a gentler accent after this treatment.

IN COOKING If a recipe requires chopped onion, and I have the time, I chop it by hand because it has better texture. I cut the onion in half going from top to bottom. I lay the flat side on a cutting board and, starting parallel to the root end, I slice the onion thin, stopping short of cutting all the way through. Then I slice it as thin as I can, all the way through this time, putting my cuts at a right angle to the previous ones, thus producing a pile of small dice. I then chop these up as fine as I need them to be.

When I am short of time or energy, I resort to the food processor. I use one that has a small bowl nestled inside the large one because I don't want to process too much at one time, turning it into mush. I put in a piece of onion the size of a lime and pulse the blade no more than three or four times. It is quite sufficient for most dishes, but if I should need more, I remove what I have processed and chop another batch.

If a recipe calls for sliced onion to be sautéed rapidly, I slice the onion any which way comes most easily. If, however, I want the sliced onion to "sweat," to cook down slowly and evenly, I slice it in the manner detailed above where I describe how I prepare onion that we eat raw.

Parsley

The only parsley we use is the flat-leaf variety known as Italian. We might use parsley stems in a few dishes such as *ossobuco* or broth, but generally we use only the leaves. I pull off the quantity of leaves I need and wash them in two or three changes of cold water. I then spread them out loosely on paper towels. I roll up the towels and press the moisture out. The parsley must be dry before you chop it or it will turn to pulp, which cannot be sautéed. You can chop it immediately or put it, still wrapped in the paper towel, in a plastic bag and store it in the vegetable drawer of the refrigerator where it will keep fresh for 3 or 4 days.

Peppers

There are two approaches to peeling peppers, one is charring the skin off over direct fire or in the oven, the other is skinning them raw with a vegetable peeler. If, like my mother, I should live to be 101 I would still be frustrated by how difficult it is to persuade other cooks that the two methods are not interchangeable and that there are well-grounded reasons for choosing the first one sometimes and at other times the second.

When the skin is charred off a bell pepper, the flesh becomes partly softened and releases moisture. If you are sautéing peppers for a pasta sauce or as the flavor base of a risotto, they must be peeled and they must be raw dry. They must be peeled because the skin is bitter and interferes with the extraction of the peppers' sweetness. They must be raw dry otherwise the sautéing—the process of *insaporire*, making tasty, that is described on page 15—cannot be carried out fully. You cannot sauté moisture. In those dishes where the peppers are not sautéed, but braised or baked, the charred skin method is acceptable, although I find it is a great deal faster to skin them raw with a peeler.

CHARRED-SKIN PEELING

✦ If you are planning instead to use the peppers without any additional cooking as an appetizer or in a sandwich, char them over or under direct heat, on a gas burner or in a broiler. Direct heat scorches the skin quickly and the peppers' flesh stays firm. In an oven the pepper becomes limp, which is not a problem if it is going to be baked or braised afterward.

✦ When the pepper is over the gas or right under the live flame of the broiler, check it frequently. Just as soon as one part of its skin is blackened, turn it; continue to do so until it has been blackened all over. Stand it on end, then, to char first one end, then the other.

✦ Place the hot, charred pepper in a plastic bag and close it tight. As soon as the pepper feels cool enough to handle, remove it from the bag and pull all the skin off, bit by bit.

✦ Split the pepper, remove the stem, seeds, and pithy core. If you are going to use it as an appetizer or in a sandwich, lay it flat in a deep dish, sprinkle lightly with salt, and drizzle with olive oil.

PEELING PEPPERS RAW

✦ Cut the pepper lengthwise along its creases. Remove the stem, seeds and pithy white core.

✦ Use a swivel-blade vegetable peeler to remove the skin. Employ a very light touch, moving the peeler from side to side in a seesaw motion as you skim it over the skin.

Potatoes

For roast or fried potatoes, potatoes in a stew, a braise, a soup, or a dish of baked vegetables, the skin comes off. Then I wash the cut potatoes in cold water to remove the gummy surface starch. If I am not ready to use them immediately, I let them soak in a bowl of cold water to prevent their discoloring. For boiled potatoes, the skin stays on. Potatoes boiled disrobed of their skin become leathery.

Rapini

The stems of the vegetable Italians call *cime di rapa* are, like broccoli stalks, tender within, but sheathed by a hard-to-chew bitter rind. Peel it away from all but the spindliest stalks, then wash the vegetable in several changes of water.

Tomatoes

TO USE THEM RAW FOR A SALAD I peel them with a swivel-blade vegetable peeler. Peeled tomatoes taste riper and are more digestible. Depending on the salad, I either slice them or cut them into very irregular wedges. A perfectly ripened tomato has a more luscious feel when it is cut into meaty lumps rather than sliced. Slices are more attractive and they are the traditional cut for a Caprese salad of tomatoes, mozzarella, and basil.

PEELING THEM FOR COOKING If I am making a dish for which the tomatoes have to cook down a long time and it doesn't matter how mashed up and runny they may be at the start, I drop them into a pot of boiling water and I let them cook until I see the skin coming loose. Then I drain them, let them cool off, and finish peeling them.

When I need the tomatoes to be fairly firm and to cook down rather sooner than later, I cut a little cross with the point of a sharp knife at the stem end, where they used to be attached to the vine. I drop them into boiling water, wait for the water to return to a boil, and if the tomatoes are on the soft, ripe side, I count to 12 before draining them. If they are slightly underripe and very firm, I add another 4 seconds. As soon as they are cool enough to handle comfortably, I pull off the peel. If I am looking for really sweet tomato taste, I split the tomato and scoop out the seeds. I never crush it or pulp it because I don't want to break down its consistency.

If my sauce calls for the tomatoes to be sautéed briskly and briefly, I use plum tomatoes that are both ripe and firm. I skin them with a swivel-blade vegetable peeler to preserve their compactness, then cut them into wedges and gently pick out their seeds. I cook them in a skillet in very hot oil over high heat so that the flesh retains much of its firmness. A tomato sauce that is made this way would be described in Italy as *al filetto di pomodoro,* with tomato fillets.

Zucchini

No matter the method by which I may be cooking zucchini, I first always soak the vegetable in cold water, for 20 to 30 minutes, to loosen any grit embedded in its tender skin. Afterward I rinse it under cold running water. If it should still feel grainy to the touch, I might just rub it with a coarse cleaning cloth, or even scrape it lightly with a knife

A boiled zucchini or two is invariably included in one of the great, pure Italian salads, a salad of mixed cooked vegetables that is seasoned with sea salt, red wine vinegar, olive oil, and cracked black pepper. To boil zucchini, I cook them whole after I have soaked and rinsed them. I do not trim their ends because they would absorb water if cut and then become sodden.

For all other preparations—sautés, braises, stews, or for frying—I trim both ends off after their obligatory soak, and then cut or slice the zucchini as the recipe instructs me.

Pecorino Cheese

Along with olive oil and wine, Pecorino cheese reaches the deepest place in the collective food consciousness of the peoples of the eastern Mediterranean, the sea into which Italy pokes its toe. Pecorino comes from the Italian word for sheep, *pecora*. It is an animal whose domestication antedates Christianity by millennia and whose husbandry has inspired some of the most affecting metaphors in Christian liturgy, such as one may find in the Agnus Dei prayer and in Psalm 23, which begins, "The Lord is my Shepherd."

Cheese is milk, rennet, and salt. To these fundamentals, Pecorino adds one more element, the open sky. Unlike other farm animals, sheep do not submit to incarceration. They live out their lives neither in pens nor in barns, but in the open where they graze. Of all foods, milk may be the one that is most expressive of the conditions wherein it is engendered. Ewe's milk speaks to us of the grasses, the weeds, the scrub, and the wildflowers that its producer crops, of the air that it breathes, of the valleys and meadows where it roams. That the taste of Pecorino is deeper and fuller than that of any cow's milk or goat's milk cheese of comparable maturity can be explained by its substantially richer composition. Sheep's milk outstrips every other in its protein content, in particular, in a protein called casein. The word casein comes from the Latin *caseus*, from which comes the oldest Italian word for cheese, *cacio*. It is also the ultimate root of the English word cheese, as well as of the Italian word for cheesemaker, *casaro*. Casein is the very substance of cheese and because Pecorino has so much of it, one might say that it is the cheesiest of cheeses. You sense it in its tactile thrust, in the satisfyingly viscous grip that it lays on the palate.

There are other ways in which Pecorino differs from cow's milk cheese. It is a strictly seasonal product. A cow's milk is collected every day of the year, while the ewe parts with hers only when she is not feeding a newborn, a period that usually goes from fall to spring. With the exception of a cream cheese such as mascarpone, cow's milk cheese is made partly or wholly from skim milk. Pecorino is always made from whole milk.

The Three Stages of Pecorino—Soft, Firm, and Hard

✦ Soft Pecorino—*molle* in Italian—comes in a small, flattish, cylindrical shape called *caciotta* that rarely weighs as much as four pounds, often considerably less. The cheese undergoes the briefest aging of any Pecorino, between two and six weeks, and is salted very lightly. Its moist, simple flavor is mild and sweetly milky. Most famous are the *caciotte* of central Italy, from Tuscany and the Marches, but there is richer taste in the ones from Piedmont, where they are called *tume,* of which the best-known example is the *tuma di Murazzano.*

✦ In the firm Pecorino category, dry cheese that may have been aged four to six months, we find some of Italy's most hallowed and exciting table cheeses. Pecorino di Pienza, Formaggio di Fossa, Fiore Sardo, Pecorino di Crotone, Pecorino del Sannio, Canestrato Siciliano, and Pecorino Abruzzese di Campo Imperatore are some of the more prominent names among those of the several score of firm cheeses from as many different sites throughout Italy. The variability in the traditions and techniques by which each Pecorino is produced and the precisely articulated character of the habitat it represents endow each cheese with its own separate and unmistakable style. At the same time they all share in the fundamental tasting dynamics of Pecorino: its spiciness, its adhesive impact on the palate, its steadily expanding deployment of flavor, its ability to find and fill every one of the mouth's secret places, its seemingly everlasting finish.

✦ Pecorino becomes a hard cheese suitable for grating when it has lost most of its moisture through a period of maturation that may last eight months or even more than a year. The best-known example is Pecorino Romano, Italy's oldest cheese, produced in Rome since pre-Christian times. Romano was originally a product of the Roman countryside but today most of it comes from Sardinia. The producer Locatelli has become so familiar a name that it is almost synonymous with Romano, but there are better makers around, foremost among them one still working in the Roman *campagna,* Sini Fulvi. Eighty to ninety percent of Romano's output is exported to the United States and Canada, a taste legacy that we owe to Italian-American cooking. Chalky white and crumbly, Romano addresses the palate with what to me is excessive bluntness. There are hard Pecorinos that that have a more nuanced spectrum of flavors, such as, for example, Fiore Sardo *stagionato.*

No hard Pecorino should be thought of as interchangeable with Parmigiano-Reggiano, the monarch of Italian cow's milk cheeses. A chunk of three-year-old Parmigiano-Reggiano is one of the necessary staples of an Italian kitchen and when it is called for you want nothing else. A hard Pecorino, such as Romano or Fiore Sardo, has a more limited, but nonetheless important role. Macaroni pasta tossed with olive oil-based sauces made with such vegetables as broccoli, rapini, or cauliflower, may or may not need grated cheese, but if it does a hard Pecorino is the one to choose. It is indispensable to an *amatriciana* sauce and a little of it must go into pesto as well, although there it must be paired with Parmigiano-Reggiano. Where a hard Pecorino really triumphs is with some seafood dishes, particularly with clam and fish soups where I would never use Parmesan cheese.

✦ *Aging terms* You may come across such terms as *fresco, maturo, stagionato. Fresco* means young, which indicates the cheese will be soft and moist. *Maturo*—mature—is quite firm and possibly grating hard. *Stagionato,* equivalent to seasoned in the sense of periods of time having gone by, usually applies to a hard cheese, but it may also be a very firm one still suitable as table cheese.

D.O.P., The Italian Food Appellations

D.O.P stands for Denominazione di Origine Protetta. It means that the production of an ingredient such as cheese or olive oil that has been listed by the law is controlled and protected as to its methods and place of origin. The intention of the law is a noble one inasmuch as it is intended to protect and guarantee the pedigree of Italy's traditional food products. Like a similar law for wine, however, it has cast too broad a net for it to be fully effective, being more inclusive than exclusive. The names of the sheep's milk cheeses that have so far been gathered under the D.O.P. umbrella are Canestrato Pugliese, Caciotta d'Urbino, Fiore Sardo, Murazzano, Pecorino Romano, Pecorino Sardo, Pecorino Siciliano, Pecorino Toscano. Over time more names are to be added.

Pecorino at Table

Honey has been from very early times one of the most congenial matches for Pecorino cheese. If you can bring together a moderately firm Sardinian Pecorino with one of the island's peerless honeys such as those produced by Leccu Manias you may not be tempted by any other coupling. Fresh fruit has always been recognized as a natural accompaniment to cheese, and it is probably better with Pecorino than with any other kind. In Italy the preferred fruit is a juicy, ripe pear and there is a rhyme that goes with it: *Al contadino non far sapere quant'è buono il pecorino con le pere.* Translation: Don't let your farmer discover how delicious Pecorino is with pears. It harks back to the old days of sharecropping, when a landowner and a farmer on his land had conflicting views on what constituted the other's just portion. A tiny dollop of a slightly bitter or spicy jam such as bitter orange or onion marmalade is also a combination well worth trying.

Firm or even some hard Pecorinos are delicious when drizzled with fruity olive oil and topped with cracked black pepper. In the spring, when sweet, young fava beans first arrive in the market, they are shelled and served with slivers of very firm or hard Pecorino that may, or may not, have been drizzled with olive oil.

Sources

It is gratifying to see how the availability of Pecorino cheese, which until not too long ago was dominated almost exclusively by Romano, has expanded to include many of Italy's tastiest examples. Even if your neighborhood specialty food shop does not carry a good selection of these cheeses, there are mail-order houses and Web sites that do, some of which are listed in the Appendix.

The Kitchen I Live In

During my adult life, and specifically after my marriage, I have spent an unusually large proportion of time in kitchens. My food career has had something to do with that, of course, but only to a degree. I have cooked very nearly all the meals my family has eaten, whether or not I was teaching or working on recipes for a cookbook, and even whether or not we were at home, as long as I had the use of a kitchen. Moreover, my mind is so often engaged in speculations on flavor that I seem to inhabit the kitchen even when I am not in it. Designing and building a kitchen is a process I have gone through seven times, often enough that it has felt like a secondary, albeit unremunerated, career.

The space configurations within Venetian dwellings, most of which are between 400 and 600 years old, are frozen by law to safeguard their historical character. It means that you cannot tear down walls and alter rooms at will. In the apartment of our 500-year-old house in Venice we could not enlarge the kitchen to accommodate all of the cooking and dining paraphernalia, so we created space for the overflow in a narrow but skylit cubicle at the opposite end of the hall that we called the miracle room. When we had drawn up the list of the things we wanted to put in there—in addition to cupboards and equipment, we included laundry facilities, several wardrobes, a linen closet, storage for the floor polisher and other large appliances, and a vanishing spare bed—our architect exclaimed, "You don't want a storeroom, you want a miracle!" Entering the miracle room was one of the favorite stops for my students when we showed them the apartment's various sights. I invite you now to enter another miracle room, this time in Florida, a room that was once dreary and inhospitable to work in and that has since been transformed into the most efficient and comfortable kitchen I have ever had.

It is neither the smallest or largest kitchen I have owned. The smallest was in the compact eighteenth-century attic apartment we had in Bologna, close to where my school was located. It had been carved out from under the roof beams and the space allotted to cooking was so small that there was just enough room for one solidly built person, me, to turn either to the left or to the right. If I backed away more than a couple of steps I was out of the kitchen. There was room for only the absolutely indispensable in equipment and ingredients, but I could reach everything I needed practically without having to move, which is the great advantage of tight cooking quarters. My largest kitchen was also in Bologna. It was my school kitchen where we accommodated as many as twenty-eight students and several assistants. In addition to a dining room with four tables for eight, we had over 1,000 square feet of working space, but even so, when a full class would press around me at the stove, I had moments of claustrophobia.

I work alone now, with no assistants except for my always willing, if occasionally contentious husband. The kitchen is in a condominium on an island off Florida's west coast. It overlooks our building's well-groomed grounds, several species of palms, and beyond them the wild vegetation of a white beach, sea oats, sea grasses, sea grapes, and beyond the beach the usually languid waters of the Gulf of Mexico, sometimes parted by the rising and dipping of a dolphin's back. Had the kitchen faced a dark, inside courtyard I might not have been prompted to do anything about it. However, it did have that glorious view, but the stove was backed against a wall. Here is something I cannot understand about most of the kitchens I have seen: why, when you could have before you the colors, the light, the variety of life of a natural or urban landscape, must you cook turned to a wall, as though you were doing penance?

Once we decided the stove had to go, the whole kitchen went, cabinets, sinks, appliances, floor, wallpaper, lighting, everything except the inalterable structure of the room. When my husband and I, together with our consultant, Deborah Krasner—who flew down to Florida from Vermont—sat down to draft the design of the kitchen-to-be, the first order of business was to create a peninsula for the cook top, so that whenever I looked up from my skillet, I could see the beach and the Gulf. To my everlasting regret, gas is not available in our building, so we had to install electric burners. We chose an exceptionally responsive yet compact ceramic cook top, in fact we took two of them, laying them side to side. In that narrow peninsula I now have six burners of different diameters and a lava-stone grill on which I can grill everything from peppers to two-inch-thick beefsteaks for *tagliata* to a side of salmon.

Like most Italian cooks, I do nearly everything, including roasts, on top of the stove. It is an active style of cooking whose fumes need a hood to convey them to the exhaust duct that will carry them out of the room. Unfortunately, even the most stylish of modern hoods is an encumbrance, blocking light and eating up space. Rather than settling for such an awkward apparatus, we borrowed an idea that we had originally developed in the apartment we had in Venice, whose kitchen ceiling was supported by magnificent hand-hewn sixteenth-century beams. There, to avoid covering up the beams, we had designed a totally transparent hood made of plate glass panels. Now there is another one over the Florida cook top, a sparkling plate glass pyramid whose openmouthed bottom engulfs and disposes of all my grilling and sautéing fumes.

In the peninsula under the cook top there are steel-lined shelves on which I can rest a pan that needs to be taken off the heat or keep dirty pots out of sight until they can be washed. Below those shelves there are vertical dividers for stowing both large and small pot lids. To the end of the peninsula that projects into the kitchen we added a rounded steel drop-leaf shelf that snaps up flush with the cook top when extra workspace is required at that station. The oven is nearby, installed under the counter so that the baking preparations can be performed right above it on the countertop.

The kitchen had originally been equipped with a double-door side-by-side refrigerator-freezer of monstrous and useless size. We gave that one away and replaced it with a much smaller unit, a refrigerator with a freezer drawer and icemaker at its base. I use the freezer for ice cubes, homemade meat broth, an occasional soup, gelato and, because you never know when someone might send you fresh caviar, a bottle of vodka. The refrigerator itself has shelves wide enough to accommodate a pan of lasagne, but it is not colossal, which suits me because I prefer frequent marketing to long-term food storage.

I wonder if mine is the only kitchen left in America without a microwave. I gave away the one I found. It doesn't take me that long to reheat things the old-fashioned way, over the stove, and not only do I have so much better control, I am persuaded that flavors come through better, having suffered less perceptible alterations than they do when bombarded by those waves. I enjoy, moreover, getting a whiff of what's cooking.

I eliminated the garbage disposal for reasons both aesthetic and practical. I use the sinks to make things clean, not as a catch-all for garbage. Also gone are a soap dispenser and an instant boiling water faucet. I have two deep undermounted stainless steel sinks whose drain holes are set back so that the space underneath is almost wholly unencumbered. In the space that would have been occupied by centered drainage pipes, the garbage disposal, and the other unlamented gadgets we disposed of are now two pull-out perforated steel bins, one under each sink. One is to keep tomatoes at room temperature until they are ripe enough to use, and the other is for root vegetables.

In my last kitchen, in Venice, the cabinets were faced in Venetian sand-speckled, waxed plaster, matching the walls. There are no walls visible in the Florida kitchen. The cabinets go all the way to the ceiling and the space between them and the counters is entirely covered by a backsplash of the same granite that was laid on the counters. It is a South American stone, *juperana colombo,* whose broad swirls of ochre, sand, and blue-gray evoke the colors and undulations of the beach and sea just outside.

I have several drawers, but there are many tools that I don't want to have to hunt for when I am cooking: spatulas, long spoons, long forks, ladles, measuring spoons, tongs, Microplane graters, strainers, pastry brushes, very small skillets, among others. They are all organized according to their function and they hang in full sight along a long rod mounted at the top of the backsplash on the cook top and oven side of the kitchen.

The cabinets are American-made by the Wood Mode company, constructed without ornamentation in plain, golden American maple. The doors of the upper cabinets are of opaque glass framed also in maple. They slide so that they open without intruding into the kitchen's air space or colliding with one's head. The lower cabinets are all pullout drawers of various depths designed to contain items as disparate as spare dish towels and large stockpots. At their base, where most cabinets usually rest on a recessed toe kick faced by a fixed panel, mine have broad, shallow drawers that are ideal for stowing large items such as platters and baking pans. There are several vertical openings where we have inserted pullout bars for towels and pot holders or vertical dividers for cutting boards and trays. Because I like to do as much of my prepping as possible sitting down, I have a butcher block table that, when I am not using it, disappears into a cabinet so as not to impinge on the kitchen's limited floor space. It pulls out at the end of the kitchen by the terrace, one more workplace from which I can look up and enjoy the view of the Gulf. The garbage can fits into a maple cart that wheels in and out of its "garage" so that I can roll it close to me at the prepping table or to wherever else I am working.

The gifted and industrious crew who built this kitchen is American. The materials are American. It enjoys one of America's loveliest views. But the way my new American kitchen puts its space to work reminds me of another site and another time. When I contemplate how it exploits every usable flat and cubic inch within it, I think, "We have done all of this before." Where we did it was in the apartment that I lived in for two decades before I came to Longboat Key. It was on a different island, a very much smaller one, where space was so hemmed in by water that it became too precious for any part of it to be wasted. That island was one of the many that are strung together to form the ancient, sea-battered jewel that I once called home, my town, my Venice.

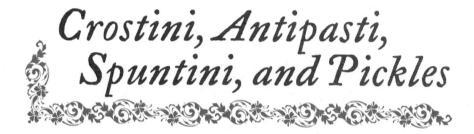

Crostini, Antipasti, Spuntini, and Pickles

I Crostini

What dips are to the American cocktail hour, crostini are to the Italian table. As in those shows where someone appears on the stage to warm up the audience before the star comes on, crostini keep the palate entertained while it waits for the main courses to arrive. Crostini may also be served as a snack during the long interval between lunch, which in Italy is the main meal of the day, and dinner, which in some parts of the country may not start before 9 P.M. That snack is called *merenda,* and it is usually intended to pacify the active metabolism of young children. Italian children also have a mid-morning *merenda,* consisting of a piece of focaccia or a small prosciutto sandwich or biscotti that they take to school to help them bridge the gap between next-to-no-breakfast and late lunch.

The word *crostini* means small crusts of bread, and a slice of grilled or toasted bread provides the foundation for all crostini. The topping can be a raw or cooked vegetable, cheese, or any other savory product that can be spread on the bread or otherwise rest securely on it so that the crostini can be maneuvered safely from hand to mouth. All of the crostini below satisfy this description. The practice of serving tidbits before dinner along with a glass of wine or other light aperitif has infiltrated Italian custom, and crostini are admirably suited to that purpose. All of the ones that follow below can also be served at table as appetizers.

Crostini may also be Soup Croutons, for which there is a recipe on page 112.

Victor's Parmesan and Olive Oil Crostino

❧ *La Merenda di Victor*

When my husband was a schoolboy in Bologna, his favorite afternoon merenda was a crusty slice of grilled bread that his grandmother would top with Parmesan cheese and olive oil. It doesn't need a recipe, just a description:

✦ Cut slices from very good, crusty white bread. Grill them to a light brown.

✦ Place the slices on a plate or a tray, keeping one or two aside.

✦ Blanket thickly with freshly grated Parmigiano-Reggiano cheese, letting some cheese drop onto the plate or tray.

✦ Pour enough olive oil over the cheese to soak it thoroughly, letting some oil spill onto the plate or tray.

✦ When you have eaten the cheese and oil crostini, use the reserved slices to wipe the plate or tray clean. These may taste even better than the first.

Your fingers will get sticky handling this. Italian children lick theirs clean.

RAPINI AND PECORINO CHEESE SPREAD FOR CROSTINI
⌁ Crostini di Cime di Rapa e Pecorino

1 cup rapini leaves and florets, no stems (For more information, see page 79 of The Why and How of Prepping Vegetables.)

Fine sea salt

1 tablespoon extra virgin olive oil

1 teaspoon garlic, chopped very fine

2 tablespoons grated Pecorino Romano or other sheep's milk grating cheese

Black pepper ground fresh from the mill

16 small slices from a narrow baguette-style loaf or 4 slices very thin white toasting bread

YIELD: *16 crostini*

1 Wash the rapini in cold water. Bring a pot of water to a boil, add salt, and when the water returns to a brisk boil, drop in the rapini. Cook until quite tender, drain, and as soon as you are able to handle it, squeeze to force out as much water as possible.

> *Marcella Says:* **Do not be tempted to skip this blanching step and proceed directly to the sautéing. Like other greens that are to be sautéed in olive oil, rapini will cook more completely and taste sweeter if blanched first.**

2 Pour the oil into a small skillet, add the garlic, turn the heat on to medium, and cook the garlic, stirring it from time to time, until it becomes colored a pale blond. Add the rapini and cook for 1 minute, turning the vegetable over a few times to coat it well.

3 Transfer the rapini to a cutting surface and chop it as fine as possible. Put it in a bowl and add the cheese and several grindings of black pepper.

4 If you are using the baguette-style bread, grill the slices lightly or toast them in the oven. If you are using the thin white bread, toast it medium dark, trim away the crusts, and cut each slice in four. Spread the rapini mixture over the toasts and serve at once.

Avocado and Parmesan Crostini

꒰ Crostini di Avocado e Parmigiano

4 tablespoons diced peeled ripe avocado

Fine sea salt

1 teaspoon freshly squeezed lemon juice

Black pepper ground fresh from the mill

3 tablespoons freshly grated Parmigiano-Reggiano cheese

2 tablespoons extra virgin olive oil

8 thin slices good white bread

YIELD: *8 crostini*

1 Put the avocado in a small bowl with all of the remaining ingredients except for the bread, and use a fork to mash them to a creamy and uniform consistency.

2 Toast the bread and cut it into 2-inch squares.

3 When ready to serve, spread the avocado mixture over the toasted bread squares.

AHEAD-OF-TIME NOTE: You can prepare the avocado and Parmesan a few hours before serving, preferably keeping it at normal room temperature so that it will be both more spreadable and flavorful.

Baked Mozzarella, Tomato, Capers, and Parmesan Crostini

Crostini al Forno di Mozzarella, Pomodoro, Capperi, e Parmigiano

8 slices (each ½ inch thick) from a baguette-style loaf

3 tablespoons extra virgin olive oil

2 ripe, firm, round tomatoes, each about the size of an apple

8 thin slices mozzarella

3 tablespoons capers, preferably the small nonpareils, drained and rinsed in cold water if packed in vinegar, OR if packed in salt, rinsed, soaked in cold water for 10 minutes, then rinsed again

8 teaspoons freshly grated Parmigiano-Reggiano cheese

YIELD: *8 crostini*

1 Turn the oven on to 550°.

2 Lightly toast the bread.

3 Drizzle just a few drops of olive oil on each slice of bread.

4 Skin the raw tomatoes with a swivel-blade vegetable peeler, then cut each one into 4 round slices that should be no thicker than ⅓ inch.

5 Cover each slice of bread with a slice of mozzarella.

Marcella Says: **You should not need salt, but some mozzarella producers put next to no salt in their cheese. Taste the one you are using. If it is very insipid, sprinkle a tiny pinch of salt over it.**

6 Distribute the capers over the mozzarella, 8 or so if they are tiny, 5 or 6 if they are larger.

7 Top with a slice of tomato.

AHEAD-OF-TIME NOTE: You can prepare the crostini up to this point 2 to 3 hours in advance.

8 Sprinkle 1 teaspoon of grated Parmesan over each crostini.

9 Put the crostini on a baking sheet and place in the preheated oven for just a few minutes. They are ready when the mozzarella melts. Serve piping hot.

SARDINIAN MULLET ROE CROSTINI
Crostini di Bottarga di Muggine

Sardinian bottarga is the pressed and dried roe of a particular variety of gray mullet—*muggine*—caught in the brackish waters of a large pond on the western coast of the island. The roe has a penetrating flavor that is like nothing else coming from the Italian pantry, sweetish yet densely briny. It makes an irresistible appetizer when sliced paper thin and placed between two shards of Sardinian sheet music bread that is slathered thickly with soft sweet butter. The genuine article from Sardinia is, after white truffles and traditional aged balsamic vinegar, one of the most expensive of Italian food products. It is becoming available in some food stores that stock high-end Italian products, but if it is not sold where you shop, it is obtainable from online sources, some of which are listed in the Appendix. It is possible to buy grated bottarga, which has a sharper flavor and more limited use than the whole roe.

Mullet *bottarga* is made elsewhere besides Sardinia. Excellent *bottarga* is made in Turkey, and while it doesn't quite scale the peaks of flavor of the Sardinian version, its price stops considerably short of the other's lofty height. In Sicily, *bottarga* is made from tuna roe. It is relatively inexpensive and it is certainly tasty but compared with mullet *bottarga*, its flavor is blunter, single-faceted.

1 ounce very thin slices Sardinian mullet *bottarga*

Sardinian sheet music bread, *carta musica,* or 8 unsalted fine-quality crackers

> *Marcella Says:* **The wafer bread that Sardinian women bake from semolina flour and that they call sheet music is occasionally available from stores or Web sites specializing in Italian foods. One source is listed in the Appendix. If you want to make it yourself—and it is such delicious bread with so many uses that you may well enjoy trying it—my recipe for it is in *Marcella Cucina,* my preceding book.**

3 tablespoons unsalted butter, softened at room temperature

YIELD: *8 crostini*

1   Turn on the oven to 300°.

2   Sardinian mullet *bottarga* is vacuum-packed in little plastic bags, while mullet *bottarga* from Turkey or other sources is encased in paraffin. The natural membrane of the roe's sac still adheres to it. It isn't difficult to pry it off before slicing and I prefer to do it, although it is not indispensable. To strip it away, slip the point of a sharp thin knife under the membrane and, grasping it between your thumb and the flat of the knife, pull it off. It won't all come away in one piece, so you will have to repeat the procedure a few times. If the roe is encased in paraffin, you must chip it completely away before slicing the *bottarga.* Slice the *bottarga* into thin, thin strips using a swivel-blade vegetable peeler, a truffle slicer, or a thin but very sharp knife. Do not discard the crumbs. Divide the *bottarga* into eight parts, crumbs included.

3   Place a couple of large pieces of the sheet music bread or the 8 crackers on a baking sheet and place in the preheated oven. Toast for 5 minutes. Watch the sheet music bread to make sure it doesn't become too dark.

4   If you are using sheet music bread, break it up into 16 irregular pieces, each about 2 inches long and wide. Spread butter over 8 of the pieces. Cover each with 1 part of the *bottarga.* Top it with another piece of sheet music bread. If you are using crackers, use just one cracker for each crostino, buttering it and topping it with *bottarga.* Serve within 1 hour of assembling.

BOTTARGA AND ARUGULA SALAD

🐚 *Insalata di Bottarga e Rucola*

¼ pound arugula, about 8 cups

> *Marcella Says:* In its wild state, arugula is pungent and richly nutty, precisely the qualities required to keep up with the exuberant taste of *bottarga*. The common limp, round-leafed variety of arugula that I find in the markets here has had all its pungency and most of its nuttiness bred right out of it. But there is some good news. Arugula grown—sometimes hydroponically—from seeds of the wild Italian *rucola* has begun to make its appearance. Its leaves, while larger than those of wild *rucola,* are similarly firm and sharply pointed and its flavor, while somewhat tamer, is considerably feistier than what we have been getting heretofore. I strongly urge you to search for it, not just for this *bottarga* salad, but for the potent boost it can give to the flavor of other salads.

A pinch of fine sea salt

2 tablespoons freshly squeezed lemon juice

5 tablespoons olive oil

> *Marcella Says:* To some, 5 tablespoons may sound like a lot of olive oil. Believe me, no less will accomplish the flavor potential of this salad.

Black pepper ground fresh from the mill

¼ pound *bottarga,* sliced very thin, as described on page 96 of the preceding recipe, about ⅔ cup

For 4 persons

1 Detach the longest and thickest stems of the arugula and discard them. Soak the arugula in a basin of cold water for about 15 minutes, retrieve it, rinse it, and either spin it dry or pat it dry gently in a clean dish towel.

2 Put the arugula in a bowl and toss it with a pinch of salt, the lemon juice, olive oil, and liberal grindings of black pepper.

3 Distribute the tossed green among 4 individual salad plates and scatter the *bottarga* slices over it.

Baked Squash and Parmesan Cheese Pudding
Tortino di Zucca

There are many wonderful Italian dishes with squash, but I had held back from working with them in my classes or for the cookbooks because they usually call for *zucca barucca*, an orange-fleshed pumpkin of exceptional sweetness and silky texture that I have never seen outside of Italy. After looking for but never finding an American equivalent for *zucca barucca*, I resigned myself to keeping my squash recipes in the drawer. When I moved to Florida, my son, who lives here, urged me to try butternut squash. I did and I am glad of it. It may not be quite as flavorful as *zucca barucca*, but it is very similar to an excellent Neapolitan squash that can be exceptionally versatile. In this book you'll find butternut squash used in four radically different ways, in the appetizer below, in a soup with rapini on page 120, in a risotto with leeks and clams, page 143, and in a luscious baked Neapolitan dessert with raisins and pine nuts on page 362.

This very simple little pudding is one of the tastiest dishes I have made with the squash. The recipe has landed here among the antipasti because it provides such an encouraging way to start a meal, and in addition, it lends itself to smart presentations. I hope, however, that when you are serving meat or chicken you will try it as a tasteful alternative to potatoes.

1 medium butternut squash, about 1 pound or slightly more

½ cup freshly grated Parmigiano-Reggiano cheese

1 egg

1 teaspoon fine sea salt

Black pepper ground fresh from the mill

3 tablespoons butter softened at room temperature plus additional for greasing the ramekins

¼ teaspoon freshly grated nutmeg

4 5-ounce ramekins

2 tablespoons fine, dry, unflavored bread crumbs

For 4 persons

1 Turn on the oven to 400°.

2 Put the squash in a baking dish and, when the oven reaches the preset temperature, put it in the oven. After 1 hour remove it from the oven, but do not turn off the oven. Split the squash in half lengthwise, and use a spoon to scoop away and discard the seeds and strings. Scoop out the pulp. There should be about 1 cup.

3 Put the pulp, the grated Parmesan, the egg, salt, black pepper, 2 tablespoons of softened butter, and the nutmeg in the large bowl of a food processor. Run the blade just long enough to produce a homogenous but not overly creamy mixture.

4 Thickly grease the inside of the ramekins with butter and sprinkle about half of the bread crumbs over the butter.

5 Divide the squash mixture equally among the ramekins. Sprinkle the remaining bread crumbs on top, then dot with the remaining tablespoon of butter, cut into 4 pieces.

6 Bake in the still-hot oven for 20 minutes. Let the ramekins rest for 6 minutes after you remove them from the oven. Turn each ramekin over onto a separate plate and give it a little shake to loosen the pudding, letting it drop onto the plate.

AHEAD-OF-TIME NOTE: You can serve this *tortino* while it is still warm, or several hours later at room temperature.

A Suggested Mode of Presentation

You can dream up your own way to dress up the *tortino* should you want it to launch your dinner on a slightly formal note. When I do this, while looking for an aesthetically pleasing solution, I try to bear in mind the flavor values that are involved. I find that the naturally sweet taste of the squash benefits from a sprightly contrast with elements that are moderately bitter and sour. In the presentation suggested below, Belgian endive contributes a slight touch of bitterness and the tomatoes or olives some tartness.

> *For 4 tortini*
>
> 2 plump Belgian endive
>
> Fine sea salt
>
> 1 tablespoon extra virgin olive oil
>
> ½ tablespoon wine vinegar
>
> Black pepper ground fresh from the mill
>
> 6 grape tomatoes OR 8 Greek olives

✦ Trim off the butt end of the endives, wash the heads in cold water, and cut them across—not lengthwise—into strips as thin as possible. Put them in a small bowl and toss with salt, the olive oil, wine vinegar, and black pepper.

✦ If you are using grape tomatoes, slice them in half. Set aside half of the cut tomatoes and slice the remaining halves into thin strips. If you are using olives, leave 4 of them whole, pit the other 4, then cut them into thin slices.

✦ Place each *tortino* on an individual appetizer or salad plate. Ring each with the tossed endive strips. If you are using tomatoes, top the center of each *tortino* with a tomato half so that it looks like a little red button or cupola, and distribute the sliced tomatoes over the endive. If you are using olives, gently nudge one whole olive into the *tortino,* centering it on the top, and scatter the olive slices over the endive.

BREAST OF CHICKEN PÂTÉ WITH BLACK OLIVES
๑ *Paté di Petto di Pollo e Olive Nere*

This paté makes a crostino with greater delicacy and finesse than the familiar Tuscan crostino with chicken livers. Spread it over warm, grilled rounds or squares of bread, or use it in a salad, cutting it into strips, arranging them over shredded greens and garnishing with halved cherry tomatoes or wedges of hard-boiled eggs.

1 small carrot, peeled

¼ of a medium onion

1 celery stalk

1 pound skinless boneless chicken breast

Fine sea salt

6 ounces black Greek olives, about 30 olives

1 tablespoon extra virgin olive oil

4 tablespoons butter softened at room temperature

½ teaspoon freshly grated nutmeg

The grated peel of 1 medium lemon, the outer yellow layer only with none of the bitter white pith beneath

Black pepper ground fresh from the mill

YIELD: *About 12 portions*

1 Pour 3 cups of water into a saucepan, add the carrot, onion quarter, and celery stalk, and bring to a boil.

2 Trim the chicken breast clean of any bits of skin and fat and drop it into the pot with 1 teaspoon salt. Cook over moderate heat at a slow boil for 10 minutes, then retrieve the breast with a slotted spoon or with tongs and make an incision in the thickest part of it to see whether it is fully cooked or still slightly raw. In the latter case return it to the pot and cook at a leisurely boil for another 3 or 4 minutes. Remove the breast and set it aside to cool, but do not discard the broth it has produced although you won't be using for this recipe.

> *Marcella Says:* **To keep the chicken broth for future use in a soup or in making risotto, fill ice cube trays with it and freeze it. When frozen solid, unmold the cubes and store them in the freezer in plastic bags with an airtight zipper closure.**

3 Pit the olives, put them in the bowl of a food processor with the olive oil, and process to a creamy consistency. Do not remove the olive paste from the bowl.

4 Cut the chicken breast into 1-inch pieces and add them to the processor bowl with the butter, the nutmeg, the grated lemon peel, and liberal grindings of black pepper. Process to a creamy consistency. Taste and correct for salt.

5 Scoop the mixture out of the processor bowl and onto a plate, and mold it into a thin brick shape. Wrap with plastic film and refrigerate for at least 24 hours or no longer than 5 days.

The Versatile Frittata

When I moved from Italy to America to join my husband in New York, the Brooklyn Dodgers were playing the Yankees in the World Series and I immediately became a fan of the most beautiful of games, baseball. I stopped watching many years ago when we moved back to Italy, but I seem to remember that there was a type of player called the utility infielder, adept at playing various positions. I think of the frittata as the utility course of the Italian menu, adept at filling many blanks. I want something colorful and easy to handle and really tasty to offer guests with drinks? Give them frittatas sliced into little squares. I am hosting a major dinner party and after the first course I am ducking back into the kitchen to finish the second course, how do I help my guests bridge the interval? With a wedge or two of a frittata prepared earlier and kept at room temperature. It is hot, I had a heavy restaurant meal the previous day, I am not in the mood for pasta or meat or fish or anything equally demanding: A frittata is just right, not too much bulk and a lot of fresh flavor. What can I take to have on the plane or on a stop during a long car trip or on a picnic? Wedges of one or two different frittatas will be delicious cold on slices of good bread.

The first of the two recipes that follows illustrates the basic technique that I have employed in making all of the frittata recipes in my previous books. Grasp the simple three-part method and you can call on every appropriate combination of vegetables to produce a nearly limitless variety of frittate. The vegetables for the batter have first to be made tasty, *insaporiti,* and so you sauté them in butter or olive oil, with or without onions as the case may suggest. Add salt and pepper, and mix them with eggs and grated Parmesan cheese. Second step: Pour the batter over very hot butter in a skillet with an ovenproof handle. If you use a small skillet, you will have a thick frittata, a large skillet will produce a thin, and to my mind, finer frittata. Third step: When the frittata turns firm at its rim, place the skillet in a preheated oven. Cook just until the top sets.

Do butter and Parmesan cheese always have to go with frittata? On the whole, I would say yes, but I was curious to see if it could be done differently, which led to the second of the two recipes that follow. I took as my base for the batter some zucchini cooked as for pasta sauce— with olive oil, onion, and garlic—and when I mixed it with the eggs I added basil, as I would have done on pasta. I think I will still be making most of my frittatas with butter and cheese, but I am glad to have such an agreeable alternative available when I feel like a change.

LEEK AND SCALLION FRITTATA
⟿ *Frittata di Porri e Cipolline Verdi*

A 10- or 12-inch nonstick skillet with an ovenproof steel handle

2 tablespoons butter

1 tablespoon extra virgin olive oil

The white portions of 1 (or more) bunches of leeks, sliced into very thin strips, about 2 cups (You may want to look up Leeks on page 76 of The Why and How of Prepping Vegetables.)

The green tops from a bunch of scallions, cut into ½-inch pieces or smaller, about 1 cup

Fine sea salt

Black pepper ground fresh from the mill

3 large eggs

⅓ cup freshly grated Parmigiano-Reggiano cheese

An oven mitt or thick pot holder

For 4 persons

1 Put 1 tablespoon of the butter and the olive oil in the skillet together with the leeks and scallions and turn on the heat to medium. Cook, stirring from time to time, and when the vegetables are about halfway soft add ¼ cup of water. Continue cooking until the leeks and scallions are completely soft and the water has totally evaporated. Transfer the contents of the skillet to a bowl and add salt and pepper, turning over the vegetables to season them well.

2 Break the eggs into the bowl, add the Parmesan, and turn the contents over several times to produce a uniformly blended mixture.

AHEAD-OF-TIME NOTE: You can make the frittata batter several hours in advance up to this point. Refrigerate it, but return it to full room temperature before cooking the frittata.

3 Turn on the oven to 400°.

4 Wipe the skillet clean with paper towels. Add the remaining tablespoon of butter and turn on the heat to medium high. Give the mixture in the bowl a turn or two with a wooden spoon and when the butter has melted and its foam begins to subside pour the contents of the bowl into the skillet, leveling it with the spoon.

5 When the rim of the frittata begins to be firm, put the skillet in the preheated oven. Cook for just a few minutes, until the top is firm all over and the frittata no longer feels runny to the touch. Remove the skillet from the oven using an oven mitt or thick pot holder, and slide the frittata onto a round platter. Serve the frittata cut into wedges.

THE NO-BUTTER, NO-CHEESE ZUCCHINI AND BASIL FRITTATA
↫ *La Frittata di Zucchine Senza Burro, Senza Formaggio*

3 firm, glossy medium zucchini

A 10-inch nonstick skillet with an ovenproof steel handle

3 tablespoons extra virgin olive oil

1 cup thin-sliced onions

Fine sea salt

1 large garlic clove, peeled and sliced very thin

3 tablespoons chopped Italian flat-leaf parsley

3 extra-large eggs

Black pepper ground fresh from the mill

Fresh basil leaves, about 15 if small to medium in size, cut into fine shreds

An oven mitt or thick pot holder

For 4 persons

1   Soak the zucchini in water for about 30 minutes, scrub them with a rough cloth, slice off both ends, then slice the zucchini into very thin disks either by hand or using the food processor's slicing disk.

2   Turn on the oven to 400°.

3   Pour 2 tablespoons of the oil into the skillet, add the sliced onions and salt, and turn on the heat to low. Cook until the onion is partly done, then mix in the garlic. Continue to cook until the onion is very soft and has become colored a pale blond.

4   Add the parsley, stir once or twice, and after a minute put the zucchini in the pan. Sprinkle them with salt, turn them over to coat them well, and cook over low heat until they are fully tender and lightly browned. When the zucchini are done, empty the contents of the skillet into a medium bowl and wipe the pan clean with paper towels.

5   Break the eggs into the bowl, add generous grindings of pepper, mix thoroughly, and add the shredded basil, turning it into the frittata batter a few times.

6   Pour the remaining tablespoon of olive oil into the skillet you have just wiped clean and heat it over high heat until hot. Pour the frittata batter into the skillet and level it. Cook until the edges of the batter become firm, then slip the skillet into the preheated oven. When the top of the frittata has firmed up, remove the skillet from the oven using an oven mitt or a thick pot holder, and slide the frittata onto a serving plate.

AHEAD-OF-TIME NOTE: You may choose to serve this frittata or the preceding one immediately. Frittatas are also excellent lukewarm, or hours later, at room temperature. Or, if you wish, refrigerate it under plastic film overnight and bring to room temperature before serving the next day.

Impromptu Mustard Fruit with Mascarpone
☞ La Mostarda di Frutta Improvvisata e Mascarpone

Pickling fruit with mustard has been popular for centuries in Italy and some of the local productions have become famous for their special style. The best known is *mostarda di Cremona* from the Lombard town celebrated also for its string instruments. The fruit for it—apricots, figs, plums, small pears—is candied whole before it is pickled. Although it is produced on such a commercial scale that you can find Cremona's *mostarda* even in remote corners of the country, the makers hold on to their formulas as family secrets. Its most frequent employment is as an accompaniment to mixed boiled meats to which its combination of sugar and spice brings considerable life.

A less well known *mostarda* is produced in Vicenza, and I don't know that I have ever seen it outside of the Veneto. And it was just as well because there was never enough of it there to go around. It is made of quince jam and mustard and its peerless producer is a firm called Lazzaris. It comes on the market at the beginning of fall, when freshly harvested quince becomes available for Lazzaris to process, and it is all gone by Christmastime. At the end of summer we started to wait for its first appearance, and by the beginning of December we would begin to hoard it, hoping to make it last at least until Easter.

We used the Lazzaris quince mustard on the exquisite boiled ham they make in Parma, on *musetto*—Venice's succulent version of *cotechino*, on hot dogs, called *würstel* in Venice, but most of all we found it irresistible with mascarpone. When I was stuffing the dates for the recipe on page 372, Victor and I were reminiscing nostalgically about the Lazzaris *mostarda* when I thought, "We have mustard in the house and even some quince preserve, why not see what comes of mixing them?" And so we did. The very first try was so good that Victor said, "*Strepitosa!*" which is somewhat like saying "It's a hit!"

It was encouraging enough to warrant pursuing and I tried it with several jams and preserves. Let me tell you immediately, it doesn't work with Smucker's. It does work with those jams and preserves that are not excessively sweet and that are made, as the quince preserve Lazzaris uses is made, from very high-quality fruit. My best results came with a quince preserve by the Swiss maker Hero. Also very good were an apricot jam and a fig jam from the Pyrenees, both of them obtained online through Chef Shop (see Appendix, page 373); an English hand-cut

Seville orange marmalade, also from Chef Shop; and a marvelous Dalmatian fig jam found only at Whole Foods supermarkets. I am sure that there are others in the market that are as good and you should feel free to experiment with them. I tried a sour cherry jam that I had liked very much, but it didn't work with mustard.

> Superior-quality fruit jams or preserves (See suggestions above.)

> Good, plain mustard (I used Colman's.)

> Domestic or imported mascarpone (Italian cream cheese)

1 Measure out the amount of jam you want into a small bowl.

2 For each tablespoon of jam, add 1 teaspoon mustard. Stir with a small spoon, or even better, with a butter knife, until the jam and the mustard are uniformly mixed.

3 Spoon mascarpone into individual saucers. Add a dollop of the mustard fruit, and mix lightly. Spread on grilled or toasted bread or on unsalted crackers. Serve with Prosecco or with one of the great Italian sweet wines, such as Recioto di Soave.

Other uses for mustard fruit

As I recalled in the introduction to this recipe, instead of mixing our mustard fruit with mascarpone, we have used it alone on cold boiled ham, on *cotechino*, the warm cooked Italian sausage, and on hot dogs. It is also excellent with cold chicken or turkey. While, to my knowledge, the Lazzaris *mostarda* is not yet available in America, some other fruit mustards are, but I prefer my own "impromptu" one to the ones I have tasted.

SWEET PICKLED ONIONS

✐ *Cipolline Agrodolci*

The sharpness of most pickles, even for those who tolerate acid better than I, circumscribes their use. When I came upon these gently pickled onions, in which the vinegar's bite is softened by the fruitiness of red wine and by a modest dose of sugar, I knew I had a find. They are kinder to many more foods and enjoyable in a greater variety of contexts than almost any other pickle.

The onions are very appetizing before dinner with cheese and drinks, but they also add zest at the table to simple meat and fish dishes, such as grilled chops or steaks, roast beef, boiled short ribs, a steamed salmon or bass, or with prosciutto or other cold meats whether served on a platter or in a sandwich. They are terrific too at barbecues with hamburgers and hot dogs. Sliced into thin rounds, I use them as a change of pace from the raw onions that my husband and I like to have in most of our salads. Actually I find them so irresistible that I don't need anything to go with them. I eat them right out of the jar.

12 small onions, each the size of a walnut, approximately 1¼ inches across, about ½ pound

> *Marcella Says:* **The ideal onion for this is the small, flat, yellow onion that is quite common in Italy, but I have found it only occasionally here. If you find them, buy a lot. You may not find them again too soon, and when pickled they keep a long time. Do not use pearl onions.**

½ cup red wine, preferably Barbera (see Wine Note below)

¾ cup good-quality red wine vinegar

½ cup water

2 bay leaves

3 or 4 fresh sage leaves

1 tablespoon sugar

1 tablespoon fine sea salt

A storage jar large enough to hold the onions snugly

YIELD: *1 dozen pickled onions*

1   Peel the onions and, if they are any bigger than a small walnut, reduce their size by removing one or two of the outer layers. (Do not discard these because you can use them in any recipe that calls for chopped or sliced sautéed onions.) With the tip of a paring knife, make a ¼ inch-deep cross in their root end. Rinse the onions under cold running water.

2   Put all of the ingredients except the onions in a small saucepan and bring the liquids to a boil. When they have boiled for 5 minutes, drop in the onions. When the liquids return to a boil, cook for 5 minutes more.

3   Retrieve the onions with a slotted spoon and put them in the storage jar. Remove the sage leaves from the saucepan and discard, but keep the bay leaves. Pour the contents of the pan over the onions in the jar. There should be enough liquid to cover the onions. If there is not, use a smaller jar. Cover tightly.

AHEAD-OF-TIME NOTE: The onions are ready to eat after 3 days, but they are even better if you keep them a while longer. They will keep at normal room temperature, but it does no harm to refrigerate them. They have been stored for months in a closed jar in my refrigerator with no loss of flavor, only a slight and negligible softening.

WINE NOTE: You can use any dry red wine, but the natural acidity of Barbera makes it an obvious choice for making pickles. A simple standard-quality Chianti would also work well as would any wine based on the Nebbiolo grape, if you can find one inexpensive enough for the purpose.

SOUP CROUTONS

᥎ *Crostini da Minestra*

Our crostini for soup are very plain. They are just crisply fried diced bread that make it so interesting when you find one in a spoonful of soup. You could make them in advance, but I don't see why one should. They are quick to do and taste good when freshly made. If you are determined to make them in advance, use them the same day you make them. Their flavor goes off when kept overnight.

> 4 slices good-quality white bread
>
> Vegetable oil, enough to come ½ inch up the side of the pan

For 4 persons

1 Trim off any crusts on the bread and cut the slices into ½-inch squares.

2 Pour the oil into a 10-inch skillet, turn on the heat to medium high, and heat until the oil is hot enough so that it sizzles when a square of bread is dropped in. When the oil is ready, slip in as many pieces of bread as will fit without crowding the pan. It doesn't matter if they don't all go in at one time, because you can do two or more batches. Turn the heat down, because bread burns quickly when the oil gets too hot. Move the squares around in the pan with a long spoon or spatula, and as soon as they become colored a light gold remove them using a slotted spoon or spatula. Place on paper towels or a fine-mesh wire cooling rack to shed excess oil. If you are doing more than one batch, adjust the heat whenever necessary to avoid burning the bread. Maintain sufficient heat, however, to brown the squares lightly and quickly.

Soups

BROCCOLINI AND CANNELLINI BEAN SOUP
↝ *Zuppa di Broccolini e Cannellini*

Baby broccoli, or broccolini, to call it by the catchy name coined by one of its producers, is a hybrid in which broccoli's pungency is sweetened by the gentler genes of Chinese broccoli. Its willowy stems, unlike the sturdy stalks of broccoli, do not need to be peeled. The slenderness of the vegetable is matched by the delicacy of its flavor. Look for bunches whose color is deep. They are the freshest and deliver the clearest, brightest taste.

1 cup dried cannellini beans, sea salt, and 1 tablespoon extra virgin olive oil OR
2 cups canned cannellini beans, fully drained

1 bunch baby broccoli, also known as broccolini

> *Marcella Says:* **If you are unable to find broccolini, you can make the soup with broccoli, as long as you are content with knowing that the flavor notes will be sharper and earthier. See the note at the end of this recipe for the procedure to follow.**

Fine sea salt

¼ cup extra virgin olive oil

1 large garlic clove, peeled and chopped fine

2 tablespoons chopped Italian flat-leaf parsley

Optional: homemade broth (page 48)

Black pepper ground fresh from the mill

For 4 persons

1 If you are using dried beans: Put the beans in a bowl, cover them amply with lukewarm water, add two or three large pinches of salt, and let them soak overnight or for no less than 6 hours.

2 Drain the beans, discarding the water, rinse them in cold water, and put them in a saucepan, pouring into it just enough water to rise 1 to 1½ inches above the beans. Add 2 teaspoons of sea salt and the 1 tablespoon of olive oil, cover the pan, and turn on the heat to medium. When the water begins to break into a boil, lower the heat, adjusting it so that the beans cook at a gentle simmer. Continue to simmer them gently, yet steadily, until the beans are fully tender, about 45 minutes to 1 hour. If you are ready to make the soup at this point, take the pan off the heat, reserving the cooked beans in the water in which they have simmered.

AHEAD-OF-TIME NOTE: You can make the dried beans ready for the soup 4 or 5 days in advance. When cooked, transfer them to a storage container or glass jar together with all the water from the pan, cover tightly, and refrigerate until you are ready to use them.

3   If you are using canned beans: Drain them thoroughly and set aside.

4   Trim away about ½ inch from the butt end of the broccolini stalks. Wash them in three or four complete changes of cold water.

5   Bring a large saucepan of water to a boil, add 1 tablespoon of salt to keep the vegetable green, drop in the broccolini, and cook at a moderate, steady boil until very tender, about 15 minutes.

6   Drain, discarding the water. Cut the broccolini into pieces, each 1 to 1½ inches long.

7   Rinse and wipe dry the saucepan in which you cooked the broccolini. Put the olive oil and chopped garlic in the pan, turn on the heat to medium high, and cook, stirring, until the garlic has become colored a light gold. Add the chopped parsley, stir once or twice, then add the broccolini pieces. Cook for at least 10 full minutes, turning them over from time to time to coat them well.

Marcella Says: **Sautéing the vegetable and then the beans in olive oil and garlic is a critical passage in making this dish. Don't rush through it, the step needs time and care. The more thoroughly the broccoli and beans are bonded to the aromas and texture of the garlic and oil, the deeper and more satisfying will be the flavor of the soup.**

8 If you chose to use dried beans, drain them, but save the water in which they cooked in a separate container. Put 1½ cups of whichever cannellini beans you are using into the saucepan containing the broccolini. Cook the beans for about 2 minutes, stirring thoroughly to coat them well. Add the remaining ½ cup of beans, mashing them through a potato ricer as you add them. If your ricer has interchangeable disks, fit it with the one that has the smallest holes. Stir thoroughly.

9 If you used dried beans, add enough of their reserved cooking water to achieve a moderately dense consistency. If you are using canned beans, add fresh still water from the tap or, even better if you have it available, homemade meat broth. Continue cooking until the soup is hot, but not scalding. Add several twists of the pepper mill, stir, and serve.

If Using Broccoli:

Cut off about 1 inch of the butt end of the broccoli stalk. With a small, sharp knife pare away the tough dark-green outer skin from the main stalk and the larger branches. Dig deepest where the stalk is thickest to remove the entire tough outer layer. Without detaching the florets, split the larger stalks in two or in four if larger. Cook, drain, and cut up as described above in steps 3 and 4 for broccolini and proceed with the recipe from step 5.

Two Rapini Soups

The Italian palate, and even more the palate of southern Italians, is strongly attracted to astringent flavors, which accounts for the great popularity of both wild and cultivated greens whose bitter undertones encompass varying degrees of explicitness. In the country's good home cooking, however, balance counts more than impact, and bitterness will be tempered by mildness. The two soups that follow exemplify this: Both are based on *cime di rapa*—rapini—a bitter green.

In the first soup, cannellini beans provide the mellow counterweight to rapini's astringency. I prefer to use dried beans that I can soak and then cook very slowly in olive oil and very little water. Their rich taste and fine texture are wonderful here, as they always are in any other way in which they are served. You can use canned beans if you really must, they make good soup, but if you should come across a reliable source of dried cannellini—see Knowing Beans on page 57 in AT MASTER CLASS—treat yourself well and give them a try.

In the second of the two soups, squash replaces the beans. Butternut squash, so similar to a Neapolitan *zucca,* has some of the sugary touch that, in varying degrees, is common to all squashes. The gentle conjunction of bitter rapini and sweet squash is yet another example of the subtlety and light-handedness of which southern cooking is capable and for which it is never given sufficient credit.

Without upsetting the fine balance of flavors, I have tinkered a little with the ingredients. Among them originally there was orzo pasta, shaped like large grains of rice. It's one of the rare pasta shapes that I wish had not been invented—nothing about it holds the slightest interest for me. *Orzo,* however, is also the Italian word for barley, a favorite component of soups in Friuli, in northeastern Italy, a place as diametrically opposite from Naples as it is possible to be, both geographically and temperamentally. I thought that a little northern firmness would do no harm to this soft southern soup, and so I have replaced orzo pasta, fake barley, with true *orzo,* real barley.

RAPINI, POTATO, AND CANNELLINI BEAN SOUP

⏝ Zuppa di Cime di Rapa, Patate, e Cannellini

> 1 cup dried cannellini beans, sea salt, and 1 tablespoon extra virgin olive oil OR
> 2 cups canned cannellini beans, fully drained
>
> 1 bunch rapini, about 1 pound
>
> Fine sea salt
>
> 2 medium-large potatoes
>
> ⅓ cup extra virgin olive oil
>
> 2 tablespoons garlic, chopped fine
>
> A potato ricer or vegetable mill

For 6 persons

1 If you are using dried beans, soak them for 6 hours or overnight and cook them as described in Knowing Beans on page 57. If you are using canned beans, drain them thoroughly and set aside.

AHEAD-OF-TIME NOTE: You can make the dried beans ready for the soup a day or two in advance. When cooked, transfer them to a storage container or glass jar together with all the water from the pan, cover tightly, and refrigerate until you are ready to use them.

2 Cut off the tough butt end from the rapini stems and with the paring knife peel back the dark-green rind from the stems. Wash the rapini in cold water.

3 Bring 4 to 5 cups of water to a boil in a saucepan, add 1 tablespoon of salt, and when the water returns to a fast boil drop in the rapini. Cook until tender, 5 to 7 minutes after the water returns to a boil. Retrieve the rapini from the pan with a slotted spoon or spatula, but do not discard the broth, which you want to reserve in a container to use later in the soup. Rinse out the saucepan under the faucet and wipe it dry. When the rapini are cool enough to handle, chop them very fine.

4 Drop the unpeeled potatoes into a saucepan of cold water, bring to a boil, and cook at a steady, but moderate boil until they are tender when tested with a fork.

5 While the potatoes are cooking, pour the olive oil into the same saucepan in which you cooked the rapini, add the garlic, turn on the heat to medium high, and cook the garlic, stirring occasionally, until it becomes colored a pale gold.

6 Add the chopped rapini, turning them to coat them well, and continue cooking for 10 minutes, turning the vegetable from time to time to keep it from sticking to the pan.

7 Add the fully drained cannellini beans. If you have cooked your own dried beans, reserve their broth separately for possible later use. Continue cooking for about 7 minutes, turning the beans over from time to time. Remove the pan from the heat and reserve until the potatoes are fully cooked.

8 When the potatoes are done, drain them and skin them while they are still hot or warm, depending how soon it is possible for you to handle them. Return the saucepan with the rapini and the beans to medium heat, bring the contents to a simmer, and add the potatoes, mashing them directly into the pan through the potato ricer or vegetable mill. Turn all the ingredients over two or three times and stir in the reserved rapini broth, adding just a little of it at a time, until you obtain the desired thickness for the soup. I like it the consistency of rather runny cream. It should not be necessary to add more liquid, but if it is you can use some of the broth reserved from cooking the dried cannellini beans, or water, if you used canned beans. Taste and correct for salt before serving.

AHEAD-OF-TIME NOTE: You can freeze the finished soup and serve it later, even weeks later, after thawing and reheating it fully.

Rapini and Butternut Squash Soup

Zuppa con le Cime di Rapa e la Zucca Napoletana

1 bunch rapini, about 1 pound

Fine sea salt

1 medium butternut squash, about 1 pound

¼ cup extra virgin olive oil

2 large or 3 medium garlic cloves, peeled and chopped very fine

Black pepper ground fresh from the mill

1 beef bouillon cube

⅓ cup pearl barley

Chopped dried red chili pepper, *peperoncino,* ¼ teaspoon, or adjust quantity to taste

½ cup freshly grated Parmigiano-Reggiano cheese

For 4 to 6 persons

1   Turn on the oven to 400°.

2   While the oven is heating up, trim, cook, drain, and chop the rapini exactly as described in steps 2 and 3 of the preceding recipe on page 118. You will be using the water in which you cooked the rapini, so remember to save it in any suitable container.

3   Put the squash in a baking dish and cook it in the preheated oven for about 1 hour.

AHEAD-OF-TIME NOTE: You can cook the squash up to this point a day in advance. Refrigerate it wrapped in heavy aluminum foil.

4   Split the squash lengthwise, remove the seeds and strings, scoop out the flesh, and mash it in a bowl.

5 You can make the soup in the same saucepan in which you cooked the rapini. Rinse it and wipe it clean and dry, or use another one if that is more convenient. Pour all the oil into the pan, add the chopped garlic, and turn on the heat to high. Cook the garlic, stirring it frequently. When it becomes colored a rich gold, but no darker, add the chopped rapini. Turn it over from time to time to coat them well.

6 When you have sautéed the rapini for a few minutes, add the mashed squash and salt and pepper. Turn the squash over two or three times, sautéing it with the rapini for 3 to 4 minutes.

7 Add 2 cups of the reserved water in which you boiled the rapini, adjust the heat to medium, and cook for about 15 minutes, turning the contents of the pan over occasionally.

8 Add the bouillon cube, cook for a few more minutes, stirring to dissolve the cube, then pour the barley into the pan. Add the chili pepper, stir once or twice, and cook at a moderate, but steady simmer for about 40 minutes, until the barley is tender to the bite. Add some of the remaining rapini cooking water whenever it is necessary to adjust the consistency of the soup. Taste and correct for salt. Swirl in the grated Parmesan, transfer the soup to a serving bowl, and bring to the table piping hot.

> *Marcella Says:* **If squash is too bland for you, and I know that for some it is, I suggest replacing it with potatoes to give the soup an earthier taste. Cook 2 medium potatoes with their skins in boiling salted water until tender, peel them when cool enough to handle, then mash them through a potato ricer directly into the pan with the rapini as directed in step 6. Continue with the recipe.**

GREENGROCER'S SOUP WITH ONION, PEPPER, RAPINI, AND POTATOES

ᴄ᷾ Zuppa dell'Ortolano

An Italian vegetable soup is an excellent illustration of the principle of *insaporire,* the extraction and building up of flavor that I discuss at length in At Master Class on page 15. The potatoes and onion aside, the vegetable flavors of this particular soup come from the rapini stems and bell pepper. Note how the rapini is sautéed at length with onion that has already been cooked to a golden color. Only then is the red pepper added, after the rapini has been given an opportunity to release and concentrate its flavor. Note too that the red pepper is peeled, so that there is no skin to mask its sweetness; moreover, it is skinned raw, not charred first. Unlike charred bell peppers, the flesh is dry and compact and takes the sautéing more deeply.

1½ to 2 pounds potatoes (Although it is not a variety found in Italy, the Idaho makes an excellent choice for this soup.)

1 bunch of rapini, about 1 pound

1 large meaty red pepper or 2 smaller ones

1 tablespoon vegetable oil

3 tablespoons butter

⅔ cup chopped onion

A potato ricer

Depending how thin or thick you like the soup: 2 to 4 cups meat broth, made as described on page 48 or a beef bouillon cube dissolved in water or canned beef broth diluted with 3 parts water

Fine sea salt

Black pepper ground fresh from the mill

For 4 to 6 persons

Marcella Says: **You may choose to boil the potatoes, as a cook in Italy would do, or bake them. Either way works well, but because Idahoes are such ideal baking potatoes, if you are using them, I would bake them and let that Italian cook look the other way.**

1   If you are baking the potatoes, turn on the oven to 450°. Wash the potatoes in cold running water, pierce them here and there, and put them in the preheated oven. They are done when the tines of a fork enter them easily, about 50 minutes to 1 hour, depending on their size. As soon as they are cool enough to handle, scoop out the flesh, mash it through a potato ricer, and set it aside until you are ready to add it to the soup.

If you are boiling the potatoes, bring a pot of water to a boil. Wash the potatoes in cold running water, drop them into the pot, and cook at a steady, moderate boil. They are done when they can be easily pierced with a fork, about 30 minutes or more, depending on the size and youth of the potatoes. Drain and as soon as you are able to handle them, pull off the peels and mash the flesh through a potato ricer. Set aside until you are ready to add them to the soup.

2   Cut off the tops of the rapini and put them away to use or in Sautéed Rapini with Chickpeas on page 308. Peel back the tough dark-green rind that surrounds the stems. Wash the rapini in cold water. Bring a pan of salted water to a boil, add the stems, and cook them until tender. Drain and cut into pieces about 2 inches long.

3   Cut the red pepper lengthwise along its creases, remove the stem, seeds, and pithy core, then skin it with a swivel-blade vegetable peeler. (For more details, see Peeling Peppers Raw on page 79.) Cut it into narrow strips about 2 inches long.

4   Put the oil, butter, and chopped onion in a saucepan, turn on the heat to medium high, and cook, stirring occasionally, until the onion becomes colored a pale gold.

5   Put in the rapini stems, turn once or twice to coat well, and cook for about 10 minutes.

6   Add the pepper strips and cook for 8 to 10 minutes, stirring from time to time.

7   Add the potatoes to the pan. Stir well, add salt and several grindings of black pepper. Pour enough meat broth into the pan to achieve the consistency you desire. I like it as loose as thin cream. Cook at a steady, slow simmer for 30 to 40 minutes. Taste and correct for salt.

AHEAD-OF-TIME NOTE: You can make the soup entirely in advance and serve it several hours later after reheating it at a gentle simmer. You may also freeze it.

MUSHROOM AND POTATO SOUP WITH SUN-DRIED TOMATOES

⊰ *Zuppa di Funghi e Patate con i Pomodori Secchi*

In the figurative, as well as in the literal sense, potatoes put starch into soup. When you mash them into the pot, as you do here, they flesh out the soup's body and become efficient collectors and concentrators of contiguous flavors. Mushrooms, on the other hand, are a study in flavor potential. The flavor is certainly in them, or they would not be so desirable, but with the exception of porcini—the dried variety particularly—it is not self-starting flavor, it needs to be nudged. The most effective nudging agents are olive oil, garlic, and parsley, and you will notice that they are almost invariably present when cooking mushrooms in the Italian way. I have learned, moreover, as I have observed elsewhere in this book, that when you bring two or more varieties of mushrooms together they stimulate each other to project flavor more forcefully. Here we use all these methods to loosen the mushrooms' restraint; we add a few sun-dried tomatoes and call on accommodating potatoes to be the bearers of the earthy flavors that we have drawn out.

½ pound assorted fresh mushrooms that should include white button mushrooms, portobello (either the small or large) and possibly shiitake

3 tablespoons extra virgin olive oil

1 tablespoon chopped garlic

3 to 5 sun-dried tomatoes (not packed in oil), depending on their size, cut into small dice

2 tablespoons chopped Italian flat-leaf parsley

Fine sea salt

Black pepper ground fresh from the mill

1 pound potatoes

A potato ricer or food mill

Depending how thin or thick you like the soup: 2 to 4 cups meat broth, made as described on page 48, OR a beef bouillon cube dissolved in 2 to 4 cups of water, or plain water

For 4 to 6 persons

1   If you are using shiitake, detach and discard their stems. Wash all the mushrooms rapidly under cold running water. Slice them very thin. If some of the caps are broader than 1½ inches, cut them in half and slice them perpendicularly to the long side so that no slice becomes exceedingly long.

2   Put the olive oil and garlic in a wide-bottomed saucepan, turn the heat on to medium, and cook the garlic, stirring occasionally, until it becomes colored a deep gold. Add the diced sun-dried tomatoes and the parsley, turn them over a few times to coat them well, and cook for a minute or two, watching the garlic to make sure it does not become colored dark brown.

3   Add the sliced mushrooms, turning them over two or three times to coat them well. Add salt and pepper, turn the contents over again once or twice, turn the heat down to the lowest setting possible, and cook the mushrooms for at least 30 minutes.

4   While the mushrooms are cooking, cook the potatoes in their skins in moderately boiling, abundant water. When the potatoes are tender enough that a fork can penetrate them without resistance, drain them, peel them, and mash them through the potato ricer or the food mill fitted with a small-holed disk directly into the saucepan with the mushrooms. Mix them in thoroughly.

5   Add the broth or other liquid as suggested in the ingredients list, enough of it to yield the consistency you prefer, keeping in mind that this soup ought not to be either too runny or too dense. Bring to a simmer and cook for about 15 minutes, stirring the pot from time to time. Taste and correct for salt and pepper. Serve hot.

AHEAD-OF-TIME NOTE: You can make the soup up to a day in advance and refrigerate it. Reheat it thoroughly at a gentle simmer. You may also freeze it for up to 3 months.

Jerusalem Artichokes

It was a happy day for me when David, the produce manager of Morton's market in Sarasota, agreed to special-order a case of Jerusalem artichokes for me. Why they are not on everyone's table perplexes me. I can't say enough good things about this heavenly knotty little tuber, which is the root of a variety of sunflower and, solely in appearance, resembles ginger. Once you have peeled away its leathery skin, you handle it as you would potatoes. It can be boiled, sautéed, gratinéed, fried and, as in the two examples that follow, put into soups. I have always put recipes for Jerusalem artichokes in my books and I am delighted to serve them whenever I can get them because they have never once failed to please.

Although they are not even remotely part of the artichoke family, the taste of a Jerusalem artichoke is curiously close to that of an artichoke bottom, but with a sweeter touch. Jerusalem artichokes have a distinctive texture, not the least bit starchy, rather silky, in fact. When buying them, press one between your fingers. Its texture should be very hard. If it is soft in any way, pass on it because it is no longer fresh.

Jerusalem Artichoke and Mushroom Soup
Zuppa di Topinambur e Funghi

1 pound Jerusalem artichokes, also known as sunchokes

½ pound cremini mushrooms, also known as baby bella

2 tablespoons extra virgin olive oil

½ cup white or yellow onion, chopped fine

3 medium garlic cloves, peeled and chopped fine

2 tablespoons chopped Italian flat-leaf parsley

Fine sea salt

Black pepper ground fresh from the mill

Depending how thin or thick you like the soup: 2 to 4 cups meat broth, made as described on page 48, OR a beef bouillon cube dissolved in 2 to 4 cups of water

1½ tablespoons butter

3 tablespoons freshly grated Parmigiano-Reggiano cheese

Optional: Crostini da Minestra (Soup Croutons), made as described on page 112

For 4 persons

1 Peel the Jerusalem artichokes. You can take off most of the skin with a swivel-blade vegetable peeler, then use the tip of a paring knife to peel the hard to reach places. Wash them under cold running water.

2 Drop the peeled chokes into a pot of boiling water and cook until they feel tender when pierced by a fork.

> *Marcella Says:* **It would make things simpler if all the pieces cooked at the same rate, but unfortunately they do not. When some are already tender, others may still be hard. Test them patiently and retrieve them, piece by piece, as they are done.**

Drain and allow to cool. When cool enough to handle comfortably, cut the chokes into thin slices. Parts of them may break off into small lumps, which is perfectly all right because it all goes into the soup.

3   While the Jerusalem artichokes are cooking, you can begin to work with the mushrooms. Wash them rapidly under cold running water, then slice them thin.

4   Choose a wide-bottomed saucepan that can accommodate all the vegetables and the broth. The broader the bottom the better it is for sautéeing the mushrooms. Put in the oil and the chopped onion and turn on the heat to medium high. Cook the onion, stirring from time to time, until it becomes colored a light gold. Add the garlic. Cook and stir and when the garlic's aroma begins to rise (do not let it get dark), add the parsley. Stir two or three times, then put in the sliced mushrooms.

5   Turn up the heat and cook the mushrooms, stirring and turning them, just until they are lightly browned. Add salt and liberal grindings of black pepper, turn the mushrooms over once or twice, then turn the heat down to medium. Cook, stirring from time to time, for about 15 minutes or more, until the liquid that the mushrooms will shed has evaporated.

6   Using a slotted spoon, scoop the mushrooms out of the pan and chop them. You may, if you wish, chop them in the food processor, hitting the pulse button three or four times. Take care not to overprocess them. Return them to the pan.

7   Add the sliced chokes to the mushrooms and brown them lightly over medium-high heat for 2 to 3 minutes, stirring frequently.

AHEAD-OF-TIME NOTE: You can prepare the soup base up to this point as early as the morning of the day you are planning to serve the soup at dinner, refrigerating it until you are ready to reheat it.

8   Add enough broth as suggested in the ingredients list to make the soup as runny or as thick as you prefer. Bring to a steady simmer, add the butter, and cook for 3 to 4 minutes. Turn off the heat and swirl in the grated Parmesan. Taste and correct for salt. Serve promptly. If you have chosen to make a runny soup, you may want to serve it with soup croutons.

Jerusalem Artichoke and Asparagus Soup

Zuppa di Topinambur e Asparagi

1 pound Jerusalem artichokes, also known as sunchokes

½ pound asparagus

> *Marcella Says:* **The asparagus spears are going to get all chopped up so there is no reason to buy the big, beautiful, but expensive thick ones. The cheaper, spindlier specimens, as long as they are crisply fresh, are quite good enough.**

1 bouillon cube

3 tablespoons butter

1 tablespoon vegetable oil

½ cup chopped onion

Fine sea salt

Black pepper ground fresh from the mill

⅛ teaspoon freshly grated nutmeg

½ cup freshly grated Parmigiano-Reggiano cheese

For 4 persons

1 Peel, wash, and cook the Jerusalem artichokes as described in steps 1 and 2 of the preceding recipe on page 127. Using a slotted spoon or a strainer with a handle retrieve them. Do not pour out the cooking water.

2 Trim away the hard outer skin from the asparagus stalks as described on page 74 of The Why and How of Prepping Vegetables. Cut the spears in two.

3 Bring the reserved water in which the chokes were cooked to a boil, dissolve the bouillon cube in it, then drop in the asparagus. Cook until tender, then retrieve them without pouring out the broth. Transfer the asparagus broth to a large beaker or other container and set aside for use later on in this soup.

4 Chop up the cooked asparagus and Jerusalem artichokes, cutting the chokes into pieces somewhat smaller than the asparagus.

5 Wipe clean the pot in which you boiled the chokes and the asparagus, put in the butter, the oil, and the chopped onion and turn on the heat to medium. Cook the onion, stirring it from time to time, until it becomes colored a rich gold.

6 Add the cut-up asparagus and Jerusalem artichokes and turn them a few times to coat them well. After 2 to 3 minutes, add 1½ cups of the reserved bouillon-enriched asparagus broth, or more of it if you like a much thinner soup. Simmer for 10 to 15 minutes. Taste and correct for salt, then add several grindings of black pepper and the grated nutmeg, stirring once or twice. Take off the heat and swirl in the grated cheese. Serve piping hot.

A MUSSEL SOUP FROM BOSA

Zuppa di Cozze come la Fanno a Bosa

Bosa is a town on Sardinia's western coast, where I came to know flavors that have lodged at the peak of my experience. The never cloying single-bloom honeys—in particular those of arbutus and of rosemary—constituted one group, with the unflagging freshness and fragrance of paradisiacal aromas. Another set of sensations came from the pure, golden ambrosia of a wine, Malvasia di Bosa, rare then and possibly even extinct now. To use a term that has since become chic, it was a garage wine. Literally so, and my husband and I had our first sip of it sitting on a pile of used tires in the garage where it had been produced. Italy has many such miracles, and Sardinia more than its share.

Like other coastal towns on the island, Bosa also has an excellent maritime cuisine. An example is this excellent mussel soup. Two ingredients unique to it are the grated sheep's milk cheese that cooks along with the mussels, deepening their flavor, and the bread crumbs—some Sardinian cooks use couscous instead—that add texture and density to the mussel juices.

2 pounds live mussels

⅓ cup extra virgin olive oil

1 heaping tablespoon chopped garlic

2 tablespoons chopped Italian flat-leaf parsley

2 tablespoons fine, dry, unflavored bread crumbs

⅓ cup grated Fiore Sardo or Pecorino Romano or other hard, grating sheep's milk cheese

> *Marcella Says:* **You may find it useful to read about Pecorino beginning on page 81 of** AT MASTER CLASS.

1 cup dry white wine

1 cup tomatoes cut up with their juice, either ripe, firm, fresh plum tomatoes, peeled, OR canned imported San Marzano Italian tomatoes

Chopped dried red chili pepper, 1 teaspoon or more, depending on taste and on the potency of the chili

Grilled crusty bread, 1 or more slices per serving

For 4 persons

1 Cut away any protruding tufts from the mussels. Set aside any whose shells are even slightly open and tap them sharply. Check them after 2 or 3 minutes and throw out all those that are still open. Drop the mussels into a basin or large bowl of cold water, move them around a little bit, then let them settle for a few minutes. Retrieve them without stirring up the water. Pour the water out slowly to see if any sand has collected at the bottom. If any has, rinse out the container, refill it with fresh cold water, and drop the mussels into it again. Repeat this procedure until the water runs clear.

2 Pour the olive oil into a 6-quart saucepan, add the garlic, turn on the heat to medium high, and cook the garlic, stirring occasionally, until it becomes colored a light gold. Add the parsley, stir two or three times, then add the bread crumbs, stirring for a few seconds.

3 Put the drained mussels in the pot, turn them around a bit, then cover the pot. Uncover after a few minutes, add the grated cheese, stirring it in well.

> *Marcella Says:* **Ordinarily you'd add cheese after a soup is cooked, but in this case I want it to settle into the shells while the soup is still cooking.**

4 Add the white wine, let it bubble away briskly for 2 to 3 minutes, then put in the tomatoes and the chili pepper. Turn the contents of the pot over two or three times and continue to cook for about 15 minutes.

5 Place a slice or two of toasted or grilled bread in each individual soup bowl, distribute the contents of the pan over the bread, and serve piping hot.

Rice

BOILED RICE WITH BLACK AND GREEN OLIVES AND CHILI PEPPER

ⱸᕽ Riso Bollito con le Olive e il Peperoncino

Risotto is justifiably the most celebrated Italian dish made from rice, but we also like to make boiled rice, which is an entirely different thing. There is, of course, a critical difference in technique. We make boiled rice by adding it to a pot of boiling liquid and leaving it be until done. In risotto, liquid is added to the rice in small doses, and the rice is stirred constantly. But there is another fundamental difference, and it is one of sensations and mood. Italians have their risotto at the main meal, usually the midday meal. If they are making rice for guests, it will be a risotto, not boiled rice. They would be most unlikely to order boiled rice at a restaurant. Where risotto is rich and important, boiled rice is spare and casual, demanding far less energy to make and to consume. Boiled rice is a comforting, easygoing dish that addresses itself to intimate family mealtimes. It is a dish for the evening, when Italians hope to retire without major challenges for their metabolism. None of this means that it has to be dull. On the contrary, it can be lively and savory, as this recipe, I believe, demonstrates.

10 black olives, preferably the blackish-brown round ones packed in olive oil commonly known as Greek olives (See MARCELLA SAYS opposite.)

20 green olives packed in brine

Fine sea salt

1 cup rice, either Arborio or Carnaroli if, like me, you like their creamy starchiness, OR long-grain boiling rice or converted rice of any variety

A warm serving bowl

¼ cup extra virgin olive oil

2 teaspoons garlic chopped very, very fine

Chopped chili pepper, 2 teaspoons fresh jalapeño, OR 1 teaspoon dried red chili pepper, adjusting such quantities to taste and to the potency of the chili

For 4 persons

1 Pit the olives, then chop half of them and cut the other half into thin strips.

2 Bring water to a boil in a medium saucepan, add salt, and when the water is boiling fast again drop in the rice. Cook until tender, but firm, somewhere between 15 and 20 minutes. Drain the rice when done, but first retrieve about ¼ cup of the cooking water and reserve.

3 Transfer the rice to the warm serving bowl, add the olive oil, garlic, chili pepper, and all the olives, and toss well. If the rice appears to be a little too dry for you, add 2 tablespoons or more as needed of the reserved cooking water, toss two or three times, and serve at once.

> *Marcella Says:* **There are a score or more of olives packed for the table in Italy, but in cooking the most frequently used variety is the one known as Greek, a large, egg-shaped olive whose color ranges from a medium nut-brown to a brown that is almost black. It is packed in salt and olive oil, the flesh is tender, and its mild yet savory flavor appears to go well in almost any kind of dish. It is widely available: Specialty food shops carry it, but so does the delicatessen counter in every supermarket I have ever been in. You may of course experiment with other black olives, taking into consideration that any assertively spiced one might dominate the delicate balance of flavors in this boiled rice dish. One variety whose flavor I sometimes find to be out of sync with Italian cooking is the elongated purplish olive known as Kalamata.**

RISOTTO WITH RED, YELLOW, AND GREEN PEPPERS
Risotto con Peperoni di Tre Colori

Green is the color of peppers that are not yet fully ripened and for that reason cooks in Italy used to shun them as immature produce. How ripe a pepper needs to be, however, has become a matter of taste and of how it is used. There is not much that I can say in favor of roasted green peppers, but their sprightly flavor can add a welcome briskness to the sultry sweetness of red and yellow bell peppers. And that is precisely what they do in this risotto.

3 meaty bell peppers, 1 red, 1 yellow, and 1 green

3 tablespoons butter

1 tablespoon vegetable oil

½ cup chopped onion

Fine sea salt

6 cups fresh or frozen homemade meat broth, made as described on page 48, OR 1 beef bouillon cube dissolved in 6 cups simmering water

2 tablespoons chopped Italian flat-leaf parsley

1½ cups Italian risotto rice, such as Carnaroli, Vialone Nano, Baldo, or Arborio

⅓ cup freshly grated Parmigiano-Reggiano cheese

Black pepper ground fresh from the mill

For 6 persons

1 Wash the bell peppers in cold water, split them lengthwise along the creases, and remove the stem, seeds, and pithy core. Cut into ½-inch squares.

2 Choose a heavy-bottomed, heat-retaining 4- to 6-quart saucepan—such as enameled cast iron—and add 1 tablespoon of the butter, the tablespoon of vegetable oil, and the onion, and turn on the heat to medium high. Cook the onion, stirring from time to time, until it becomes colored a deep gold.

3 Add the peppers, turn up the heat a notch, turn them over two or three times to coat them well, and cook for about 5 minutes before turning the heat down to medium. Sprinkle with salt, and continue cooking for 30 to 35 minutes more, stirring from time to time.

4 While the peppers are cooking, bring the broth or the water with the bouillon cube to a low simmer in a saucepan on a nearby burner.

5 When the peppers have cooked for 30 to 35 minutes over medium heat, add the parsley and combine it thoroughly with the peppers. Remove about ½ cup of peppers from the pan and set aside for later.

AHEAD-OF-TIME NOTE: You can cook the peppers up to this point, stopping short of adding the parsley, up to a day in advance. If you choose to do so, cook the peppers in a skillet and when cool refrigerate them in a sealed container. When ready to make the risotto, heat the peppers gently in the saucepan you are using for the risotto, add the parsley, and remove ½ cup of peppers for later use as instructed above in step 5.

6 Add the rice to the saucepan and turn up the heat. Stir, turning the rice over several times to coat it well. Add a ladleful of the simmering broth and stir, using a straight-edge wooden spatula to keep the rice moving away from the bottom and sides of the pan. When the liquid in the pan has evaporated, add another ladleful or two and continue stirring. Cook in this way until the grains of rice lose their chalky centers and are firm yet tender, about 25 minutes. If you find yourself running out of broth before the rice is done, add a cup or two of water. When you near the end, do not let the rice dry out completely, but leave in enough broth to keep the risotto loose and flowing.

7 When the risotto is done, turn off the heat, add the remaining 2 tablespoons of butter and the grated Parmesan, and swirl vigorously.

Marcella Says: **This is the magic step, known as** *mantecare,* **that will give any risotto that has been made with butter a lusciously creamy consistency.**

Swirl the reserved ½ cup of cooked peppers into the risotto, taste, and correct for salt. Add liberal grindings of black pepper, mix again, and serve at once.

Marcella Says: **Do not serve any risotto mounded up in the center of the plate. Spread it thin and evenly over the whole plate. You can then eat it starting at its rim, gradually working from the perimeter to the center. The reason for eating it in this way is to allow the risotto to cool off slightly so that its flavors can settle and bloom.**

Seafood Risotti with Vegetables

It has been noted that certain dishes can jog the memory and stir the past to life. There is a particular kind of risotto, a runny risotto in which the flavors of seafood and vegetables play upon each other, that is associated with two significant times of my life when I lived in Venice, one distant, the other recent. The first time was that of my student days, when I had been shipped off to Venice to stay with my aunt so that I could commute to the university in Padua. The second was in the concluding decades of my teaching career, when I conducted a cooking school in my house in the city. Today, any time I spread out a steaming seafood and vegetable risotto on my plate to cool it and take my first forkful of it, images of my early and late Venetian years come alternately to mind, like a succession of slides clicking on and off from an internal projector. I see my young, black-tressed self at my aunt's table, a famished student laid low at the end of an implacably long and all but lunchless school day, whose recovery was powered by copious helpings of the fuming, delectable mass going round the table on a deep, blue-rimmed platter. The next images come from a lifetime later; my hair is white, the students are my own, and it's my table they are sitting at this time, passing the platter, greedily filling their plates with the risotto I had taught them to make that morning.

In the home cooking of Italy's regions there are some dishes that are such unmistakable expressions of their native territory that they could not have sprung up elsewhere. When food speaks so plainly of a special place its appeal doesn't lose freshness, not even after a lifetime of familiarity. If you have had the opportunity of becoming attuned to Venetian speech, to its lilting pitch, to its soft, consonant-dropping sounds, you could draw a parallel with the gentle taste of the risotti of which I speak here, with their flowing consistency, with their reconciliation of vegetable sweetness and tangy sea flavor. There are many possible components in this formula. A few, such as risotto with baby cuttlefish and those large juicy peas that the produce vendors at the Rialto market call *senatori,* can be a source of amazed delight, which—like that of the city itself—is to be experienced only in Venice. Others, such as the two that follow, serve as role models that you can follow anywhere.

What you particularly want to note about the risotto with asparagus and shrimp and the one with squash and clams is at what point and in what manner the vegetables and seafood become part of the risotto. Whenever you make seafood risotto, you must accommodate two apparently conflicting objectives. For the risotto to be saturated with flavor, the seafood, or some part of it, must cook with the rice from the beginning and all but dissolve in it. (To know more about this process, look up *Insaporire* on page 15 of AT MASTER CLASS.) At the same time it may be desirable to preserve in the dish the sight and unaltered texture of the shrimp or clam or lobster or crab that you are using.

The two examples that follow illustrate different ways of achieving the goal. For the shrimp risotto, most of the shrimp is chopped up, but some of it is left whole. Both the chopped and the whole are sautéed in a saucepan with chopped onion and, in the present recipe, with blanched, chopped asparagus. When it is done, you remove only the whole shrimp from the pan, you put in the rice, and begin to cook it with the chopped shrimp. During the cooking, the shrimp's consistency disappears and is replaced with the concentrated flavor of the crustacean which is essential to the risotto's style. When you serve the risotto, you garnish it with the whole shrimp. The method is applicable to other shellfish. If you want to do lobster, chop up the tail but not the claw meat, or if using lump crabmeat, keep whole a few of the meatiest lumps. You will note too that in this particular risotto, you handle the asparagus nearly the same way you do the shrimp. Chop and sauté most of the blanched asparagus and cook the rice with it, but hold back the spear tips to serve with the finished risotto.

When using clams, you do it a little differently. It would serve little purpose to subject any of the clams to long cooking because they would turn into unpleasantly chewy pellets. You do want clam flavor to permeate the risotto, however, so you will heat the clams separately, collect their juice, filter it, and add it to the liquid with which you cook the rice. To preserve the juiciness of the clams, stir them into the pot only when the risotto is done.

ASPARAGUS AND SHRIMP RISOTTO

⚘ *Risotto di Asparagi e Gamberi*

Fine sea salt

½ pound asparagus, washed and peeled as described on page 74 of The Why and How of Prepping Vegetables

10 to 12 large shrimp

1 beef bouillon cube

2 tablespoons butter for cooking plus 2 additional tablespoons for *mantecare,* the creamy finishing touch

1 tablespoon vegetable oil

½ cup chopped onion

1½ cups Italian risotto rice, such as Carnaroli, Vialone Nano, Baldo, or Arborio

1 tablespoon chopped Italian flat-leaf parsley

½ cup freshly grated Parmigiano-Reggiano cheese

Black pepper ground fresh from the mill

For 4 to 6 persons

1   Bring water to a boil in a 12-inch sauté pan or skillet, add 1 tablespoon salt, and slide in the trimmed asparagus. Put a lid on the pan and cook at a steady simmer until an asparagus spear bends easily when lifted with tongs or a fork. Using tongs or a slotted spoon or spatula, retrieve the asparagus and set aside to cool without discarding their broth. Pour the broth into a medium saucepan and set aside.

2   Shell and devein the shrimp, and wash them in cold water. Dry them off with kitchen or paper towels. Set aside 6 or 7 shrimp and roughly chop the rest into pieces no bigger than ½ inch.

3 Cut off the tips from the asparagus spears and reserve for later use. Chop the spears into ¼-inch pieces.

4 Add 3 cups water to the asparagus broth and bring it to a simmer over medium heat. Add the bouillon cube and dissolve it in the liquid.

5 Choose a heavy-bottomed, heat-retaining 4- to 6-quart saucepan—such as enameled cast iron—and add the 2 tablespoons butter, vegetable oil, and chopped onion, and turn on the heat to medium high. Cook the onion, stirring from time to time, until it becomes colored a light blond. Add the cut-up asparagus spears and all the shrimp, the whole ones and the pieces. Add some salt and cook, occasionally stirring and turning over the ingredients, until the shrimp are cooked, about 2 minutes. Remove the whole shrimp and set aside for later use.

AHEAD-OF-TIME NOTE: If serving the risotto for dinner, you can cook everything up to this point the morning of the same day and refrigerate. When resuming the cooking, bring the asparagus broth to a simmer and reheat the risotto base gently in a saucepan.

6 Add the rice to the saucepan. Stir it and turn it over several times to coat it well. Add a ladleful of the simmering asparagus broth and stir, using a straight-edge wooden spatula to keep the rice moving away from the bottom and sides of the pan. When the liquid in the pan has completely evaporated, add another ladleful or two and continue stirring. Cook in this way until the grains of rice lose their chalky centers and are firm yet tender, about 25 minutes. If you find yourself running out of broth before the rice is done, add a cup or two of water. When you near the end, do not let the rice dry out completely. Make sure there is just enough liquid in the pan to keep the risotto's final consistency loose and flowing in the fine Venetian style.

7 When the risotto is done, turn off the heat, add 1 to 2 tablespoons of the remaining butter, the chopped parsley, and the grated Parmesan. Taste and correct for salt, add generous grindings of black pepper, and swirl vigorously, distributing all the ingredients evenly. Pour the risotto onto a serving platter. Arrange the asparagus tips and the whole shrimp over the top. Serve at once.

> *Marcella Says:* **Please see my remarks about *mantecare* and about how to serve risotto on page 138.**

Risotto with Butternut Squash, Leeks, and Clams

Risotto di Zucca, Porri, e Vongole

½ pound butternut squash

1½ dozen live littleneck clams

1 large or 2 medium leeks, trimmed as described on page 76 of The Why and How of Prepping Vegetables

¼ cup extra virgin olive oil

2 tablespoons scallions, the white part only, cut into very thin rounds

Fine sea salt

Chopped marjoram, 1 tablespoon if fresh, ½ tablespoon if dried

1 cup Italian risotto rice, such as Carnaroli, Vialone Nano, or Baldo, or Arborio

1 cup dry white wine

1 tablespoon whole green peppercorns

½ cup grated Pecorino cheese (discussed at length beginning on page 81 of At Master Class)

For 4 persons

1 Turn on the oven to 350°.

2 Peel the squash, remove the seeds and strings, and cut the squash into dice no larger than ½ inch. Lay the diced squash in a baking dish that can contain it all without overlapping. Pour in ½ cup water, and put the dish in the preheated oven. Cook for 20 minutes. When cool, drain, then set aside.

3 Soak the clams in a basin of cold water, rubbing them vigorously one against the other. Repeat the procedure with several changes of water until you find that there is no sand settling at the bottom of the basin. If any of the clams open and stay open after you've handled them, discard them because they are no longer alive.

4 Pour ⅓ cup water into a 12-inch sauté pan or skillet, put in the clams, place a lid on the pan, and turn on the heat to high. Look in on the clams after 1 minute, stirring them around. As soon as they unclench their shells, transfer them to a bowl. Keep the heat going under the pan, moving quickly to retrieve any clam that has opened up.

5 When all the clams are out of the pan, line a small strainer with a paper towel, and set the strainer over a small bowl. Pour the pan juices and any juice that has collected in the bowl of clams through the strainer. The paper towel will trap any grit in the clam juice.

6 Detach the clam meat from the shells and put it in the bowl with the filtered juice. If there is not sufficient juice to cover the clam meat, add a little water.

AHEAD-OF-TIME NOTE: You can prepare the clams up to this point 2 or 3 days in advance. Tightly cover the bowl with plastic film and refrigerate it.

7 When the clam meat has steeped for 15 to 20 minutes, retrieve it with a slotted spoon from the bowl and cut each clam in half. Do not discard the juice in the bowl. Reserve the cut-up clams.

8 Wash the trimmed leeks, cut them in half lengthwise, then across into very thin slices.

9 Put a saucepan on the burner next to the one on which you shall cook the risotto. Pour about 2 quarts of water into the pan and bring it to a steady simmer.

10 Choose a heavy-bottomed, heat-retaining 4- to 6-quart saucepan—such as enameled cast iron—and pour in the olive oil, add the sliced leek and scallion, and turn on the heat to medium high. Cook, stirring from time to time, until the leek and scallion become colored a very pale gold. Add half the drained squash together with some salt, and cook for 2 or 3 minutes, turning it from time to time. Add the marjoram, and stir all the ingredients together.

11 Add the rice, turning it several times to coat it well.

12 Add half the wine, steadily stir the rice, and when all the wine has bubbled away, add the remaining half. Continue stirring, preferably using a straight-edge wooden spatula to keep the rice moving away from the bottom and sides of the pan at each turn.

13 Pour the clam juices into the risotto. Continue to stir until all the liquid has evaporated, then add a ladleful or two of simmering water from the other saucepan. Stir constantly, adding simmering water by the ladleful whenever the rice begins to dry out, threatening to stick to the pan.

14 In about 15 minutes, when the rice is still hard and chalky to the bite, stir in the remaining squash. Continue to cook, stirring steadily and replenishing the water when necessary, for another 10 to 15 minutes, until the rice has lost its chalky consistency and is tender, but still firm, to the bite. When you near the end, do not let the rice dry out completely but keep it runny enough so that its final consistency will be loose and flowing in the fine Venetian style.

15 Add the reserved cut-up clams, stirring them quickly into the risotto. Add the green peppercorns and the grated Pecorino. Remove the pan from the heat and stir vigorously. Taste and correct for seasoning. Serve at once.

Marcella Says: **Please see my remarks about letting the risotto cool on page 138.**

Pasta Sauces

Eggplant, Tomato, and Mozzarella Pasta Sauce

✒ Sugo di Melanzana, Pomodoro, e Mozzarella

The characters in that evergreen classic of Neapolitan cooking, eggplant parmigiana, give a slightly different rendition of their act, appearing here as a summery pasta sauce. It is light, fresh, and vivacious. The eggplant doesn't need preliminary steeping in salt, as it does in the parmigiana; there is a new, lively member of the troupe, chili pepper; and the Parmesan cheese has been replaced by the brasher Fiore Sardo or Pecorino.

1 medium eggplant

3 tablespoons extra virgin olive oil

1 cup tomatoes cut up with their juice, either ripe, firm, fresh plum tomatoes, peeled raw and seeded, as described on page 80, OR canned imported San Marzano Italian tomatoes

Chopped chili pepper, 2 teaspoons fresh jalapeño, OR 1 teaspoon dried red chili pepper, *peperoncino*, adjusting the quantities to taste and to the potency of the chili

Fine sea salt

¼ pound mozzarella cut into thin strips

1 pound boxed pasta: A short tubular shape, of which penne is a familiar example, will work best with the sauce. Other suitable shapes are *maccheroncini*, rigatoni, or ziti.

A warm serving bowl

¼ cup freshly grated Fiore Sardo, Pecorino Romano, or other hard sheep's milk cheese

Several fresh basil leaves, torn into two or three pieces by hand

For 4 persons

1   Wash the eggplant in cold water, cut off the green top, and cut into ½-inch dice.

2   Pour the olive oil into a 10-inch skillet and turn on the heat to high. When the oil is hot, slip in the eggplant. Cook for about a minute, turning the eggplant dice frequently, then add the tomatoes and the chili pepper. Turn the heat down to low, and cook at a gentle simmer until the fat floats free. Sprinkle with salt, stir once or twice, then take off the heat while the pasta cooks.

3   Drop the pasta into 4 quarts of salted, rapidly boiling water.

4   When the pasta is almost, but not quite, done, turn the heat back on under the skillet, and add the cut-up mozzarella, stirring it thoroughly until it dissolves in the hot sauce.

5   As soon as the pasta is done, tender yet firm to the bite, drain it, put it in the warm serving bowl, pour the sauce over it, and toss thoroughly.

6   Add the grated cheese, toss, add the torn basil leaves, toss again, and serve at once.

BOTTARGA PASTA SAUCE
❧ *Sugo di Bottarga*

I was born and raised in a fishing town and that may be one of the reasons that I am drawn to the flavors of the sea. My inclinations aside, however, it cannot be denied that there are few land products—the only ones I can think of are wild mushrooms, white truffles, some sheep's milk cheeses—that approach the intensity, depth, complexity, and variety of the products of the deep. The flesh of marine creatures, whether it is the dark one of anchovies, sardines, or mackerels, the paler one of bass or red mullet or turbot, or the firm and sometimes spicy one of an infinite variety of hard-shelled fish and mollusks, has no match in the bland meat of four-footed or two-footed air-breathing animals. When dried or otherwise preserved, the taste of the deep can become even more stirring. This is the case of *bottarga di muggine*, made in Sardinia from the pressed and dried roe of a particular variety of gray mullet. Its flavor registers so many changes, from pungent to almost sweet, that it challenges our ability to keep pace with it and, as we catch up, it becomes uniquely thrilling.

For more information about *bottarga*, please see the introductory note on page 95.

2 tablespoons extra virgin olive oil

1 whole garlic clove, unpeeled

3 tablespoons *bottarga,* dried Sardinian gray mullet roe, chopped very, very fine, OR bought ready-grated

¼ cup chopped Italian flat-leaf parsley

1 pound boxed long pasta: The most satisfactory match is with spaghettini, (thin spaghetti).

2 tablespoons butter at room temperature

A warm serving bowl

½ cup paper-thin slices of *bottarga* (cut using a swivel-blade vegetable peeler, a mandoline, or a truffle slicer as described in step 2 on page 96)

For 4 persons

1   Put the olive oil, garlic clove, and chopped or grated bottarga in a small skillet and turn on the heat to medium low.

2   Cook for about 2 minutes, stirring frequently. Take off the heat, remove the garlic, and stir in half the chopped parsley.

3   Drop the pasta into 4 quarts of salted, rapidly boiling water. While the pasta cooks, return the skillet to medium-low heat, and reheat the contents thoroughly, stirring from time to time. Ladle about ¼ cup of the boiling water from the pasta pot, and add it to the skillet. Cook for about 2 minutes, stirring from time to time, then take off the heat and swirl in the butter until it melts fully into the sauce.

4   When the pasta is tender but very firm to the bite, drain it immediately, and slip it into the warm serving bowl. Add the sauce, toss thoroughly, and add the remaining chopped parsley and the thin-sliced *bottarga*. Serve at once. If you are keen on presentation, toss the pasta with half the *bottarga* slices and half the parsley, then top with the remaining *bottarga* and parsley.

Pasta Sauce with Dried Porcini, Fresh Shiitake Mushrooms, and Clams

ᵺ *Sugo di Funghi e Vongole*

To explore the attraction that some vegetables and certain varieties of seafood have for each other can be one of the most rewarding matchmaking exercises in Italian cooking. You will find examples of it in the seafood and vegetable risotti beginning on page 139. Here it is a pasta sauce that joins the tangy, sea-bottom flavors of clams with the scents of two mushrooms. The combination exploits the earthiness of fresh shiitake and releases the mysteriously potent palate-arousing powers of dried porcini. To know more about porcini, turn to The Taste-Altering Power of Dried Porcini on page 62.

½ ounce dried imported Italian porcini mushrooms

1 pound fresh shiitake mushrooms

1 dozen live littleneck clams (See my suggestion below for keeping them fresh if you can't use them immediately.)

4 tablespoons extra virgin olive oil

1 tablespoon shallot, chopped fine

Chopped chili pepper, 1 teaspoon fresh jalapeño, OR ½ teaspoon dried red chili pepper, *peperoncino*, adjusting the quantities to taste and to the potency of the chili

¼ cup dry white wine

2 cups tomatoes cut up with their juice, about 1 pound ripe, firm, fresh plum tomatoes, peeled raw, seeded, as described on page 80, OR canned imported San Marzano Italian tomatoes

Fine sea salt

2 tablespoons chopped Italian flat-leaf parsley

Fettuccine or *tonnarelli,* made with 3 whole eggs as described on pages 40 to 42 of Why and How You Should Be Making Your Own Egg Pasta OR 10 ounces boxed fettuccine

Marcella Says: **The choice of pasta is not necessarily engraved in stone. It is a question of judgment, and in my judgment it's the sauce-thirsty nature of good egg pasta that we should try to capitalize on here.**

A warm serving platter

For 4 persons

1 Pour 1½ cups lukewarm water into a small bowl, drop in the dried porcini, and let them soak until you need to use them in this recipe, by which time, 30 minutes or more, they should have absorbed enough water to become soft.

2 Detach and discard the shiitake stems, wash the caps rapidly under cold running water, then cut them up coarsely.

3 Soak the clams in a basin of cold water, rubbing them vigorously one against the other. Repeat the procedure with several changes of water until you find no sand settling at the bottom of the basin.

4 Pour ⅓ cup of water into a 12-inch sauté pan or skillet, add the clams, place a lid on the pan, and turn on the heat to high. Look in on the clams after 1 minute, stirring them around. Remove any that have already unclenched their shells. Keep the heat going under the pan, moving quickly to retrieve any clam that has opened up. As soon as every last clam has opened—some will take longer than others—and is out of the pan, pour the pan juices into a small bowl. Detach the clam meat from the shells and put it in the bowl with the pan juices.

5 Retrieve the dried porcini mushrooms from their soak, but do not discard the liquid. Wash the mushrooms in various changes of cold water, then cut them up coarsely. Filter the mushroom soaking liquid through a coffee filter, or a paper towel folded into a funnel, into a small container. Set the liquid aside for later use.

6 Put 2 tablespoons of the olive oil and the chopped shallot in a 10-inch skillet and turn on the heat to medium high. Cook the shallot, stirring from time to time, until it becomes colored a rich gold, then put in the cut-up porcini and shiitake mushrooms, turning them over to coat them well. Cook for a few seconds, then add the reserved filtered liquid from the porcini soak.

7 When the liquid has evaporated completely, stir in the chili pepper, pour in the wine, and let it bubble gently until it evaporates completely. Add the tomatoes with some salt, stir once or twice, and turn the heat down to cook the tomatoes at a steady simmer for about 15 minutes.

AHEAD-OF-TIME NOTE: You can prepare the sauce up to this point a full day in advance. Refrigerate the clam meat in the juices until you are ready to proceed.

8 While the tomatoes are simmering, retrieve the clam meat from the juices and cut each clam into three pieces. Filter the clam juices through a coffee filter, or a paper towel folded into a funnel, into a small container. Pour the filtered juices into the pan with the mushrooms.

9 When the clam juices have cooked down some—you don't want the sauce to be too runny—add the chopped clam meat with the parsley and the remaining 2 tablespoons of olive oil. Stir well, taste, and correct for salt. Take off the heat while the pasta cooks.

10 Cook the pasta in a large pot of salted boiling water until it is tender, but firm to the bite. When it is nearly done, turn on the heat under the sauce to medium, stirring once or twice. As soon as the pasta is done, drain it, transfer it to the warm platter, and toss it with the contents of the skillet.

> *Marcella Says:* **If you cannot use the clams the same day you bought them, you can keep them alive for an additional 48 hours. When you bring the clams home check them out: If there are any that are open and do not clamp shut when handled, throw them out. Soak a large dish cloth or face towel in cold water, then wring it out. Lay it flat, pile up the clams in the center, and then pull the corners of the towel together and twist tightly to close. Place the towel on the lowest shelf of the refrigerator, toward the back if possible. If the towel is twisted tight, the clams are prevented from opening up and thus stay alive on the oxygen that their juices contain. When ready to use them, before putting them in the pan, check them again and discard any that remain open when handled.**

MUSHROOM AND MUSSEL SAUCE
Sugo di Funghi e Cozze

I owe this sauce to Pierino Jovine, a man who has cooked some of the best seafood meals of my life. The students who came to the school I had in Bologna may also have fond memories of his cooking. It was our custom, at the end of each course, to travel to Cesenatico, the fishing town on the Adriatic where I was born and where, on a stone pier that stuck straight out into the sea, Pierino had a restaurant. There, at sunset, we celebrated our leave-taking with a splendid seafood dinner whose many courses were separated by intervals that, by arrangement, were filled by the strong male voices of a local chorus singing folk songs.

I have dipped often and profitably into Pierino's repertory. A native of Amalfi, he had come to our northern town bringing culinary gifts that were both his own and those of his Neapolitan region. Pierino could turn his hand deftly to anything from soup to dessert, but he was at his most irresistible in the pasta sauces that he devised, using vegetables to set off the succulence of fresh seafood. One of the most delectable examples is the Fettuccine with Zucchini and Clams in my third cookbook, *Marcella's Italian Kitchen*. Another is this sauce of mushrooms and *cozze*, perhaps the most savory way I have ever come across to bring mussels and pasta together.

For the mushroom base

½ ounce dried imported Italian porcini mushrooms

> *Marcella Says:* **The flavor of dried porcini is what drives this sauce. Do not let any difficulty you might have in finding them lead you to omit them or look for a substitute. If there is no specialty food store where you live, you can easily obtain dried Italian porcini through the Internet or by mail order. You should always have some in your kitchen. When refrigerated in an airtight container they will last a very, very long time. Read more about dried porcini on page 62 of** At Master Class.

A 1-pound assortment of fresh mushrooms, including white button, Portobello, and preferably shiitake

2 tablespoons extra virgin olive oil

3 tablespoons *scalogno* (shallots), chopped very fine

Fine sea salt

Black pepper ground fresh from the mill

1 pound live mussels, their shells shut tight

3 tablespoons extra virgin olive oil

2 tablespoons garlic, chopped very fine

⅓ cup chopped Italian flat-leaf parsley

Black pepper ground fresh from the mill

1 pound short tubular pasta, such as penne or *maccheroncini*

A large warm serving bowl

For 4 to 6 persons

1 For the mushroom base: Put the dried porcini in a medium bowl and pour at least 1 cup of lukewarm water over them. There has to be enough water to cover them. Set them aside to steep for at least 30 minutes.

2 Detach and discard the stems of the shiitake. Wash all the fresh mushroom rapidly under cold running water, cut them in half lengthwise, then cut them across into the thinnest possible slices.

3 When the dried porcini have become soft and limp, retrieve them with your hand, squeeze as much water from them back into the bowl where, for the time being, you will save the water from their soak. Wash the porcini in several changes of cold water to cleanse away any grit, and set them aside.

4 Line a small strainer with a sheet of paper towel or with a coffee filter. Use it to strain the liquid from the mushroom soak into a clean container.

5 Pour the olive oil into a 10-inch skillet, add the chopped shallots, and turn on the heat to medium. Cook the shallots, stirring from time to time, until they become colored a deep gold. Add the reconstituted porcini and sauté them for about 1 minute, stirring frequently.

6 Pour the filtered water of the porcini soak into the pan and turn up the heat to bring the liquid to a bubbling simmer. Stir from time to time until all the liquid has boiled down, then add all the sliced fresh mushrooms to the pan. Sprinkle with salt, turn them once or twice to coat them well, lower the heat, and cover the pan. If all the mushrooms do not fit into the pan at one time, let some of them cook down a bit to make room for the rest. You will presently see the mushrooms release their vegetal liquid. When all their liquid has cooked away, cook them for another 30 minutes or more. Taste and correct for salt, sprinkle with a few grindings of black pepper, and take off the heat.

Marcella Says: **Do not undercook these or any other mushrooms. You want them tasty, not chewy, and they become tasty only after long cooking has made them soft.**

AHEAD-OF-TIME NOTE: You can cook the mushrooms up to this point a day in advance of serving the sauce. Store them in the refrigerator. When ready to resume cooking, reheat them gently in the pan, adding a tablespoon of water, if necessary.

7   For the mussels: Soak the mussels in several changes of cold water, scrubbing them vigorously each time with a stiff brush. Cut off any protruding whiskery tuft. Discard any mussel that does not clamp shut.

8   Drop the pasta into 4 quarts of salted, rapidly boiling water.

9   Pour the olive oil into a 12-inch skillet or sauté pan, add the chopped garlic, turn the heat on to medium, and cook the garlic, stirring it, until it becomes colored a pale gold. Add the chopped parsley, stir two or three times, then put in all the mussels, and cover the pan. When you see the mussels begin to open, add all the mushrooms, and uncover the pan. Sprinkle with several grindings of black pepper, turn the contents of the pan over once or twice, and continue cooking until all the mussels have opened. Taste and correct for salt. Toss immediately in the warm bowl with the hot pasta the instant that it is drained. Serve at once.

Fresh Tuna and Zucchini Pasta Sauce

✒ *Sugo di Tonno e Zucchine*

Tuna is an excellent ingredient, but it needs help. The ubiquitous and boring rare grilled tuna steak is one of the most inert things one can eat. On the other hand, take a choice cut of Mediterranean tuna, especially the blue fin, and even more especially its belly, boil it in salted water, can it in olive oil, and you have a taste you can never tire of. When it comes to fresh tuna, I like it cast in a pasta sauce where a few aromatic components—note below the presence of garlic, bay leaves, parsley, lemon zest—prompt it into giving a vibrant performance.

¾ pound fresh, young, firm zucchini, not baby vegetables nor overgrown ones

¾ pound fresh tuna

3 tablespoons extra virgin olive oil

2 or 3 garlic cloves, peeled and lightly smashed with the flat part of a heavy knife blade

2 bay leaves

¼ cup dry white wine

Fine sea salt

Black pepper ground fresh from the mill

2 tablespoons chopped Italian flat-leaf parsley

The grated peel of 1 lemon, the yellow outer layer only, none of the inner white pith

1 pound boxed pasta: A short tubular shape, such as ridged penne, seems to work best with this sauce, but so would fusilli.

2 tablespoons freshly grated Fiore Sardo, Pecorino Romano, or other hard sheep's milk cheese

A warm serving bowl

For 4 persons

1 Soak the zucchini in a basin of cold water for at least 10 minutes. Wash them well under running water, rubbing their skin with your hand to loosen and remove any embedded soil. Cut off the ends, then cut the zucchini into ½-inch dice.

2 If the tuna still has some of its skin, slice it off. Also discard any blackish portions of the flesh. Wash the fish in cold water, then pat it dry with kitchen towels. Cut the tuna into ½-inch dice like the zucchini.

3 Drop the pasta in 4 quarts of salted, rapidly boiling water.

4 Choose a 12-inch skillet, preferably nonstick. Add the olive oil, the garlic cloves, and the bay leaves and turn on the heat to medium. Cook, stirring from time to time, until the garlic becomes colored a light nut brown, then remove and discard it along with the bay leaves.

5 Turn up the heat to high and when the oil is quite hot slip in the diced tuna. Turn it two or three times, then use a slotted spoon or spatula to transfer it from the pan to a plate.

> *Marcella Says:* **You don't want to cook the tuna any longer than this because it will become dry but, as you will see, you will return it to the pan briefly before saucing the pasta.**

6 Pour the wine into the pan, scraping loose any cooked-on particles from the bottom. When the wine has bubbled away, put in the diced zucchini, and add salt, liberal grindings of black pepper, the parsley, and the grated lemon peel. Cook over very high heat, stirring constantly, for no longer than 1 to 2 minutes to keep the zucchini firm.

AHEAD-OF-TIME NOTE: If you need to, you can prepare most of the sauce several hours before you are ready to cook and serve the pasta. When you put the zucchini in the pan, stir once, then immediately take it off the heat. When ready to proceed, assuming the pasta is almost done, turn the heat under the pan on to high, and continue to cook the zucchini, stirring constantly, stopping before the pieces become too soft.

7 When the pasta is nearly cooked, season the tuna with salt and pepper, and slide it off the plate into the pan, stirring quickly.

8 Transfer the drained, cooked al dente pasta into the warm serving bowl and toss immediately with the full contents of the skillet. Sprinkle with the grated cheese and serve at once.

Veal Pasta Sauce with Red, Green, and Yellow Peppers
Ragù di Vitello col Sughetto di Peperoni Rossi, Verdi, e Gialli

"Do we really have to skin the peppers and tomatoes raw?" I have often seen the question on my students' faces even if they refrained from saying it out loud. The advantage of a live class is that afterward you can say, "Here, taste this, now do you understand why?" My reader will have to proceed on faith, and when she or he does, then the clarity and richness of flavor in this sauce will speak for me.

6 meaty bell peppers 2 red, 2 green, and 2 yellow

¼ cup extra virgin olive oil

6 or 7 whole garlic cloves, peeled

Fine sea salt

4 fresh, ripe, firm plum tomatoes

2 tablespoons vegetable oil

2 tablespoons butter

½ cup onion, chopped very finely

½ pound ground veal/ground sausage meat.

Black pepper ground fresh from the mill

Pappardelle or fettuccine, made with 3 whole eggs, as described on pages 40–42 of Why and How You Should Be Making Your Own Egg Pasta, OR 10 ounces boxed fettuccine OR 1 pound short tubular boxed pasta, preferably penne. Other shapes that would be congenial to this sauce are *maccheroncini*, rigatoni, or ziti.

For serving *pappardelle* or fettuccine: a platter; for boxed pasta: a deep bowl. In either case, it must be warm.

¼ cup freshly grated Parmigiano-Reggiano cheese, adjusting the quantity to taste

For 6 persons

1   Cut each pepper lengthwise along its creases, remove the stem, the seeds, and pithy core, then peel, as described on page 79 of The Why and How of Prepping Vegetables. Cut the peppers into strips slightly less than 1 inch wide.

2   Pour the olive oil into a 12-inch skillet, preferably nonstick. Add the garlic cloves, turn the heat on to medium high, and cook the garlic, turning it from time to time, until it becomes colored a light nut-brown. Remove from the pan and discard.

3   Add the peppers with a pinch or two of salt and turn the heat down to medium. Cook the peppers, turning them over from time to time, until they are quite tender. It should take about 45 minutes and they will be wilted and considerably diminished in bulk.

4   While the peppers are cooking you can move forward with other steps of the sauce. Skin the tomatoes using the swivel-blade vegetable peeler. (Don't skin them by scalding them in hot water because you want them to be very firm.) Chop them coarsely.

5   Pour the vegetable oil into a 10-inch skillet, and add the butter and chopped onion. Turn the heat on to medium high and cook the onion, stirring from time to time, until it becomes colored a pale gold.

6   Add the ground veal with some salt and liberal grindings of black pepper, and turn the heat down to medium. Cook the meat, turning it once or twice, until it has completely lost its raw color. Add the tomatoes with any of their juice, then turn the heat down some more to cook at a gentle simmer for about 20 minutes.

7   If the peppers are done, transfer the contents of the skillet with the veal to the pan with the peppers, turning all the ingredients over two or three times to coat them well. Cook at a gentle simmer for 15 minutes, stirring from time to time. Taste and correct for salt.

> *Marcella Says:* **The usual practice in Italian cooking is to cook everything in its proper sequence in the same pan, a practice that contributes to the immediacy and integration of flavors characteristic of the cuisine. Nonetheless there are exceptions, as in this case, where the veal is cooked separately and combined later with the peppers to preserve its juiciness.**

AHEAD-OF-TIME NOTE: You may cook the sauce through to completion 2 or 3 days in advance. Refrigerate it in a tightly sealed container. When you are ready to proceed, begin reheating it at a very gentle simmer as you begin to cook the pasta. If you find that the consistency of the sauce is not as fluid as you would like it to be, add up to 3 tablespoons water while the sauce is simmering.

8   Cook the pasta in 4 quarts of salted, rapidly boiling water. The instant it is done al dente, tender yet firm to the bite, drain it and transfer it to the warm serving platter or bowl. Pour the sauce over it. Toss quickly and thoroughly, add the grated Parmesan, and toss again. Serve at once.

VEAL PASTA SAUCE WITH FOUR DIFFERENT VARIETIES OF MUSHROOMS

Ragù di Vitello con Quattro Varietà di Funghi

When I was living in Bologna, where I had a cooking school, my next-door neighbor was a canny forager of wild mushrooms. Through much of the year, but mostly in the fall, he hiked in the woods of the hills north and west of the city and brought back, from places whose location he never disclosed, basketfuls of mushrooms, *porcini* (boletus), *gallinacci* (chanterelles), *spugnole* (morels), *sanguinacci* (pine mushrooms), and others whose names I have since forgotten. Because lovers of mushrooms prize the flavor, texture, and fragrance of porcini above those of all others I once asked him "Why, when you know where to find such magnificent porcini, do you bother looking for anything else?" "Have you ever made risotto with porcini?" he asked back. "Certainly," I replied. "And have you ever made lasagne with porcini?" he added. "Of course I have." "*Brava, brava!* And you used only porcini?" "Naturally." Wagging his finger at me, he went on ironically, "*Ma che brava!* Next time, however, just try adding two or three other varieties to the porcini, and then you'll begin to understand what mushroom flavor is about. *Quello sì ch'è sapore,* that really is taste!"

I was thankful that none of my students was around to hear that dressing down. Miffed though I was, I followed his advice, and on the many occasions since that I have done so I remember that exchange. I hear his broad Bolognese vowels. I see the knobby and soil-blackened finger wagging at me. How right he was. Marvelous though porcini are, when they are joined in a pasta sauce or in a risotto by other kinds of mushrooms that single bass note of theirs grows to a full chorus of harmonizing flavors.

In my Florida supermarket there are no fresh porcini, no chanterelles, no morels, no *sanguinacci*, but there are fresh shiitake, cremini, portobello, and white button mushrooms. And I can get choice imported dried porcini—whose aroma is far more effusive than the reticent one of the fresh—from either local sources or online specialty food sites. I bring them together in a *ragù*, to use the Italian term for meat sauce, that I think might well cause my Bolognese friend's finger to stop its wagging.

One of this *ragù*'s great virtues is its versatility. Use it as a meat sauce for homemade egg pasta—*pappardelle* or *tagliatelle* would be my choice—or as the filling for lasagne, see page 187. Or use it with boxed dry pasta—chunky shapes, such as rigatoni, or as a base on which to build the most savory of risottos. Please see page 192 where a scaled-down version of the *ragù* becomes a tasty filling for ravioli.

For the mushrooms

2 ounces imported dried porcini mushrooms (See the full discussion of dried porcini on page 62 of AT MASTER CLASS.)

6 ounces fresh shiitake mushrooms

6 ounces cremini mushrooms, also known as baby bella

½ pound fresh white button mushrooms

Two 12-inch nonstick skillets or sauté pans or one of each kind

> *Marcella Says:* **If you have two 12-inch skillets or sauté pans—there never seem to be too many such pans in an Italian kitchen—I suggest that you use both as a timesaving measure. You can cook the mushrooms, which are done in olive oil, and the veal, which is best with butter, simultaneously. Of course, if you have only one pan, you can first do the mushrooms, wipe the pan clean, and then cook the meat. For this kind of cooking I find that nonstick coatings make the pot-washer's life a lot easier, but of course you can cook quite well on conventional surfaces, too.**

4 tablespoons extra virgin olive oil

1 cup onion, chopped fine

Fine sea salt

For the veal sauce

4 tablespoons butter

1 cup onion, chopped fine

1 pound ground veal

1 cup dry white wine

Black pepper ground fresh from the mill

6 fresh, ripe plum tomatoes, peeled, seeded, and cut up

2 teaspoons freshly grated nutmeg

YIELD: *about 10 cups of veal and mushroom* ragù, *enough for 12 servings*

1 For the mushrooms: Pour 1½ cups lukewarm water into a small bowl, drop in the dried porcini mushrooms, and let them soak until you need to use them in this recipe by which time, 30 minutes or more, they should have absorbed enough water to become soft.

2 While the porcini are soaking, detach and discard the shiitake stems. Briskly wash all of the mushrooms in cold running water and slice them very thin, using a knife or the slicing disk of a food processor, if you prefer.

3 Retrieve the dried porcini mushrooms from their soak, but do not discard the liquid. Wash the mushrooms in various changes of cold water and cut any extra-large pieces into two or three smaller ones. Filter the liquid from the mushroom soak through a coffee filter or a paper towel folded into a funnel, into a small container.

4 Pour the olive oil into one of the 12-inch pans, add the 1 cup chopped onion, and turn on the heat to medium high. Cook the onion, stirring from time to time, until it becomes colored a deep gold.

5 Add the softened reconstituted porcini, cook them for 1 minute, turning them two or three times, then add the filtered liquid from their soak.

6 When the porcini soaking liquid has evaporated completely, add as many of the sliced fresh mushrooms to the pan as will fit cozily, sprinkling them with salt. Turn them over once or twice to coat them well, then turn the heat down to medium. When the mushrooms have released some liquid and shrunk in bulk, add the remaining mushrooms. Cook, turning the mushrooms over from time to time, for about 1½ hours, until they have become very soft and all the liquid they have released has evaporated. Take off the heat.

7 For the veal sauce: While the mushrooms are cooking, put the butter and the 1 cup chopped onion in the second pan and turn on the heat to high. Cook the onion, stirring from time to time, until it becomes colored a deep gold. Add the ground veal, crumbling it with a fork, and turn it once or twice to coat it well. When all the meat has been browned lightly and uniformly, pour the wine into the pan, and add salt and several grindings of black pepper.

8 When the wine has bubbled away completely, add the tomatoes, turn the heat down to the lowest setting possible, and cook for about 45 minutes, stirring the contents of the uncovered pan from time to time.

9 When the meat and the mushrooms are done, empty the contents of both pans into a large bowl, and, with a wooden spoon, turn the contents over several times to combine them into an evenly distributed mixture.

10 Wipe both pans clean with paper towels. Divide the contents of the bowl evenly between the two pans, turn on the heat under both to medium low, and cook for 20 minutes, stirring frequently. If you are not going to use the sauce the same day, empty the contents of both pans into the bowl you had just used, cover with plastic film, and refrigerate. Reheat gently but thoroughly before using.

AHEAD-OF-TIME NOTE: You can refrigerate the finished sauce in a tightly sealed container for 5 days, or you can freeze it for up to 3 months. Bring to actual room temperature before reheating.

SICILIAN PESTO
✑ *Pesto alla Siciliana*

That Sicily has its own take on pesto I had long known, but I had never tasted it until my husband and I stopped overnight in Erice, the ancient and mysteriously beautiful mountain town that is perched seemingly a mile high, overlooking the city of Trapani on the island's northwestern tip. Trapani is in fact the birthplace of this sauce, which has little in common with Genoa's far more celebrated pesto except for the name and for the fact that it too is a sauce served raw on pasta. Trapani's pesto contains one of Sicily's most typical products, almonds, instead of pine nuts; the herb in it is not basil but mint; chili pepper is among its ingredients, and the color of the sauce—derived from a generous dose of fresh tomatoes—is southern red rather than northern green. I like both pestos equally, but they satisfy me differently: The Genoese is more herbal, it registers cool on the palate; the sensations the Sicilian one delivers are sultry and ripe.

2 ounces, about ½ heaping cup, peeled almonds

1 whole garlic clove, peeled

4 tablespoons extra virgin olive oil

2 tablespoons grated Pecorino cheese, preferably one milder than Romano

½ cup tightly packed washed fresh mint leaves

¼ teaspoon dried red chili pepper, or more to taste

3 or 4 ripe, firm, fresh plum tomatoes, peeled raw, split open, seeds scooped away, and cut up, about 1 cup

1 teaspoon fine sea salt

YIELD: *enough pesto for 1 pound boxed pasta, preferably spaghettini (thin spaghetti, serving 6 persons)*

Put all of the ingredients in a food processor and process to a creamy consistency. Taste and correct for salt. Toss with pasta that has just been drained and is still piping hot in a warm bowl. Serve at once.

AHEAD-OF-TIME NOTE: The sauce may be refrigerated in a tightly sealed container for up to a week.

Pork or Veal and Zucchini Pasta Sauce

~ *Sugo di Maiale o di Vitello e Zucchine*

One might not think that the choice of pork or veal could affect the sauce too much, yet from each you will end up with distinctly different pasta dishes. If you choose pork, the cooking fat should be olive oil, and the most satisfactory pasta match for the sauce would be the firm-bodied dried, boxed factory-made pasta in a tubular shape, such as penne or small maccheroni, or a shape with nesting hollows for the sauce, such as *ruote di carro* or *conchiglie*. The finished dish should be tossed with grated Pecorino, hard sheep's milk cheese. If it were available to you, a Sardinian Fiore Sardo or a well-aged Tuscan Pecorino would be a more desirable choice than Romano.

If you choose to use veal, sauté it in butter instead of olive oil, and toss the sauce with a light-bodied homemade egg pasta, such as *tagliatelle* or fettuccine. The Parmesan cheese in this version can only be Parmigiano-Reggiano.

5 or 6 firm and glossy medium zucchini

5 or 6 fresh, firm plum tomatoes

4 tablespoons extra virgin olive oil if using pork, 3 tablespoons butter if using veal

⅔ cup onion, chopped very fine

8 ounces ground pork or veal

Fine sea salt

Black pepper ground fresh from the mill

YIELD: *enough pork and zucchini sauce for 1 pound factory-made pasta, serving 4 to 6 persons* OR *veal and zucchini sauce for 2-egg homemade* **tagliatelle** *or fettuccine, approximately ¾ pound, serving 4 persons. (See pasta and cheese recommendations in introductory note above.)*

1   Soak the zucchini in a basin of cold water for about 20 minutes, then rub their skin clean under cold running water. Trim away the ends, then cut the zucchini into the thinnest strips that you can.

2   Use a swivel-blade vegetable peeler to skin the tomatoes. Refer, if you wish, to Tomatoes on page 80 of The Why and How of Prepping Vegetables. Split them, scoop away the seeds without mashing the shells, and cut them into ¼-inch dice.

3   Put the fat you have chosen in a 10-inch skillet with the chopped onion and turn on the heat to medium high. Cook the onion, stirring from time to time, until it becomes colored a deep gold.

4   Add the ground meat together with salt and several grindings of pepper. Turn the meat over with a wooden spoon, crumbling and coating it well. Cook until it is browned, then add the zucchini. Turn up the heat and cook the zucchini over lively heat, turning them over from time to time, until they become lightly browned.

5   Add the diced tomatoes, turning them over with the wooden spoon until coated well. Cook for about 2 minutes. If the pasta is ready, drain it, transfer it to a warm serving bowl, and toss immediately with the hot sauce.

AHEAD-OF-TIME NOTE: The fresh flavor of this sauce does not improve with reheating.

LELE RIVOLTA'S LEEK SAUCE
☞ *Il Sugo di Porri della Lele*

Lele, short for Rachele, is a Milanese artist who lives with her husband Piero, a ship-builder and developer, on a neighboring island to ours on the Gulf of Mexico. When we were over for dinner one evening, she said she had made pasta with leeks. "Just leeks?" I asked.

"*Certo*—of course—just leeks" was the answer. How can that be, I thought. Leeks alone can be so cloying. But then, as it turned out, there was garlic, and lots of black pepper, and a heap of grated Parmesan, and the flavors balanced out. A lovely sauce it was, indeed, with both finesse and gusto.

6 large leeks

1 tablespoon vegetable oil

3 tablespoons butter

6 whole garlic cloves, peeled

Fine sea salt

½ cup heavy whipping cream

Black pepper ground fresh from the mill

1 pound very good-quality imported Italian macaroni

> *Marcella Says:* Lele tosses her sauce with *strozzapreti,* a short shape with a twist to it. Fusilli would also be a good choice. My preference goes to penne in the shorter of the two versions that are usually available.

A hot serving bowl

Freshly grated Parmigiano-Reggiano cheese

For 4 to 6 persons

1 Cut away the root end on each leek. Slice the white bulbous part into rounds about ¼ inch thick. When you get to the green tops, discard the first and even the second layer of leaves to expose more of the white leek flesh, which you should also slice into rounds. Put all the slices in a colander, run cold water over them, and shake off the excess water, but do not dry off the leeks.

2 Pour the oil into a 10- to 12-inch skillet, add the butter and the garlic cloves, and turn on the heat to medium. Cook the garlic briefly, stirring it, and when it becomes colored a very pale blond, remove it from the pan. Add the sliced leeks to the pan, sprinkling them with salt. Cook the leeks, stirring them from time to time, until they become very soft, almost creamy in consistency. If you find that at some point there is insufficient liquid to continue the cooking and the leeks are not quite done yet, add 3 or 4 tablespoons water.

3 When the leeks are completely soft, raise the heat to high, and continue cooking them until they become colored a pale nut color, turning them over from time to time. Sprinkle with generous grindings of pepper to counterbalance their potentially cloying sweetness.

4 Add the cream and reduce it over high heat to a moderately dense consistency.

5 As soon as the pasta is done to a firm, al dente consistency, drain it and toss it immediately in the hot serving bowl with the sauce. Add a generous amount of freshly grated Parmesan, toss thoroughly five or six times, and serve at once.

Late-Night Pasta Sauce with Pine Nuts and Raisins

✒ Spaghettata della Mezzanotte con Pinoli ed Uvetta

At the hour that some of my neighbors in Florida are already halfway into their night's sleep, many Italians are beginning to feel a gnawing emptiness that needs to be filled with a quick plate of spaghetti. The main meal in Italy usually comes early in the day, at noontime, so that it's not uncommon for those who stay up late, and not a few do, particularly in the South, to experience hunger when night is at its zenith. It is these sensations that have given rise to *la spaghettata della mezzanotte*, which might be translated informally as the midnight spaghetti bash. The sauces for a *spaghettata* have to fulfill two requirements: They must be of the quickest to make because no one wants to start cooking something lengthy at midnight, and they must taste lively. The one below fills the bill on both counts.

½ cup golden raisins

½ cup pine nuts

¼ cup extra virgin olive oil

1 large OR 2 small garlic cloves, peeled and chopped fine

2 tablespoons of the pasta cooking water

Fine sea salt

1 pound boxed pasta, preferably *spaghettini* (thin spaghetti), or very small penne

A warm serving bowl

For 4 to 6 persons

1 Let the raisins steep in lukewarm water to cover until they swell. Drain them and chop them coarsely.

2 Chop the pine nuts coarsely, then mash them slightly, using the flat side of a knife blade or a meat pounder.

3 Put the olive oil and chopped garlic in a small skillet, turn on the heat to medium, and cook just until the garlic becomes colored a pale gold, but no darker. Add the chopped pine nuts and cook, stirring, for about 1 minute. Add the chopped raisins, stir well, and cook for just a few seconds. Turn off the heat.

4 Cook the pasta in 4 quarts of salted, rapidly boiling water. When almost done, turn on the heat under the skillet containing the sauce to medium low, retrieve about 2 tablespoonfuls of the pasta cooking water, and add it to the sauce together with some salt, stirring rapidly.

5 Drain the pasta the moment it is cooked al dente, tender but firm to the bite. Immediately transfer it to the warm serving bowl and toss it with the sauce. Serve at once.

Blasut's Chicken Thigh Pasta Sauce with Herbs, Tomatoes, and White Wine

Il Sugo di Cosce di Pollo di Blasut

Dante Bernardis uses the name Blasut both for himself and for his restaurant in Lavariano, a Friuli farmland town. Dante makes this pasta sauce with young roosters, which are tastier than hens. To achieve comparable flavor with what is available in the meat counter of most markets, I have used chicken thighs, the tastiest part of the bird. The liberal use of herbs, unusual in most Italian cooking, makes the sauce intensely aromatic and endows it with a depth of flavor that one generally associates with game. It is excellent on sturdy pasta shapes, such as penne, and I also find it to be a very congenial match with the grilled pasta known as *Mlinci*—find it on page 198—which is sublimely presented at Al Cacciatore restaurant in Friuli.

4 chicken thighs, about 1½ pounds

2 tablespoons vegetable oil

3 tablespoons butter

⅓ cup onion, chopped fine

⅓ cup carrot, chopped fine

½ cup celery, chopped fine

Fine sea salt

Black pepper ground fresh from the mill

7 large or 10 small fresh mint leaves, chopped

1 cup dry white wine

2 cups tomatoes cut up with their juice, using either ripe, firm, fresh plum tomatoes, peeled raw, split, and seeds scooped out OR canned imported San Marzano Italian tomatoes

A mixture of 1 teaspoon fresh rosemary leaves, 1 tablespoon fresh sage leaves, and 3 to 4 strips of lemon peel, just the yellow skin with none of the white pith beneath, chopped together fine

YIELD: *enough sauce for 6 servings of pasta*

1 Remove the skin and all the fat from the chicken thighs, wash them in cold running water, and cut all the flesh away from the bone. Grind the meat fine in a food processor or a meat grinder.

2 Put the oil, butter, and chopped onion in a medium skillet, turn on the heat to medium high, and cook the onion, stirring from time to time, until it becomes colored a light gold.

3 Add the chopped carrot and celery and cook for a minute or so, turning the vegetables over from time to time to coat them well.

4 Add the ground chicken, turn the heat up, and cook for 6 to 7 minutes, turning the meat over frequently.

5 Add salt, pepper, the mint leaves, and the white wine, turning the contents of the skillet over two or three times.

6 When the wine has bubbled away, add the tomatoes, turn the contents of the skillet over, and lower the heat. Let the tomatoes cook at a gentle but steady simmer for 30 to 45 minutes in the uncovered pan until, when you skim the surface of the sauce with the side of a wooden spoon, the fat following the spoon's trail runs clear.

7 Add the mixture of chopped rosemary, sage, and lemon peel, turn it over with the contents of the skillet to distribute it thoroughly, and cook at a gentle simmer for 10 minutes.

AHEAD-OF-TIME NOTE: You can cook the sauce a day or two in advance. Refrigerate it until you are ready to use it.

Spaghetti "Rotolo" with Zucchini and Bacon

Il Rotolo di Spaghetti con il Sugo di Zucchine e Pancetta Affumicata

Just outside S. Giovanni al Natisone in southeastern Friuli, there used to be, and there still may be, a small tennis and horseback riding resort called Shangri-la. The food was happily more Italian than the unlikely name, but the exceptionally accomplished kitchen turned away from regionally accented cooking to generically Italian dishes that they deftly executed. For their spaghetti *rotolo*, each single portion of pasta is rolled up with its sauce on a long fork to make what looks like an elongated skein of wool. Aside from its appetizing visual appeal, it has the considerable merit of imposing on whoever prepares it a full integration of pasta and sauce, a goal that cooks don't always pursue as diligently as they might.

1 pound fresh, young zucchini

2 tablespoons vegetable oil

2 tablespoons butter

2 or 3 whole garlic cloves, peeled

A 5- to 6-inch sprig fresh rosemary

A 12-inch skillet

Fine sea salt

Black pepper ground fresh from the mill

½ cup fine julienne strips of thick-sliced or slab bacon

½ cup dry white wine

1 pound high-quality imported Italian spaghetti OR spaghettini OR ¾ pound fettuccine

⅔ cup freshly grated Parmigiano-Reggiano cheese

A meat or kitchen fork with 2 long tines

A warm shallow serving platter

For 4 to 6 persons

The Sauce

1 Soak the zucchini for about 20 minutes in a basin of cold water. Scrub them under running cold water using a brush or rough cloth. Cut off both ends.

2 Cut the zucchini into fine shreds, either by hand or in a food processor. If using a food processor shredding disk, which does a very good job, first cut the cleaned zucchini into pieces that will fit into the processor feeding tube.

3 Put the oil, butter, garlic cloves, and rosemary in the 12-inch skillet and turn on the heat to medium high. Cook for about a minute or less, stirring frequently, being careful not to let the garlic become colored. Remove and discard the garlic cloves and rosemary sprig.

4 Add the shredded zucchini, salt, and pepper. Turn the zucchini over frequently to coat them thoroughly. After about a minute, add the bacon strips, turning them over two or three times.

5 Add the wine and let it bubble away at medium heat, stirring from time to time. When the wine has evaporated completely, the sauce should have acquired a creamy consistency and is ready to use with pasta.

> *Marcella Says:* **It is very important that the consistency of the sauce be quite creamy so that it can subsequently pull the pasta together to form the** *rotolo*.

AHEAD-OF-TIME NOTE: You can make the sauce several hours in advance and reheat it gently before tossing it with the pasta, but don't keep it overnight because the zucchini will acquire a slightly sour taste.

The Rotolo

1 If you are proceeding immediately to cook the pasta, leave the zucchini sauce in the skillet, warming it gently while the pasta cooks. If you have made the sauce in advance, put it in a 12-inch skillet to warm while the pasta cooks.

2 Cook the pasta in liberally salted boiling water until it is done to a very firm al dente consistency. Just before draining it, ladle 2 or 3 tablespoons of the cooking water into the skillet with the sauce.

3 Add the drained pasta to the skillet with the sauce, turn it over once, remove the skillet from the heat, and add the grated Parmesan, rapidly turning the strands in the sauce to coat them thoroughly.

4 With the long-tined fork, spear just enough pasta, and no more, to make a single serving portion and roll it up, lifting it from the skillet every other turn of the fork. Curl the spaghetti up and around the fork, making a shape like an elongated skein, about 2 inches wide and 4 to 5 inches long. Working quickly, transfer the *rotolo* to the warm serving platter, using a spoon to slide it off the fork. Repeat the operation, lining up the rolls side by side on the platter. When you have rolled up all the pasta, distribute any sauce remaining in the skillet over the pasta, and serve at once. Each *rotolo* should constitute a single full portion.

Homemade Pasta and Gnocchi

FETTUCCINE WITH PROSCIUTTO, CREAM, AND NUTMEG

✑ *Fettuccine con Prosciutto, Panna, e Noce Moscata*

An Alfredo sauce is the clearest example of the kind of sauce the open pores of good homemade egg pasta are greedy for. They are ideal collectors of butter and cream, which is basically all that the celebrated Roman sauce consists of. To that familiar foundation I have added the taste of my native Emilia-Romagna, prosciutto. At home, prosciutto quickly sautéed in butter was the quick alternative to a long-simmered meat sauce and that is what we often used on our hand-rolled *tagliatelle*. I like what prosciutto contributes to the Alfredo formula, the way its spiciness relieves the palate-coating denseness of all that butter and cream. This is one sauce you need no salt in because it draws it principally from the ham and partly from the Parmesan cheese.

3 tablespoons butter

Prosciutto cut into narrow strips to measure ⅔ cup

½ cup heavy cream

¼ teaspoon freshly grated nutmeg

⅓ cup freshly grated Parmigiano-Reggiano cheese

Fettuccine made with 3 whole eggs, as described on pages 40–42 of Why and How You Should Be Making Your Own Egg Pasta, OR 10 ounces boxed fettuccine

> *Marcella Says:* **You can use an enameled cast-iron pan both to make the sauce and serve the pasta, but if you don't have one, make the sauce in a 10-inch skillet, preferably nonstick, and serve the pasta on a very warm serving platter.**

For 4 persons

1 Put the butter and the prosciutto in whichever pan you are using, enameled cast iron or any skillet, and turn on the heat to low. Lightly brown the prosciutto, stirring from time to time, being careful not to overcook it and dry it out.

2 Add the cream and nutmeg, and cook down the cream, stirring from time to time, reducing it by a third. Remember that egg pasta is thirsty for sauce, so do not reduce it too much. Should you inadvertently reduce it more than you would have liked, do not add more cream, but extend it with 2 or 3 tablespoons of the pasta cooking water when tossing the fettuccine. Turn off the heat until the pasta is cooked.

3 When the fettuccine is done, tender but firm to the bite, turn on the heat to medium under the pan with the sauce. Drain the pasta at once, reserving a few tablespoonfuls of the cooking water in case of need, and slide it into the pan. Toss thoroughly, adding some of the cooking water if required to loosen the sauce. Add the grated Parmesan, toss again, and serve promptly directly from the enameled cast-iron pan, if that is what you used. If you used a skillet, empty its contents onto a warm serving platter and serve at once.

LASAGNE TREVISO-STYLE
WITH RADICCHIO AND BELGIAN ENDIVE

Il Pasticcio come Lo Fanno a Treviso con il Radicchio Tardivo

Eighteen miles north of Venice, the beautiful and gluttonous town of Treviso has given its name to the two most alluring versions of radicchio. The wine-red one known succinctly as *radicchio di Treviso* has soft, elongated leaves like those of a small head of romaine lettuce. It can be better described as early Treviso radicchio because it matures at the beginning of fall. In local markets, it is called *radicchio variegato di Treviso*. A rarer, far costlier sibling matures at the end of the fall season and consequently it is called late Treviso radicchio or, in Italian, simply *radicchio tardivo*. The leaves that shoot out flame-like from its root are almost all rib, pearly white with a vivid purple fringe. Its luscious flavor and delicate yet bracing bittersweet finish make it the paramount radicchio for cooking.

Almost as fine an ingredient when making risotto or pasta is the romaine-shaped early radicchio, which at this writing is the only one of the two available in America. The round radicchio whose cabbage-like head has become ubiquitous in supermarkets is known to Italians as *rosa di Chioggia*, Chioggia rose. It is the most frankly bitter of all red radicchios, a bitterness that in cooking asks to be tempered by a milder-mannered member of the chicory family, Belgian endive, as I have done in this recipe.

For the filling

1½ pounds good-quality thick-cut bacon

12 heads Belgian endive

2 round heads Chioggia or long Treviso radicchio (see the introductory note above)

2 tablespoons butter plus additional for greasing the lasagne baking dish and for dotting the lasagne

1 tablespoon vegetable oil

Fine sea salt

Black pepper ground fresh from the mill

Lasagne pasta made with 5 whole eggs, as described on pages 40–42 of Why and How You Should Be Making Your Own Egg Pasta

For the béchamel sauce

3 cups whole milk

6 tablespoons butter

4½ tablespoons all-purpose flour

¼ teaspoon freshly grated nutmeg

Fine sea salt

⅓ cup freshly grated Parmigiano-Reggiano cheese

A rectangular oven-to-table baking dish approximately 18 by 12 by 2½ inches high or its equivalent

For 8 to 10 persons

1   For the filling: Cut the bacon into strips no wider than ½ inch, but preferably as thin as ⅛ inch, to measure 4 to 4½ cups.

2   Slice off the root end of each endive and cut the tops lengthwise into narrow strips.

3   Pull away any bruised or wilted leaves from the radicchio, trim the root end, and slice the head into strips as narrow as the endive strips.

4   Put the 2 tablespoons butter and the oil in a 12-inch sauté pan or skillet, turn the heat on to medium high, add the bacon strips, and cook without letting them become crisp.

5   Put as much of the sliced endive and radicchio as will fit, piled up, in the pan, add salt, turn the vegetables over a few times to coat them well, and turn the heat down to medium. As soon as the vegetables have wilted down making room for more, add the remainder, turning them all over a few times. Proceed in this way until all the endive and radicchio are in the pan. Continue cooking them, turning them from time to time, until they are so tender to be almost creamy. Grind fresh black pepper over the cooked vegetables, turn them over once or twice, and take off the heat.

Marcella Says: At this point, the vegetables can be turned into a delicious sauce for pasta, serving 6 people. To do so, add 2 more tablespoons of butter to the vegetables before they finish cooking, and add 1 tablespoon butter to the pasta when you toss it.

AHEAD-OF-TIME NOTE: You can cook the vegetables for the filling 3 or 4 days in advance. Store them in refrigerator in a tightly sealed container, and bring back to full room temperature before using as a filling for the lasagne.

6 For the béchamel sauce: Prepare the sauce following the directions on pages 300 to 301, using the amounts in the ingredients list.

7 Turn on the oven to 400°. Lightly smear the bottom and sides of the lasagne dish with butter.

8 Turn the contents of the sauté pan into a large bowl and mix the béchamel sauce into them.

9 To assemble the lasagne: Having made the pasta strips and blanched them as described on pages 40 to 42 of Why and How You Should Be Making Your Own Egg Pasta, line the buttered baking dish with one layer of pasta. Do not overlap the pieces, but trim the pasta to fit. Spread some of the vegetable mixture thinly and evenly over the pasta, sprinkle with grated Parmesan, and top with another layer of pasta. Proceed in this manner until you have used up all the pasta and nearly all filling, arranging five or more layers of lasagne in the dish. Top with the remaining filling and a sprinkling of Parmesan and dot with butter.

AHEAD-OF-TIME NOTE: You can prepare the lasagne up to this point 2 or 3 days in advance. Cover with plastic film and refrigerate. Bring to room temperature before baking.

10 Bake the lasagne in the preheated oven for 15 to 20 minutes, until the top becomes colored a rich mottled gold. Let the dish settle out of the oven for 5 to 8 minutes before serving.

EIGHT-LAYER SPINACH LASAGNE WITH VEAL AND FOUR-MUSHROOM FILLING

✒ Lasagne Verdi ai Quattro Funghi

Shortly after my husband and I left Venice to settle in Longboat Key on Florida's West Coast, we began to receive invitations from people who wanted to cook dinner for us. I was grateful for the hospitality that opened the doors of a community so new to us, but I was aware that within the warmth of the welcome there nestled the hope to check out my own cooking credentials at some future time. It soon became evident that the number of dinners I was going to have to reciprocate far exceeded the capacity of a single sitting. When the time came, I set up an extra table at each dinner so that I could discharge my obligations over not too many evenings, and I devised a menu that could mostly be cooked in advance, finished while the guests were settling in, and served buffet style. I wanted to start off the dinner with a first course that would combine elements both of familiarity and of revelation. The dish that I chose was lasagne.

There can't be many people who are unacquainted with lasagne, which are likely to go by their Neapolitan name, lasagna. But few are familiar with true Bolognese-style lasagne whose several layers of paper-thin homemade pasta bear a filling judiciously composed of a minimum number of ingredients. To most people the pasta itself is of negligible importance. I was looking forward to demonstrating the reverse—that what makes lasagne a triumph of Bolognese pasta mastery is the ephemeral lightness of the dough building up to many layers of nearly impalpable pasta interleaved by equally thin layers of luscious, but not overbearing filling.

The filling for these lasagne, adapted from the veal and four mushroom pasta sauce on page 164, is based on the principle that there is more flavor to a combination of different mushrooms than there is to any one single variety. The lasagne I served at my dinners were made with yellow dough. When I retested the recipe for this book, I switched to spinach dough as a birthday gift to my husband for whom green lasagne is at the very pinnacle of homemade pasta dishes.

For the mushrooms

3 ounces imported dried Italian porcini mushrooms

1 pound fresh shiitake mushrooms

1 pound fresh cremini mushrooms, also known as baby bella

1 pound fresh white button mushrooms

Two 12-inch nonstick skillets or sauté pans or one of each kind

> *Marcella Says:* **There are 3 pounds of fresh mushrooms that you must cook down until they are very soft, which will take about 1½ hours. I recommend dividing them between 2 large pans because it will shorten the procedure considerably. If you don't have 2 large pans, use 1 large and 1 smaller one, distributing the mushrooms in proportion to the size of the pan. Bear in mind that one batch may need more cooking than the other. You could also pile up all the mushrooms in one large pan, but that will really lengthen the cooking time.**

6 tablespoons extra virgin olive oil

1½ cups onions, chopped very fine

Fine sea salt

Black pepper ground fresh from the mill

For the veal sauce

3 tablespoons butter

⅔ cup onion, chopped very fine

1 pound ground veal

Fine sea salt

Black pepper ground fresh from the mill

1 cup dry white wine

1½ cups tomatoes cut up with their juice, either ripe, firm, fresh plum tomatoes, peeled and seeded, OR canned imported San Marzano Italian tomatoes

For the spinach pasta

6 ounces fresh spinach, preferably baby spinach, but if mature detach the stems

Fine sea salt

Cheesecloth

3 extra-large eggs

Approximately 2½ cups unbleached all-purpose flour

For the béchamel sauce

1½ quarts whole milk

¾ cup (1½ sticks) butter

9 tablespoons all-purpose flour

½ teaspoon freshly grated nutmeg

To assemble the lasagne

A 16 by 10 by 2-inch lasagne pan, about 20 cups

Butter for greasing the lasagne pan and dotting the lasagne

1 cup freshly grated Parmigiano-Reggiano cheese

YIELD: *12 servings*

1 For the mushrooms: Pour 1½ cups lukewarm water into a small bowl, drop in the dried porcini mushrooms, and let them soak until you need to use them in this recipe by which time, 30 minutes or more, they should have absorbed enough water to become soft.

2 Detach and discard the shiitake stems.

3 Briskly wash all of the fresh mushrooms in cold running water, then cut them into thin slices. For speed, you can use a food processor fitted with the slicing disk.

4 Retrieve the dried porcini mushrooms from their soak, but do not discard the liquid. Wash the mushrooms in various changes of cold water and cut any extra-large pieces into two or three smaller ones. Filter the liquid from the mushroom soak through a coffee filter, or a paper towel folded into a funnel, into a small container.

5 If you are using two pans of the same size, divide the olive oil and the chopped onions equally between them. If one is larger than the other, divide the ingredients proportionately. Turn on the heat to high and cook the onions, stirring from time to time, until they become colored a light gold. Add the reconstituted porcini, again dividing the ingredient between the pans. Cook for about 2 minutes, stirring frequently, then pour the filtered liquid from their soak into the pans. When the liquid has bubbled away completely, add all the fresh mushrooms, sprinkle with salt and pepper, turn the mushrooms over once or twice, and lower the heat to medium low. At first the mushrooms will shed liquid profusely, but it will be reabsorbed. Cook at a quiet simmer for about 1½ hours, stirring and turning the mushrooms over every once in a while. They are done when they become very soft.

6 For the veal sauce: While the mushrooms are cooking, put the butter for the sauce in a 10-inch skillet, add the ⅔ cup chopped onion, and turn on the heat to high. Cook the onion, stirring frequently, until it becomes colored a light gold. Add the ground veal, breaking it up with a wooden spoon, and sprinkle with salt and pepper. Cook, turning the meat a few times, until it loses its raw color.

7 Pour the wine into the pan and let it bubble until it evaporates completely. Add the tomatoes, turn them over once or twice, lower the heat to medium low, and cook at a gentle but steady simmer for about 30 minutes.

AHEAD-OF-TIME NOTE: The good news is that these two preparations can be done up to 3 days in advance. Store the mushrooms and the veal sauce separately in tightly closed containers in the refrigerator.

8 When you are ready to proceed with the making of the pasta, combine the mushrooms and the veal sauce in a single sauté pan or skillet, and cook them together over medium heat for 15 minutes, turning them over every so often.

9 Make the spinach pasta: Soak the spinach in a basin of cold water. You should wash the spinach even if it has been prewashed, but in that case you only have to do it once. If it hasn't been prewashed, change the water until you find no soil deposits on the bottom of the basin.

10 Bring 2 quarts of water to a boil in a saucepan. Add 1 tablespoon salt, and then drop in the spinach. Baby spinach will be cooked within 5 minutes after the water returns to a boil; mature spinach will take a little longer. Drain the spinach as thoroughly as you can, then put it in the piece of cheesecloth or gather it up in a clean dish towel, and twist the cloth tightly to force out all the liquid you can. Remove the spinach from the cloth, and chop it very fine with a knife, not in the food processor because it would become too soggy.

11 Referring to the directions on page 40 of Why and How You Should Be Making Your Own Egg Pasta, knead the eggs, flour, and spinach together in the large bowl of a food processor fitted with the steel blade.

12 Stretch the dough through the pasta machine, a step at a time, until it is thin enough to see newsprint through it. Follow the directions on page 41 to 42, laying out the pasta strips on clean dry towels as described there.

13 For the béchamel sauce: Prepare the sauce following the directions on pages 300 to 301, using the amounts listed on page 189. Keep the saucepan in which you made the béchamel over a pot or a bowl filled with hot water. Check the temperature of the water from time to time, and if it cools off replace it with more hot water.

14 Combine the mushrooms and veal sauce in a large bowl and fold in the béchamel sauce, incorporating it uniformly.

15 Turn on the oven to 450°. Lightly grease the lasagne pan with butter.

16 To assemble the lasagne: Following the basic lasagne instructions on pages 43 to 44, blanch the pasta strips, 4 at a time, in salted boiling water, rinse them, wring them out, and lay them out on dry cloth towels. When all the strips are done, line the buttered baking dish with one layer of pasta. Do not overlap the pieces, but trim the pasta to fit. Spread some of the mushroom and veal mixture thinly and evenly over the pasta, sprinkle with grated Parmesan, and top with another layer of pasta. Proceed in this manner until you have used up all the pasta and nearly all the filling, ending with eight thin layers of lasagne in the dish. Finish with the remaining filling and a sprinkling of Parmesan and dot the top with butter.

AHEAD-OF-TIME NOTE: You can prepare the lasagne up to this point a day or two in advance. Cover with a double thickness of plastic film and refrigerate. Bring back to room temperature before baking.

17 Bake in the preheated oven for 15 minutes, until the top of the green lasagne becomes mottled with crusty-looking brown spots. Allow the dish to settle out of the oven for 5 to 8 minutes before serving.

RAVIOLI FILLED WITH VEAL AND MUSHROOMS
Ravioli con il Ripieno di Vitello e Funghi

If Italian cooking were all homemade ravioli and lasagne, one might well look elsewhere for culinary inspiration. But while there are scores of Italian dishes one can make quickly or with little labor, cooking can't be judged solely by how little time it takes to do. It is also a question of certain profound satisfactions that are the reward of an investment in time and effort. In the experience of most cooks there must come days when such an investment becomes both feasible and desirable. On those occasions, I know of few dishes that pay such a handsome return as the homemade pastas of northern Italy, of which these savory ravioli and the preceding lasagne are examples.

The filling

6 ounces fresh shiitake mushrooms

6 ounces cremini mushrooms, also known as baby bella

2 nonstick skillets or sauté pans, one preferably at least 12-inches wide, but neither less than 8 inches across

2 tablespoons extra virgin olive oil

1 cup onion, chopped fine

Fine sea salt

2 tablespoons butter

½ pound ground veal

½ cup dry white wine

Black pepper ground fresh from the mill

3 fresh, ripe plum tomatoes, peeled, seeded, and cut up

2 tablespoons whole-milk ricotta

1 teaspoon freshly grated nutmeg

1 egg

½ cup freshly grated Parmigiano-Reggiano cheese

The pasta

Pasta dough made with 2 extra-large eggs and approximately 1¼ cups unbleached all-purpose flour, as described on page 38 to 40 of Why and How You Should Be Making Your Own Egg Pasta

YIELD: *one hundred 1½-inch ravioli to serve 6 adequately, 4 abundantly*

1 For the filling: Detach the stems of the shiitake and discard them. Wash all the mushrooms rapidly in cold running water and slice them very thin, using the knife or the slicing disk of a food processor, as you prefer.

2 If your pans are different sizes, pour the olive oil into the larger one, add ½ cup of the chopped onion, and turn on the heat to medium high. Cook the onion, stirring from time to time, until it becomes colored a deep gold. Add as many mushrooms to the pan as will fit cozily, sprinkling them with salt. Turn them over once or twice to coat them well, then turn the heat down to medium. When the mushrooms have released some liquid and shrunk in bulk, add the remaining mushrooms. Cook, turning the mushrooms over from time to time, until all the liquid they have released has evaporated and they have become very soft, about 1 hour or more. Take off the heat.

3 While the mushrooms are cooking, put the butter and the remaining ½ cup chopped onion in the second pan and turn on the heat to high. Cook the onion, stirring from time to time, until it becomes colored a deep gold. Add the ground veal, crumbling it with a fork, and turn it once or twice to coat it well. When all the meat has been browned lightly and uniformly, pour in the wine, and add salt and several grindings of black pepper.

4 When the wine has completely bubbled away, add the tomatoes, turn the heat down to the lowest setting possible, and cook, uncovered, for about 45 minutes, stirring from time to time.

5 When the veal mixture and the mushrooms are both done, empty the contents of both pans into a large bowl and, with a wooden spoon, turn them over several times to combine them into an evenly distributed mixture.

6 Wipe the pans clean with paper towels, divide the contents of the bowl evenly between the two pans, turn the heat on to medium low under both, and cook, stirring frequently, for 20 minutes. Empty the contents of both pans into the bowl just used.

AHEAD-OF-TIME NOTE: At this moment, you can refrigerate the filling in a tightly sealed container for 4 or 5 days, or you can freeze it for up to 3 months. Bring fully to room temperature before proceeding.

Marcella Says: **With the mushroom and veal filling done up to this point, you don't need to add anything to it to turn it into a delicious sauce both for homemade egg pasta, such as tagliatelle or pappardelle, and for boxed dry pasta shapes, such as rigatoni, ridged penne, or** *conchiglie.*

7 When ready to stuff the ravioli, add the ricotta, nutmeg, egg, and Parmesan to the bowl and stir them thoroughly and evenly into the mixture. Taste and correct for salt, mixing once again.

Making the Pasta

1 Knead the eggs and flour in a food processor as described on page 40 until it masses into compact, elastic dough.

2 Pull about ½ cup of dough from the kneaded mass and run it through the machine's rollers, thinning it gradually step by step, as instructed in the basic directions on pages 41 and 45, producing pasta strips thin enough to be able to distinguish through them large print or the pattern in a dish towel. While rolling out one strip, keep the rest of the dough wrapped tightly in plastic film.

3 When you have rolled out the pasta strip to the required thinness, lay it perfectly flat on the work counter. Dot the strip with 1 heaping teaspoon lumps of the mushroom and veal filling, setting them down in a row 1 inch apart and about ¾ inch away from one of the long edges of the strip.

4 When you have distributed as many lumps of the filling as will fit, bring the far edge of the strip down over and overlapping the other edge. Press the spaces between the lumps to force the air out. Press the upper part of the pasta strip firmly against the edge of the half resting on the counter, creating a long tube that bulges with stuffing at regularly spaced intervals. Run a fluted pastry wheel over the whole length of the cut side of the tube to trim it evenly and seal it securely, then use the wheel to separate the ravioli, cutting across the tube between the bulges formed by the filling. Knead the trimmings into a ball that you will add to other trimmings and eventually roll out to make more pasta strips.

5 Spread the ravioli out in a single layer on cloth kitchen towels spread flat on the work counter or on a table. Make sure they do not touch because they will become glued to each other on contact and when you try to separate them the pasta tears, spilling the filling. Turn them over every 20 to 30 minutes.

6 When you have stuffed one pasta strip and made ravioli from it, pull another ½ cup lump of dough from the kneaded mass and repeat the procedure just described.

Cooking, Saucing, and Serving the Ravioli

A stockpot containing at least 4 quarts or more of generously salted boiling water

A colander spoon or large Chinese wire skimmer or any large perforated ladle

A warm deep serving platter, not a pasta bowl

2½ tablespoons butter

6 to 8 fresh sage leaves

⅓ cup freshly grated Parmigiano-Reggiano cheese

1 When the ravioli are dry enough so that they do not stick easily to each other, drop them into the salted boiling water. The traditional way of doing it is to gather them all in one of the towels on which they have been drying, cinching one end closed and releasing the other end over the pot. Another way is to collect the ravioli in a lightweight metal or plastic bowl and turn them out into the pot.

2 The ravioli should be done, depending on how thoroughly dry they were, how thick the pasta is, and how much water you are cooking them in, in about 3 to 5 minutes after the water returns to a boil. To know for sure, retrieve one and bite off a corner of the pasta. It should be tender, yet firm to the bite. When ready, scoop out the ravioli a few at a time with the colander spoon or other suitable implement and transfer them to a pasta colander where they can shed the water still clinging to them. Slide them out of the colander and into the warm serving dish.

Marcella Says: **Do not empty the pasta out all at once from the pot into a standing colander because when the ravioli fall hard upon each other they may split.**

3 While the ravioli are cooking, put 2 tablespoons of butter and all the sage leaves in a small skillet and turn on the heat to medium high. Lightly brown, but do not blacken, the sage, turning the leaves from time to time.

4 As soon as the ravioli are in the serving dish, pour the hot sage butter over them. Toss gently, preferably with wood or bone implements, being careful not to break the ravioli. Add the remaining ½ tablespoon of butter and all the grated Parmesan, toss gently again once or twice, and serve at once.

FRIULI'S GRILLED PASTA
↰ *Mlinci*

I learned to make *mlinci* in Friuli, in Cormòns, at a place called Al Cacciatore. It is the creation of Josko Sirk who put a restaurant on the ground floor of the restored farmhouse where he was born and where he and his wife Loredana still live. On the plate, *mlinci* looks somewhat like *pane frattau*, the pasta dish Sardinians make with briefly boiled pieces of their wafer-thin sheet music bread. The taste and texture, however, are entirely different and unique, recalling, unlike any other Italian pasta, tortillas in both texture and aroma. The traditional sauce for *mlinci* would be one made with game, boar, hare, or wild duck. I have served *mlinci* with a chicken thigh sauce I adapted from a recipe from the restaurant Blasut—find it on page 176—and the union was delicious.

> 1½ cups unbleached all-purpose flour
>
> ⅔ cup polenta, cornmeal flour
>
> 3 extra-large eggs at room temperature
>
> A hand-cranked pasta machine
>
> A flat griddle or unglazed cast-iron skillet

YIELD: *8 servings of pasta*

1 Combine the flour, cornmeal, and eggs, working the mixture into a homogeneous mass of dough. You may do it entirely by hand, or use a food processor or a standing mixer. Even if you do start it in the processor or the mixer, knead it afterward by hand for 2 to 3 minutes on a wood or laminated smooth work surface.

2 Cut the dough into 8 equal slabs and run them one at a time through the pasta machine to thin them, narrowing down the thinning settings notch by notch, until the dough is as thin as that of fine noodles. Cut the fully thinned-out strips of dough to a length that will fit comfortably on the griddle or cast-iron skillet and lay them flat on a counter covered with cloth dish towels. Make sure the strips do not touch or overlap or they will become stuck to each other.

3 Preheat the griddle or place the skillet over medium-high heat.

4 Place one or more strips of dough—they must not overlap—on the hot griddle or skillet. Hold the dough down flat with a metal spatula to keep it from curling and toast it briefly first on one side, then on the other. It should take about 1 minute for the first side and a little less for the second, just long enough for the dough to stiffen and become lightly speckled with reddish-brown spots. Remove the dough as soon as it is done, replacing it with a fresh strip. After the strips are grilled they can be stacked.

5 *Mlinci* strips, once grilled, are cooked in salted boiling water like pasta. You can cook them immediately or store them in a box until you are ready to do so. They can last for weeks in a dry cupboard.

Cooking mlinci

1 Break the grilled *mlinci* up into irregular pieces 2 inches large, more or less.

2 Bring 4 quarts of water to a boil, add 1½ to 2 tablespoons salt, and when the water returns to a fast boil, drop in the *mlinci*. Drain after about 1 minute and toss immediately with sauce. The robust taste of the *mlinci* naturally calls for a rich-tasting sauce, particularly one made with game.

CARROT GNOCCHI

ᝰ I Gnocchi di Carote

One of the bonuses for an Italian cook whose wine-writing husband roams the vineyards of the country is to discover unexpected dishes. We were in Friuli, whose cooking I knew I had a soft spot for. But I was not prepared to find carrot gnocchi. I fell for them at first bite. Their color, their tenderness, their mildly sweet flavor reminded me of the pumpkin gnocchi they make in Venice, but these are more tender and lighter and more prettily shaped.

½ pound carrots, about 5 or 6 of medium size

3 tablespoons butter

1 tablespoon onion, chopped fine

3 tablespoons all-purpose flour

1 egg yolk

5 tablespoons freshly grated Parmigiano-Reggiano cheese

Fine sea salt

Black pepper ground fresh from the mill

A pinch freshly grated nutmeg

3 fresh sage leaves

An oven-to-table baking dish

For 4 persons

1 Wash and peel the carrots and trim the ends. Drop the carrots into boiling water and cook until tender, 15 to 17 minutes.

2 Drain the carrots and slice them into 1-inch-thick rounds.

3 Put 1 tablespoon of the butter and all the chopped onion in a medium skillet and turn on the heat to medium. Cook the onion, stirring from time to time, until it becomes colored a pale gold.

4 Add the sliced carrots and cook for 6 to 8 minutes, turning them over occasionally, then put them in a food processor and purée to a creamy consistency. Don't mind if minute bits of carrot remain. Turn the purée out into a bowl and let cool completely.

5 When the purée is completely cool, add the flour, egg yolk, 3 tablespoons grated Parmesan, salt, pepper, and nutmeg and mix thoroughly to combine all the ingredients into a uniform batter.

AHEAD-OF-TIME NOTE: You can prepare the recipe up to this point several hours in advance.

6 Turn on the oven to 400°.

7 Bring water to a boil in a broad shallow saucepan, and add 2 to 3 tablespoons of salt. Set a bowl of water with ice nearby.

8 With a soup spoon, scoop up some of the carrot mixture. Holding a second spoon in your other hand and pointing the narrow tip of its bowl against the broad base of the bowl of the first spoon, scoop up the carrot mixture sideways. Repeat the operation

using the first spoon now to scoop up the carrot mixture, forming a three-sided, oval-shaped lump. Slide the lump off the spoon into the boiling water. Working quickly, add another 4 or 5 carrot lumps to the pan. Cook for 6 or 7 seconds, until all rise to the surface. Retrieve them with a slotted spoon and transfer them to the bowl of ice and water. Proceed in this manner until all the carrot mixture has been used.

9 Choose an oven-to-table baking dish that can contain all the carrot gnocchi in one layer without crowding. Lightly smear the bottom with a little of the remaining butter. Retrieve the gnocchi from the ice water and arrange them on the bottom of the buttered dish. Tear the sage leaves into small pieces and scatter them over the gnocchi. Sprinkle the gnocchi with the remaining grated Parmesan and dot with the remaining butter. Bake on the upper shelf of the preheated oven for about 10 minutes. Serve directly from the baking dish.

Fish

SHRIMP BRAISED WITH TOMATO, CHILI PEPPER, AND CAPERS

Gamberi in Umido con Pomodoro, Peperoncino, e Capperi

As I look over this recipe, I think how typical it is of the Italian way with seafood, how quick and clear, how sparkling fresh its flavors. How many times I have cooked dishes like this is beyond counting, past remembering. I never tire of them.

At the end of the recipe are directions for developing the dish into either a delicious pasta sauce or as the flavor base for a risotto.

3 tablespoons extra virgin olive oil

½ cup onion, chopped very fine

1 tablespoon chopped garlic

2 tablespoons chopped Italian flat-leaf parsley

Chopped chili pepper, ½ tablespoon fresh jalapeño, OR 1½ teaspoons dried red chili pepper, adjusting the quantities to taste and to the potency of the chili

1 cup tomatoes cut up with their juice, either ripe, firm, fresh plum tomatoes OR canned imported San Marzano Italian tomatoes

20 large shrimp (or fewer if you decide to make a pasta sauce or risotto base; see my recommendation at the end of this recipe)

Fine sea salt

½ tablespoon capers, drained and rinsed in cold water if packed in vinegar, OR if packed in salt, rinsed, soaked in cold water for 10 minutes, then rinsed again

For 4 persons

1 Put the oil and chopped onion in a 12-inch skillet, turn on the heat to medium high, and cook the onion, stirring it from time to time, until it becomes colored a pale gold. Add the chopped garlic, stir once or twice and, when the aroma of the garlic begins to rise, add the parsley and chili pepper. Stir once or twice, then add the tomatoes. Turn all the ingredients over once or twice, turn the heat down to medium, and cook at a steady simmer.

2 While the tomato sauce is cooking, shell and devein the shrimp, rinse them under cold running water, and pat them dry with a dish towel or paper towels.

3 When the oil floats free from the tomato (to learn more about this moment in the making of a tomato sauce, see page 48 in How to Cook a Pasta Sauce), slip the shrimp into the pan, adding salt and the capers. Turn the shrimp over several times to coat them well. After 2 or 3 minutes, when they have lost their shiny raw color, they are done. Serve at once with all the juices from the pan.

> *Marcella Says:* **The shrimp are terrific just as they are, with good crusty bread to sop up their juices. At home, I sometimes serve them over polenta or rice cooked pilaf-style, or with boiled Italian rice tossed with a pinch of salt and 1 or 2 tablespoons of olive oil.**

Utilizing the Shrimp for a Pasta Sauce or for a Risotto Base:

FOR A PASTA SAUCE SERVING 4 TO 6 PERSONS When the shrimp are cooked, retrieve them from the skillet using a slotted spoon. Chop half of them very fine, put them back in the pan, cook for another minute or two, and take the pan off the heat. Cut the remaining shrimp into 3 pieces each and put them in the skillet. When the pasta is nearly done, turn on the heat to medium under the skillet. As soon as the pasta is cooked to al dente, firm to the bite, drain it and toss it in a warm serving bowl with the shrimp sauce.

FOR THE FLAVOR BASE OF A RISOTTO SERVING 4 TO 6 PERSONS Follow the directions for making the pasta sauce described above, chopping half of the shrimp very fine, and cooking them for a short while in the skillet. Cut up the remaining shrimp and set aside. In a saucepan, sauté some chopped onion in olive oil until it becomes colored a deep gold. Add the rice, stirring at a lively heat to coat it well. Then add the shrimp base from the skillet and follow the basic procedure described in the risotto recipes on pages 136, 141, and 143, adding simmering water from time to time and stirring until the rice is done. At the end, when the rice's consistency is loose and flowing, add the reserved cut-up shrimp, swirl in a few drops of olive oil, and serve.

NOTE: If you choose to make a pasta sauce or risotto base with this recipe, half the shrimp, 10 large, will be sufficient.

Shrimp Fried in Spicy
Flour-and-Water Pastella Batter

⅗ *Gamberi Fritti con la Pastella*

To my basic frying batter I have added chili pepper because it so enlivens the flavor of seafood. If you would like to know more about this marvelous batter and about clean, greaseless frying, please turn to Frying on page 22 of At Master Class.

1 pound small-to-medium shrimp

For the batter

1½ cups lukewarm water

1¼ cups all-purpose flour

Chopped chili pepper, 1 teaspoon fresh jalapeño, or ½ teaspoon dried red chili pepper, adjusting such quantities to taste and to the potency of the chili

1 cup all-purpose flour in which to dredge the shrimp

Vegetable oil

A steel-mesh drying rack placed over a sheet of aluminum foil

Fine sea salt

For 4 persons

1 Shell the shrimp and devein them to remove their dark, gritty intestinal tube. Wash them in several changes of cold water, then pat them thoroughly dry between three or four layers of paper towels.

2 For the batter: If you want to mix the batter in the food processor, please refer to the directions on page 26. To make batter the good old-fashioned way, pour the 1½ cups of lukewarm water into a bowl. Sift the 1¼ cups of flour over it, shaking it through a strainer a little at a time. As you add the flour, whisk it into the batter with a fork to incorporate it evenly, without lumps. The batter's consistency should resemble that of buttermilk. When the flour has been incorporated, mix the chili pepper into the batter.

3 Pour the 1 cup of flour into a bowl, add the shrimp to the bowl, and turn them over a few times to coat them all well.

> *Marcella Says:* **When I omitted this preliminary flouring of the shrimp, I found that the batter did not cling so firmly to the shrimp.**

4 Pour enough vegetable oil into a 10-inch skillet to come at least 1 inch up the sides of the pan and turn on the heat to high. When the oil is hot enough to make a drop of batter sizzle instantly, pick up a shrimp by the tail, shake it to make it shed surplus flour, dip it into the batter, and slip it into the pan. Proceed in this manner, working swiftly, until there are about 10 shrimp in the pan, or as many as will fit without crowding.

5 By the time the last shrimp has gone into the pan, the first ones will have begun to be colored golden. Turn them and all the other shrimp when their color is a rich gold. As soon as they are done on both sides, after about a minute or less, transfer them to the drying rack to drain. Replace them in the pan with another batch and repeat the procedure until all the shrimp are done. Sprinkle with salt and serve at once while still piping hot.

LOBSTER TAILS TUSCAN COAST-STYLE, WITH PEAS, TOMATOES, AND CHILI PEPPER

Code di Aragosta alla Moda della Costa Toscana

There is a splendid old Tuscan recipe for cuttlefish—*seppie*—that is stewed with tomatoes and fresh peas. A cuttlefish, which some confuse with squid, is all but unknown in America except for its gritty bone that captive birds are given to sharpen their beaks on. I have adapted the recipe to spiny lobster tails, which are abundant and fairly inexpensive. I have replaced the fresh peas with frozen peas not only to shorten and simplify the cooking, but because the fresh peas that come to market are rarely sweet enough to go with seafood. If you can obtain sweet, fresh, young peas, you should of course use them, bearing in mind that they will take longer to cook than the time indicated for the frozen ones.

A pair of poultry shears or any sturdy kitchen scissors

4 pounds frozen warm-water lobster tails, thawed

1 pound fresh, ripe, firm plum tomatoes

3 to 4 tablespoons extra virgin olive oil

½ cup chopped onion

1 teaspoon chopped garlic

2 tablespoons chopped Italian flat-leaf parsley

Chopped chili pepper, ½ teaspoon fresh jalapeño, OR ¼ teaspoon dried red chili pepper, adjusting such quantities to taste and to the potency of the chili

Fine sea salt

1 ½ cups frozen small peas, unless very young, very fresh ones are available

A warm serving platter

For 4 persons

1 Use the shears or kitchen scissors to cut the tail shells along the sides so that you can separate the top and bottom of the shell, releasing the tail meat. Lay the meat on a work surface with the belly side facing down. Using a sharply pointed, thin-bladed knife, slide the edge under the tough and hard-to-chew membrane that sheaths the back on each tail. Detach the membrane from the flesh and discard it.

> *Marcella Says:* **You can skip the removal of the membrane, an operation that no restaurant that serves lobster tails performs. That membrane, however, is leathery and remains so in the cooking, interfering with the pleasurable tenderness of the flesh. It only takes a couple of minutes to do and it's worth the trouble.**

Wash the lobster tails under cold running water, pat well dry with kitchen towels, then cut into pieces approximately 1½ inches long.

2 Skin the tomatoes using a swivel-blade vegetable peeler, and cut them into small dice.

3 Add the olive oil and chopped onion to a 10-inch skillet, turn on the heat to medium high, and cook the onion, stirring from time to time, until it becomes colored a very pale brown. Add the garlic, turn it three or four times, then add the parsley and chili pepper. Cook for a few seconds while turning the ingredients over once or twice.

4 Add the diced tomatoes with some salt and cook at a lively simmer for about 15 minutes, stirring from time to time.

5 Fill a strainer with the frozen peas, rinse them under warm water for less than a minute, empty the strainer into the skillet, and turn the peas over once or twice. Cook for at least 8 minutes. Any less and they will not develop flavor. If using shelled fresh peas, cook for 20 to 25 minutes, until they are slightly wrinkled and very tender.

AHEAD-OF-TIME NOTE: You can make the tomatoes-and-peas base several hours in advance or even the night before. Refrigerate in a tightly sealed container until you are ready to reheat the base and proceed with the recipe. If following this procedure, prepare the lobster only when you are ready to finish making the dish.

6 When ready to serve, heat up the sauce in the skillet, put in the lobster pieces, turn them over occasionally, cooking them no more than 5 to 6 minutes, taste and correct for salt. Transfer the seafood mixture to the warm platter and serve promptly.

COLD LOBSTER CATALAN STYLE

Aragosta alla Catalana

Whether to serve lobster cold or hot is a discussion that my husband and I have from time to time. We usually end up having it hot because when I pull a lobster out of the steamer, its scent warm and spicy, to wait for it to cool down is more of a challenge than my powers of self-restraint can meet. Yet, whenever we have waited, I have not regretted it. As Victor maintains, lobster flesh has a finer texture and more developed, less cloying flavor when it is cold than when it is hot. Sardinians, whose lobster has few equals, are of Victor's persuasion and they almost always have it cold. Their most famous version, *alla catalana*, in which cold sliced boiled lobster is tossed with diced raw tomatoes, raw onion, parsley, lemon juice, and olive oil, acknowledges in its title the influence of a Spanish period in the island's past. It is a past that you can experience if you visit Sardinia's most beautiful city, Alghero, whose street signs are in Catalan, the language its citizens still continue to speak.

The magnificent orange-red Sardinian lobster is of the clawless, spiny variety. Its juicy, silken flesh is ideally suited to the Catalan preparation, but live cold-water lobster from the northeast Atlantic is no less delicious. You may also use the warm-water lobster tails that are widely available frozen. They are somewhat drier than a Maine lobster, but still very enjoyable.

Marcella Says: I have worked out the condiments in this recipe on the basis of a 1½- to 1¾-pound live lobster per person. If you find that you'd like a little less or more of the onion or tomato or olive oil or lemon juice, adjust the quantities to suit your taste. Also bear in mind that when served this way, a single lobster goes a long way, in the context of an Italian-style meal that could include a preliminary first course—a cold minestrone or a light pasta, say—with one less lobster, you would still have enough food for four persons.

Other eminently suitable uses for this dish are as a cold appetizer that precedes a hot seafood course or as part of an elegant buffet. When using it as an appetizer, you may want to reduce the quantities if you are making dinner for four or else stay with them and serve six.

3 cups onion sliced very thin, choosing if possible a sweet variety such Vidalia, Florida Sweet, Maui, or Bermuda Red

3 tablespoons vinegar

2 tablespoons sea salt plus additional salt for the condiment mixture

Four 1½- to 1¾-pound live lobsters or 4 pounds frozen lobster tails, thawed

¼ cup freshly squeezed lemon juice

Black pepper ground fresh from the mill

⅔ cup extra virgin olive oil

¼ cup chopped Italian flat-leaf parsley

4 cups fresh, ripe, firm tomatoes, preferably plum tomatoes, split, seeds scooped— not squeezed out—and cut into dice no larger than ½ inch

For 4 persons

1 Place the sliced onions in a bowl and pour in enough cold water to cover them. Squeeze the onions in your hands, turning the water cloudy. Drain, then pour fresh water over the onions again to cover. Set aside to steep.

If You Are Using Live Lobsters

◆ Fill a lobster pot or large stockpot halfway with cold water and bring to a boil. Add the 3 tablespoons vinegar and 2 tablespoons salt, and when the water boils drop in the lobsters. Cook for 12 to 13 minutes after the water returns to a boil. Drain.

◆ When the lobsters are cool enough to handle comfortably, detach the heads and claws. Use kitchen shears to cut the tail shell along its sides so that you can separate the top and bottom of the shell, releasing the tail meat.

◆ If the lobster has roe, extract it and crumble it in a mixing bowl.

◆ Cut the tail meat into rounds about 1 inch thick and set aside.

✦ Crack the claws and extract the flesh. Pick out any pieces of shell and cut the claw meat into two pieces, adding them to the sliced tail meat.

> *Marcella Says:* **You won't be using the tomalley (the creamy green matter found mostly in the head) in this dish, but it is too good to throw away. Spoon it out and reheat it later with a little bit of butter and a pinch of salt. Serve it over toasted rounds of bread, topping it with a few drops of lemon juice and ground pepper.**

If You Are Using Lobster Tails

✦ Cook the lobster tails in boiling water following the procedure above for cooking live lobsters. Cook for 6 to 8 minutes, depending on their size. Drain.

✦ When the tails are cool enough to handle comfortably, use kitchen shears to cut the shells along the sides so that you can separate the top and bottom of the shell, releasing the tail meat. Lay the meat on a work surface with the belly side facing down. Using a sharply pointed, thin-bladed knife, slide the knife's edge under the tough and hard-to-chew membrane that sheaths the back. Detach the membrane from the flesh and discard. Wash the tail meat under cold running water, pat well dry with kitchen towels, then cut into pieces approximately 1 inch thick. Set aside.

3 To the bowl containing the roe from the cooked live lobsters or in an empty bowl if you are using lobster tails, put some salt, then add the lemon juice, pepper, and olive oil, and beat thoroughly with a fork or whisk, emulsifying the mixture.

4 Add the parsley and mix once or twice again.

5 Squeeze the onions in your hands, drain them, and press them dry between paper towels. Add them to the bowl, turning them over once or twice.

6 Add the diced tomatoes, stirring them into the mixture.

7 Add the cut-up lobster meat, turning it over several times to coat it well. Cover the bowl and allow the mixture to macerate at room temperature for at least 30 minutes. Serve at room temperature with good crusty bread for sopping up the delicious juices.

Baked Lobster with Mustard and Oregano

🐟 *Aragosta Arrosto con la Senape e l'Origano*

When Victor and I were married, he had no work, I was fresh out of the university and I had taken the first job I'd found, a very poorly paid one teaching science in a private school. We were staying with my parents, who had let us have the large bedroom in their house in Cesenatico, the Adriatic fishing village where I was born. My mother had been visiting her sister who lived in Venice in circumstances considerably more comfortable than those of my family. As my mother was preparing to return home, my aunt called to ask what we wanted as a wedding gift that she could send with her. Victor and I talked it over and agreed that inasmuch as we had no place of our own and no early prospect of having one there was no point in asking for one of the customary household items. Yet we did hope for something festive to celebrate our union and Victor, for whom food has always ranked high among his desires, suggested a lobster. Lobsters are not plentiful in Italy and they were then an extravagance well beyond the reach of an average salary, not to speak of the pittance that was mine. "A lobster, please" we said, and not long after that my mother came back from Venice with a magnificent live one, of the coral-red spiny variety native to Italian waters.

I had not yet begun to meddle in the kitchen and neither of my parents had ever cooked a lobster, so Victor took over. In a used books shop he had bought a copy of an early edition of Ada Boni's great work, *Il Talismano della Felicità*, and in it he found just the recipe he thought would suit the lobster and us. It was simple enough for him to tackle on his own and the seasonings—olive oil, fresh oregano, and mustard—seemed very appetizing. It turned out, in fact, to be quite delicious. A set of crockery might eventually have been more useful, but it could not have enjoyed such an affectionate place in the recollections of our early days together as does the memory of that improbably extravagant celebratory feast.

4 pounds frozen lobster tails, thawed

> *Marcella Says:* **For this recipe the lobster should be one whose meat is all in the tail, as it is with the Italian spiny lobster. That is the reason I suggest you make it with frozen lobster tails, although if you are fortunate to live where live spiny lobsters are available you could certainly use them. The big, meaty claws of cold-water lobsters from the northeastern Atlantic would go unutilized in this preparation.**

2 tablespoons butter

3 tablespoons extra virgin olive oil plus additional for drizzling on top

3 tablespoons chopped Italian flat-leaf parsley

Oregano, 1 tablespoon if fresh, 2 teaspoons if dried

1 tablespoon Dijon mustard

Fine sea salt

Black pepper ground fresh from the mill

1½ tablespoons dry, fine, unflavored bread crumbs

For 4 persons

1 Turn on the oven to 400°.

2 Split the lobster tails—or the whole spiny lobsters if that is what you have—in half lengthwise. Work the meat loose from the shell in one piece. The back of the meat is sheathed by a tough, chewy membrane that when cooked detracts from the lobster's tenderness. To remove it before cooking, lay the lobster meat on a work surface with the belly side facing down and, using a sharply pointed, thin-bladed knife, slide the knife's edge under the membrane. Working the knife from the head end toward the tail, detach the membrane from the soft flesh and discard it.

3 Wash both the meat and the shells, pat them dry with paper towels, and put the lobster's meat back into its shell. Set all the tails in a baking dish.

4 Put the butter, olive oil, parsley, oregano, mustard, salt, and pepper in a small saucepan, turn the heat on to medium low, and heat the sauce just long enough for the butter to melt, stirring from time to time.

5 Spoon the sauce, distributing it evenly, over the lobster tails. Sprinkle the bread crumbs over the sauce, pressing them down lightly with the back of a spoon to fix them in place. Drizzle a few drops of olive oil over the crumbs.

6 Put the baking dish in the preheated oven and bake for 12 to 14 minutes, depending on the thickness of the lobster tails. Serve hot with good crusty bread for sopping up the exceptionally tasty juices.

RED SNAPPER OR OTHER FISH FILLETS SAUTÉED WITH PROSCIUTTO AND WHITE WINE

Filetti di Pesce in Tegame con il Prosciutto e Vino Bianco

Pork is an old friend to cooks. A ham hock, a rib with a piece of meat on it, pancetta, salt pork—they can all help to deepen the flavor of your dishes. I like to use prosciutto because, since it is air-cured, it brings no distracting smokiness into the food with which it is cooked. It is not exceedingly salty, as Southern country ham is, but it has the spice of the mountain air to which it was exposed. It can tease the shyness out of any ingredient, and it really does a job on such mild-mannered fish as snapper and bass and even on sole.

2 pounds fresh red snapper fillets or fillets from grouper, striped bass, or another mild-tasting white-fleshed fish

> *Marcella Says:* I am not an admirer of North American sole, but many people are, including some who are not otherwise all that fond of fish. Because I was concerned about the flakiness of its flesh I worked out a procedure that would hold it together better. See the special directions in the note below.

3 tablespoons butter

1 tablespoon vegetable oil

Flour, spread on a large dinner plate

½ cup dry white wine

Fine sea salt

Black pepper ground fresh from the mill

Thyme, 1½ tablespoons if fresh, 1 tablespoon if dried

¼ pound prosciutto, sliced thin, preferably with all its fat still on

A warm serving platter

For 4 persons

1   Wash the fish in cold running water, then pat the fillets dry with kitchen towels.

2   Put the butter and oil in a 12-inch skillet or sauté pan and turn on the heat to high. When the butter foam begins to subside, dredge the fish fillets in flour on both sides, shake off the excess, and slip them into the pan. Cook at a lively heat for 2 minutes on one side, turn them carefully, cook for 2 minutes, then carefully lift them from the pan with one or two broad spatulas and transfer them temporarily to a plate.

3   Pour the wine into the pan. When it has partially bubbled away, return the fillets, skin side down, to the pan, sprinkle with salt, pepper, and the thyme, and cover the fillets with the prosciutto. Turn the heat down to medium, spoon the juices in the pan over the fish, put a lid on the pan, and cook for 2 more minutes.

4   Carefully lift the fish fillets from the pan, and transfer them to the warm serving platter. Pour all the pan juices over the fillets, and serve at once.

NOTE: If you want to use sole, follow steps 1 and 2, then at step 3, after the wine has partially bubbled away, lay half the sole fillets flat on the bottom of the pan. Add salt, pepper, and the thyme, cover with the prosciutto, and top with the remaining sole fillets, thus forming a sandwich. Proceed with the recipe as instructed in steps 3 and 4.

One Small Sea, Many Cuisines

The Adriatic is a small sea that would fit loosely inside a stretch of the New England coast, but on the Italian side at least—I know nothing of the formerly Yugoslav side facing it—it teems with a multitude of cuisines. If you travel from Trieste in the north down the coast to Brindisi in the south, you could find a different style of cooking every time you stop for lunch. A small example—the two baked fish recipes that follow—will illustrate my point. The first comes from the city where I have lived a substantial part of my life, Venice. The second is from the fishing town where I was born, Cesenatico, just over 100 miles south of Venice and facing the same sea. The Venetian seasonings are lemon juice and thyme, as weightless as air. In the recipe from my town, the flavors are of the earth: The fish is robustly baked, like a meat roast, with potatoes, garlic, and rosemary.

FISH FILLETS MARINATED AND BAKED WITH LEMON AND THYME
⚜ *Pesce in Teglia al Limone e Timo*

2 pounds fish fillets with the skin on

> *Marcella Says:* **Choose a firm, white-fleshed variety such as red or yellow-tailed snapper, redfish, sea bass, or wild striped bass. It ought to be of a size that will yield a long fillet with skin on one side, not a fish steak. Do not use sole or fluke because its flesh would flake when baked, or any of the oily dark-fleshed fish such as mackerel or bluefish.**

An oven-to-table oval or rectangular baking dish

¼ cup extra virgin olive oil

3 tablespoons freshly squeezed lemon juice

2 tablespoons fresh thyme leaves

Fine sea salt

Black pepper ground fresh from the mill

For 4 persons

1   Wash the fish fillets under cold running water, pat them dry with paper towels, wrap in a couple of sheets of dry towels, and set aside for the moment.

2   Pour the olive oil into the baking dish, and add the lemon juice, thyme leaves, salt, and pepper. With a fork or small whisk, whip the mixture into an emulsion.

3   Put in the fish, skin side down. Use a brush or spoon to bathe the fillets with the thyme and lemon mixture. Let the fish stand at room temperature for at least 30 minutes.

4   While the fish is marinating, turn on the oven to 450°.

5   Bathe the fillets from time to time with the marinating liquid and give them one or two complete turns that end always with the skin side down. Sprinkle lightly again with salt and grind some more pepper over the fish.

6   When the oven is hot, put in the baking dish. Cook for 12 to 15 minutes, depending on the thickness of the fillets. When serving, spoon some of the juices over the fish. These are juices that beg to be sopped up with a piece of good, crusty bread.

BAKED COLUMBIA RIVER SOCKEYE SALMON WITH BELL PEPPERS AND CAPERS
☙ *Salmone Sockeye al Forno con Peperoni e Capperi*

If you had lived in Venice as long as I did, you too might now be looking askance at salmon, a consequence of the inflexible caste system that rules the glorious Rialto seafood market. Only local fish caught within the past twenty-four hours, and preferably still alive, can aspire to the loftiest rank, hence to the steepest price. The highest numbers usually appear on the tag stuck in the baskets of live *moleche*, soft-shell crabs no larger than a silver dollar, whose cultivation Venetians originated. Only slightly less expensive than the crabs would be the live scampi; then *branzini*, sea bass; *orate*, bream; and Adriatic sole. Further down on the scale comes the fresh catch from the southern Mediterranean, among which swordfish and *cernia*—grouper—from Sicily, and *scorfano*—scorpion fish or *rascasse*—from Turkey are well regarded. The lowest rung is for frozen fish of any provenance, and just a step above it the farmed fish from northern Europe, a group that includes fresh Norwegian salmon. I don't remember any Venetian cook of our acquaintance ever serving it, nor any of the restaurants that we frequented, hotel restaurants excepted.

It may be more opprobrium than farmed salmon deserves, but it's a preconception hard to shake. Even now we never order salmon when dining out and never shop for it. Never that is, except for that short period late in the spring when wild salmon from the Columbia River is landed. Were it to be available at the Rialto market it would seduce the skeptical Venetian palate as it has mine. Thanks to our friends at the ChefShop Web site in Seattle, last June an overnight delivery brought several pounds of the most luscious of the Columbia's denizens, the sockeye, most of which we froze. As we gradually worked our way through our hoard, grilling, baking, poaching, I thought that the sockeye's rich-tasting flesh would be particularly responsive to an Italian approach, welcoming the savory challenge of olive oil, garlic, capers, and peppers.

Other fresh wild salmon, including those from Alaska that run late into September, would take well to this preparation. What to do when the season ends? Well, steelhead trout are always available, and Arctic char, and, of course, farmed Atlantic salmon. As for me, to borrow that old cry out of Ebbets Field, I'll wait till next year.

2 red and 1 yellow bell peppers

2 pounds wild salmon, preferably cut as a long fillet, not steaks

3 tablespoons extra virgin olive oil

2 tablespoons capers, drained and rinsed in cold water if packed in vinegar OR if packed in salt, rinsed, soaked in cold water for 10 minutes, then rinsed again; if their size is much larger than nonpareils, cut them up a little bit

4 whole garlic cloves, peeled

Fine sea salt

Black pepper ground fresh from the mill

For 4 persons

1 Char the peppers, skin them, split them, and remove their core and seeds as described on page 78 of The Why and How of Prepping Vegetables. Cut them into strips less than 1 inch wide and 1½ inches long. You can prepare the peppers early on the same day that you are making the fish for dinner.

>*Marcella Says:* **Why bother to char the peppers and why skin them at all? Charring tenderizes them so that they can be fully cooked by the time the salmon is done. The pepper skins are superfluous to begin with and more important, their bitterness isn't flattering to the salmon's mellow flavor.**

2 Turn on the oven to 375°.

3 Wash the fish in cold water and pat it dry with paper towels.

4 Coat a baking dish with 2 tablespoons of the olive oil. Lay the salmon in the dish, skin side down if you have long fillets. Distribute the pepper strips, capers, and the whole garlic cloves all around the salmon. Sprinkle liberally with salt and freshly ground pepper. Drizzle the remaining olive oil over the fish. Put the dish in the preheated oven and bake for 16 minutes. When done, the fish, at its thickest part, should be moist, but not gelatinous. Let the salmon settle for a few minutes before serving it directly from the baking dish.

BAKED FISH AND POTATOES WITH ROSEMARY AND GARLIC
Pesce Arrosto al Forno con Patate all 'Aglio e Rosmarino

1 pound new potatoes, peeled, washed, and cut into wedges

An oven-to-table baking dish that can accommodate both the fish and the potatoes in one layer

4 tablespoons extra virgin olive oil

4 or 5 fresh rosemary sprigs

4 whole garlic cloves, peeled

Fine sea salt

Black pepper ground fresh from the mill

A 2-pound fillet from a firm-fleshed fish, such as grouper, striped bass, red snapper, or mahi mahi

2 tablespoons fine, dry, unflavored bread crumbs

For 4 persons

1 Turn on the oven to 400°.

2 Place the potato wedges in the baking dish, pour 2 tablespoons of the olive oil over them, add 2 sprigs of rosemary, all the garlic cloves, and salt, and pepper. Toss thoroughly. Put the dish in the preheated oven.

3 After 15 minutes, remove the dish to turn the potatoes over, then put it back in the oven. Cook until the potatoes feel tender when tested with a fork, another 10 minutes or so.

4 Remove the dish from the oven. Push the potatoes to the sides, making room in the center for the fish fillet to lie flat.

5 Wash the fish fillet, pat it dry with paper towels, and lay it flat in the dish, skin side down. Strip the leaves from the remaining rosemary sprigs, scatter them over the fish, add salt and pepper, and sprinkle the bread crumbs and the remaining 2 tablespoons olive oil over the fillet. Return the dish to the oven and bake for 14 minutes. Let the dish settle out of the oven for 3 to 4 minutes before bringing it to the table.

Baked Fish High Sicilian Style with Anchovy and Orange Juice
Pesce al Cartoccio con l'Acciuga e il Succo d'Arancia

Let me give you at least one of the reasons that it takes me five years or more to do a book. It isn't because I am a lazy cook. I am in the kitchen every day, usually twice a day, in fact. But I am moved to cook what I feel like eating, and often it is likely to be an old, familiar, and long-since published dish. The recipes for dishes I have tasted during my travels and about which I have had conversations with other cooks may lie undisturbed for years within the sheaves of notes I have amassed. As I periodically riffle through them, however, I chance upon one from time to time and say, "Oh, that was so good, I think I'll make it this morning." And so it was with this exceptionally flavorful yet simple baked fish. It's an example of a sumptuously flavored cuisine, the cooking of one of those traditional home kitchens in Sicily, where the culinary wonders of the island are still familiar fare.

Anchovies and oranges, ingredients that make frequent appearances in Sicilian seafood cookery, are the two agents responsible for the fragrance of this preparation. The fish, which is baked in parchment paper or heavy foil, may be of any mild-flavored, sweet- and moist-fleshed variety. In Florida I have used the local yellowtail snapper, which is rather close to the *pagello* a cook in Sicily would use. Any other snapper will do, as will porgy, black sea bass, or striped bass. Dry fish steaks or dark-fleshed oily fish, such as swordfish, tuna, bluefish, or mackerel are less suitable.

2 pounds whole fish with light, moist flesh (please see the introductory note above for suggestions), or a pair of fillets under 1 inch thick

> *Marcella Says:* **Using a single small or medium-size fish is the way a cook in Sicily would do it and it certainly makes an attractive way to present the dish for people who are comfortable serving themselves from a whole fish. If you prefer fillets, don't let that stop you from making the dish because they work quite well, too. In the case of a large fish like a wild striped bass, a fillet is more practical. It ought not to be thicker than 1 inch to allow the seasonings to penetrate deep into the flesh.**

6 flat anchovy fillets

2 tablespoons butter

Cooking parchment or heavy-duty aluminum foil

3 tablespoons extra virgin olive oil

Fine sea salt

Black pepper ground fresh from the mill

3 tablespoons chopped Italian flat-leaf parsley

½ cup freshly squeezed orange juice

For 4 persons

1 Turn on the oven to 400°.

2 If using a whole fish, make sure it is fully scaled and gutted, and score its skin with three or four deep parallel diagonal cuts. Wash the fish, or the fillets, under cold running water and pat dry with kitchen towels.

3 Chop the anchovy fillets to a pulp and mash them with the butter to produce a spreadable homogeneous mixture.

4 Choose a baking pan large enough to accommodate the fish. Line it with the parchment or heavy-duty aluminum foil, then extend it to make overhangs to fold over the fish. Use a little bit of the olive oil to lightly grease the paper or foil, availing yourself of a pastry brush if you wish.

5 Lay the fish or one of the fillets in the pan and spread the anchovy mixture either inside the whole fish or on the top side of the fillet. If using fillets, lay another fillet on top of the one in the pan. Sprinkle with salt, pepper, and the chopped parsley. Pour the remaining olive oil and all the orange juice over the fish. Bring the sides of the parchment or foil over and crimp the edges to make a tightly sealed packet.

6 Bake in the preheated oven for about 40 minutes. Cut the parchment or foil and fold it back to open. Open it away from you, averting your face to keep it from being hit by steam. Serve directly from the baking dish with a spoon for scooping up the very delicious juices.

ADDITIONAL SERVING NOTE: You can accompany the fish with small, new, boiled potatoes, which take quite well to the cooking juices.

A Trio of Fish Steak Recipes

Fish steaks—*pesce da trancio*—do not often find their way into an Italian kitchen. One reason is that there is not that much local fish large enough to cut into steaks and the other is that Italians like to have their fish brought to the table whole, head and tail on. A few large fish do come to the market, however, and two of these are similar to fish that you can find at an American seafood counter, swordfish and shark.

It is no coincidence that all the recipes that follow are reminiscent of veal recipes: There is a scaloppini, a cutlet, a saltimbocca. At a fish market in Italy, shark is called *vitello di mare,* sea calf, and cooks handle it as though it were veal. Bearing that in mind, whatever the fish steak you are using may be, swordfish or shark or another large fish with compact flesh, you must start with slices that are thinner than the standard steak an American fishmonger cuts. You can either ask your fishmonger to slice the fish thin for you or take a thick steak home and divide it in half horizontally. It is not as daunting as it may seem if you follow the directions in the recipe carefully. Thin is important. Steak fish is likely to turn dry in the cooking. If you keep it juicy on the outside, it will be undercooked and gelatinous on the inside; if you cook it all the way through, the outside becomes juiceless. A thin steak is cooked quickly—just as though it were veal—so that it stays juicy even as it is cooked through.

BREADED SWORDFISH OR OTHER FISH STEAK CUTLETS
ᶜᵌ *Cotolette di Pesce Spada*

A 1-pound slice of swordfish, shark, or other firm-fleshed steak fish

A long, sharp, thin-bladed slicing knife

1 egg

1 cup fine, dry, unflavored bread crumbs spread on a plate or a sheet of aluminum foil or wax paper

3 tablespoons extra virgin olive oil

A steel-mesh drying rack placed over a sheet of aluminum foil

Fine sea salt

Optional: black pepper ground fresh from the mill

Lemon wedges

For 4 persons

1   Slit the skin that encircles the fish, detach it with a sharp paring knife, and discard it. If the slice is 8 inches long or more, cut it into two smaller pieces. Slice the pieces horizontally in half to obtain thinner slices, each about ½ inch thick. To do this, hold the fish flat against a cutting board with the palm of your hand, hold the knife parallel to the board, and guide the blade with a slow, firm back-and-forth motion through the middle of the fish steak. An obliging fishmonger may do the job for you, but I have found that when I do it myself my slices are more evenly cut and thus will cook more uniformly. Remove any exceptionally dark portions on the fish steak. Wash the fish in cold water, then pat thoroughly dry with paper towels or dish towels.

2   Beat the egg in a bowl about 5 inches wide until the yolk and the white are well combined.

3   Pick up one of the fish slices by an end and dip it in to the beaten egg, coating both sides. Hold it up, allowing any excess egg to flow back into the bowl. Dredge it in the bread crumbs. When both sides are coated with crumbs, press the fish slice down into the crumbs with the palm of your hand to adhere the crumbs to the surface of the fish.

Marcella Says: **Here is an important point to follow when making any kind of breaded cutlet: Make sure that the side you are pressing against with the palm of your hand already has breading on it, because if it only has egg, the egg will stick to your palm and come off on it.**

AHEAD-OF-TIME NOTE: You can prepare the fish to this point an hour or two before completing and serving the dish.

4 Pour the oil into a 10-inch preferably nonstick skillet and turn on the heat to high. When the oil is hot, slip in as many of the fish slices as will fit in a single, non-overlapping layer, which means that you will to cook them one batch at a time. Cook for about 2 minutes until the side facing the bottom of the pan forms a crust, then turn the slices and cook for 1 more minute to form a crust on the other side. Transfer the slices to the drying rack to drain. The aluminum foil beneath serves to collect and dispose of the drippings. Paper towels do not work as well as a drying rack because as the towels become soggy so does the crust on the fish.

5 When all the fish is cooked, sprinkle it with salt and, if you have opted to use it, the ground pepper. Transfer the slices to the warm platter and serve at once with lemon wedges.

Variation with Tomatoes and Capers

All of the ingredients, except for the lemon wedges, listed in the preceding recipe for breaded fish cutlets, plus:

> 1 tablespoon extra virgin olive oil

> 1 cup peeled fresh ripe tomatoes OR canned imported Italian San Marzano tomatoes, seeded, drained of juice, and cut into small dice

> 1½ tablespoons capers, drained and rinsed in cold water if packed in vinegar, OR if packed in salt, rinsed, soaked in cold water for 10 minutes, then rinsed again

For 4 persons

1 Fry the fish steaks as described in the recipe above. When you have transferred them to the drying rack to drain, turn the heat under the skillet down to medium, add 1 tablespoon olive oil, the diced tomatoes and the capers, stir once or twice, add salt and liberal grindings of black pepper, and cook at a steady simmer for 6 to 7 minutes, stirring from time to time.

2 Slip in the fried fish cutlets, one at a time, turning it in the sauce.

3 Transfer the cutlets to a warm serving platter, pour the contents of the skillet over them, and serve at once.

BREADED SWORDFISH SCALOPPINE SAUCED WITH GARLIC, PARSLEY, AND LEMON JUICE
Scaloppe di Pesce Spada col Sughetto di Aglio, Prezzemolo, e Limone

1½ pounds swordfish slices, each about 1 inch thick

1½ cups or more fine, dry, unflavored bread crumbs spread on a plate or a sheet of aluminum foil or wax paper

⅓ cup vegetable oil

A double layer of paper towels laid out on a large platter

Fine sea salt

Black pepper ground fresh from the mill

4 tablespoons butter

1½ tablespoons chopped garlic

3 tablespoons chopped Italian flat-leaf parsley

¼ cup freshly squeezed lemon juice

A warm serving platter

For 4 persons

1   Slit the skin that encircles each swordfish slices, detach it with a sharp paring knife, and discard it. Lay each slice on a steady cutting board. Place one hand flat on the slice, and, using a long-bladed thin slicing knife, cut the slice horizontally in half through the middle to obtain two slices, each about ½ inch thick. Cut with a sawing motion, keeping the knife parallel to the cutting board. Wash the fish in cold water and pat dry with kitchen towels.

2   Dredge the fish slices in the bread crumbs, patting them down on the plate with the palm of your hand to make the crumbs adhere well.

3   Pour the vegetable oil into a 12-inch skillet and turn the heat on to high. As soon as the oil is hot, slip in the swordfish slices, as many as will fit in the pan without crowding at one time. Brown them well on one side, then turn them over and cook the other side, not more than 1 or 1½ minutes per side. Use a slotted spatula to transfer the slices to the paper towels to blot away what oil may cling to them. When you have cooked one batch, do the next batch in exactly the same manner.

4   If you don't have another 12-inch skillet, pour the oil out of the pan. (It is still too hot to pour into a garbage bag, so use a tin can or another heat-resistant container to collect it.) Rinse out the skillet and wipe it dry. Add the butter and chopped garlic and turn on the heat to medium.

5   As soon as the garlic becomes colored a very pale gold, add the parsley, stir for a moment or two, then pour in the lemon juice. Stir quickly, then lower the heat to minimum.

6   Slip a breaded swordfish slice into the pan, turn it over in the pan juices, then move it to the side of the pan to make room for another slice of fish. Repeat until you have sauced all the slices.

7   Lift the slices, one by one, with a spatula and transfer them to the warm serving platter. Pour the pan juices over the fish and serve at once.

GRILLED SWORDFISH OR OTHER FISH STEAKS STUFFED WITH RED BELL PEPPER

❧ *Saltimbocca ai Ferri di Pesce Spada e Peperone*

An outdoor grill

Vegetable oil

2 red bell peppers

2 pounds swordfish or other fish steaks

⅓ cup extra virgin olive oil

2 tablespoons freshly squeezed lemon juice

Fine sea salt

Black pepper ground fresh from the mill

2 tablespoons chopped Italian flat-leaf parsley

1 teaspoon dried oregano

2 garlic cloves, peeled and smashed lightly with a knife handle

Uncolored wooden toothpicks

A warm serving platter

For 6 persons

1 Thinly brush the grill grid with vegetable oil, then light the grill. Place the peppers on the grid to char. When one side is done, turn them with tongs to char the next side. Repeat the procedure until the peppers are charred on all sides. Drop the charred peppers into a plastic bag, and twist it tightly closed. When the peppers have cooled down just enough for you to handle them, pull off their skins. Split the peppers along their creases and scoop out the seeds and white pith.

AHEAD-OF-TIME NOTE: It is all right to prepare the peppers several hours in advance, but not the night before. If you are making them ahead of time, you may not want to light the grill just for the peppers, especially if you are using charcoal. In such an instance, you can char the peppers over the flame of a gas burner, or in your oven broiler.

2   Slit the skin that encircles the fish steaks, detach it with a sharp paring knife and discard it. If the slice is 8 inches long or more, cut it into two smaller pieces. Slice the pieces horizontally in half to obtain thinner slices, each about ½ inch thick. To do it, hold the fish flat against a cutting board with the palm of your hand, hold the knife parallel to the board, and guide the blade with a slow, firm back-and-forth motion through the middle of the fish steak. Remove any exceptionally dark portions of the fish steak. Wash the fish in cold water, then pat thoroughly dry with paper or dish towels.

3   Pour the olive oil into a small bowl together with the lemon juice, salt, generous grindings of black pepper, the chopped parsley, oregano, and garlic cloves. Use a fork to whisk the ingredients into a homogeneous mixture. Set aside.

4   Lay the fish slices flat on a work surface, matching up the pairs. In between each pair place pepper strips to cover, trimming them to fit if necessary and sprinkling them with salt. Close the two fish slices together by inserting toothpicks around the edges.

5   Place the stuffed fish steaks on the very hot grill. Cook briefly, about 1 minute per side, then transfer them to the warm serving platter. Remove the garlic cloves from the olive oil and lemon juice mixture, and whisk it over the fish. Should there be any pieces of the grilled red peppers left over, scatter them on top. Serve at once.

Chicken

CHICKEN BREASTS SALTIMBOCCA STYLE
Saltimbocca di Petti di Pollo

Roman cooks, and what is more to the point, Roman diners abhor bland food, particularly the kind that tries to pass as delicate. Forthright flavor is what grabs their palate, which explains how they came to devise a dish whose name—*saltimbocca*—means precisely "jumps into the mouth." It is a preparation intended to coax from a slice of veal somewhat more flavor than it was naturally endowed with, layering it with pancetta and sage leaves and cooking it in butter and Frascati, the off-dry local white wine. If veal can benefit from that kind of treatment, chicken breasts, that blandest of meats, need it even more. In a saltimbocca, the gentle flavor and tender texture of chicken breasts are turned to advantage because they provide the perfect foil for the fragrance of sage and the earthiness of pancetta. It is not just an irresistible way to prepare breast of chicken, it is an application of the *saltimbocca* technique that would be hard to improve upon with any other meat.

2 whole chicken breasts

1 dozen very thin slices of pancetta

18 to 20 medium fresh sage leaves

Fine sea salt

Black pepper ground fresh from the mill

Uncolored wooden toothpicks

3 tablespoons butter

1 tablespoon vegetable oil

½ cup soft dry white wine

A warm serving platter

For 4 persons

1 If the breasts are on the bone, gently work them them off the bone, using a very sharp paring knife. Pull off and discard the yellow outer layer of skin and the thin, membrane-like layer beneath. Pick off any bits of fat.

2 Each breast half is composed of two muscles, one large and the other smaller, that partly overlap. Separate them to obtain 4 individual pieces. Protruding slightly from the smaller tapered pieces you will find the tip of a white tendon that you must pull out. It is slippery, so use a paper or cloth towel to grasp it. With the other hand, press the flat side of a knife blade against the muscle at the place where the tendon protrudes, angling the blade to keep its edge from cutting off the tendon's tip. While pressing firmly with the knife, pull the tendon away in one piece and discard. Pound the muscle gently with a meat pounder or the flat of a heavy blade or other suitable tool to flatten it slightly. Repeat the procedure with the other smaller muscle.

3 Take up the larger muscle, placing the side that lay next to the bone facedown on the cutting board. Hold it in place with the palm of one hand. Take a sharp, thin-bladed slicing knife in the other hand and, keeping the blade parallel to the cutting board, slice the breast horizontally from edge to edge to divide it into 2 equal slices, half its original thickness. Repeat the procedure with the other large muscle. Repeat with the other whole breast. Out of each whole breast, you now should have 6 fillets ready for quick cooking, or a total of 12 pieces in all.

AHEAD-OF-TIME NOTE: You can cut the breasts into the pieces as described above several hours or even a day or two in advance. Wrap in plastic film before refrigerating.

4 Take one of the larger pieces, cover it with sliced pancetta, 3 or 4 sage leaves, sprinkle with salt and pepper, and top it, sandwich style, with one of the other remaining large fillets. Fasten the edges of the "sandwich" closed with a couple of toothpicks. Repeat the procedure, using the remaining fillets, pancetta, and all but a few of sage leaves.

5 Put the butter, oil, and remaining sage leaves in a 12-inch skillet or sauté pan and turn on the heat to high. When the butter foam begins to subside and the fat is hot, slip in the chicken-breast sandwiches. Brown them quickly, first on one side, then on the other, then use a slotted spoon or spatula to transfer them to a plate.

Marcella Says: **There may be nothing so easy to overcook as chicken breasts. Their scant juices can vaporize in a flash. To preserve them, don't let the meat linger in the pan.**

6 Pour the wine into the pan and let it bubble while you scrape loose the cooking residues with a wooden spoon. When the wine has evaporated, return the chicken pieces to the pan, and turn them over quickly in the little bit of sauce in the pan, then transfer them to the warm serving platter and pour the pan juices over all. Serve at once.

COLD MARINATED CHICKEN BREASTS
⤙ *Petti di Pollo in Carpione*

Cooking has been going on for a long time, refrigeration has not. In the prerefrigerator days, which account for nearly all of humanity's history, methods were devised for preserving food beyond the immediate moment of preparation, sometimes even for the duration of a sea voyage. All of these methods are essentially variations on pickling, which can produce some remarkably tasty concoctions. Venetian cooking is rich in such dishes, usually conceived for preserving fish. One of the most famous is the *saor* treatment for small sole or sardines, which I have treated at length in my previous books. *Sarde*—sardines—*in saor* is still one of the most popular offerings of Venice's wine bars. From the inland territory of the old Venetian Republic, and specifically from Lake Garda, comes another application of the principle, a method called *in carpione*. I tried it on chicken breasts, one of the most inexpressive of meats, and I was delighted with the results. Almost as thrilling was the fact that I now had a chicken dish that could be made days in advance with no impairment to its flavor, one that I could bring out for a buffet party, for a summer lunch, for a picnic, or any other time I wanted to have chicken and didn't feel like cooking it from scratch.

1 whole skinless, boneless chicken breast, about 1 pound

1 egg

1 cup fine, dry, unflavored bread crumbs, spread on a plate or a sheet of aluminum foil or wax paper

Vegetable oil

A platter lined with a triple thickness of paper towels

¼ cup extra virgin olive oil

½ cup onion, chopped very fine

Fine sea salt

1 garlic clove, peeled and chopped fine

1 celery stalk, chopped fine, about ½ cup

1 tablespoon chopped fresh sage leaves

1 tablespoon chopped fresh rosemary leaves

⅔ cup wine vinegar, preferably red, diluted with ⅔ cup water

Black pepper ground fresh from the mill

A rectangular or deep oval serving dish, approximately 8 by 12 inches, or its equivalent in different shape

For 4 persons

1 Remove and discard any bits of fat or membrane on the chicken breast. Separate the breast into two halves. Hold one half down against the cutting board with the palm of one hand. Take a sharp, thin-bladed slicing knife in the other hand and, keeping the blade parallel to the cutting board slice the breast horizontally in half, guiding the blade through the center of the breast with a slow, firm back-and-forth motion. If one slice turns out to be much thicker than the other, flatten it a little with a meat pounder or, if you don't have one, with a flat-bottomed wine bottle. Repeat the procedure with the other breast for a total of 4 nice cutlets.

2 Crack the egg into a small bowl and beat it with a fork until the yolk and the white are evenly blended.

3 Hold one of the chicken breast slices between your thumb and forefinger and dip it into the beaten egg, coating both sides. Hold it over the bowl to let any excess egg drop back into the bowl, then dredge the slice on both sides in the crumbs, pressing them on with the palm of your hand to make them adhere. Repeat with the remaining slices.

4 Pour enough vegetable oil into a 10-inch skillet to come at least ½ inch up the sides of the pan. Turn on the heat to high. When the oil is very hot, slip in the breaded chicken breasts, one slice at a time. Do not put in any more than can fit without crowding. When one side of a slice becomes colored a deep gold, turn it, and brown the other side. When both sides are done, transfer the slice with a slotted spatula or spoon to the platter lined with paper towels and drain. Repeat until all four slices are browned. It should go very quickly, if the oil is hot enough. If it takes too long, the breasts will become overcooked and stringy.

5 When you have finished frying the sliced breast, let the oil cool off for a few minutes, then carefully pour it off and wipe the skillet dry with paper towels. (It isn't necessary to wash the skillet before continuing.) Pour the olive oil into the pan, add the chopped onion, a little salt, and turn on the heat to medium. Cook the onion, stirring frequently, until it is very soft and becomes colored a light nut-brown. Add the garlic, and cook for 1 or 2 minutes, stirring frequently. Add the celery and sage and rosemary leaves. Cook, stirring from time to time, until the celery becomes very tender.

6 Pour the vinegar-water solution into the pan, turn up the heat to high, and boil down the vinegar until it is reduced by half. Meanwhile, sprinkle the chicken with salt and liberal grindings of black pepper.

7 Pour a generous tablespoon of the pan juices in the skillet into the serving dish, spreading them over the bottom. Cover with a layer of the fried chicken slices, then add more of the pan juices and another layer of chicken, and so on until you have used all 4 slices. Pour the remaining pan juices over the top.

8 Cover the dish with a tight-fitting double layer of plastic film and refrigerate. Let the chicken steep in the marinade for at least 2 days, but no more than 5. Bring to full room temperature before serving.

Chicken Fricassees

A fricassee is the most flavorful method of cooking chicken. The word—in Italian, *fricassea*—is composed of two words of Latin origin, the first one meaning "fry" and the second "break." In a fricassee, the bird is broken into pieces and sautéed in hot fat that may be butter, olive oil, or rendered pork fat. Good as birds roasted in the oven can be, and I yield to no one in my fondness for them, a properly executed fricassee has them beat. Because the chicken is cut into pieces, the dark meat and the white cook as they should, the first one at length, until it falls off the bone, the second briefly to preserve its moistness. A fricassee, moreover, permits a limitless exploration of flavors that come from the vegetables and condiments that you choose to cook alongside the bird. Look through the four recipes that follow and take note of a variety that no other method can approach: the Piedmontese fricassee with green peppers; the one with pancetta, bell peppers, anchovies, and vinegar; the Sicilian version with almonds and Marsala; and one of my all-time favorites, a recipe from Calabria with sun-dried tomatoes, garlic, rosemary, sage, chili pepper, and potatoes.

Another feature of fricassees that appeals to me is that they are cooked over direct heat on top of the stove. It's a style of cooking that puts judgment to work, and I like that a lot better than traveling through the kitchen on automatic pilot.

FRICASSEED CHICKEN WITH GREEN PEPPERS
⌒ *Pollo in Fricassea ai Peperoni Verdi*

It was not so long ago that an Italian cook picking her or his way through the produce stalls of the food market would look askance at the sight of green peppers. Peppers, like fruit, had to be ripe, and the color of a ripe bell pepper is either red or yellow or a variation on deeply colored tints. When bell peppers are green, they are unripe. Italians are still likely to favor the fruitier, sweeter taste of ripe peppers, but they have also come to enjoy the tartness, the vivacity, the explicit bell pepper aroma that only the green ones deliver. It is those qualities that contribute to the freshness of flavor of this chicken cooked over the stovetop in a contemporary version of the classic Italian fricassee.

3 large or 4 medium meaty green bell peppers

A 3-pound chicken, cut into 10 pieces: 2 drumsticks, 2 thighs, 2 wings, and 4 breast pieces. If keeping the meat of the back, add 2 more pieces.

3 tablespoons extra virgin olive oil

4 whole garlic cloves if large, 5 if medium, peeled

¼ pound sliced pancetta

> *Marcella Says:* **Ideally, you should be using pork jowl—*guanciale*—that has been cured, but not smoked. If you have a store near you that carries it, buy it instead of pancetta. Pork jowl is available online, but it is expensive unless you order a lot of other items, as it must be shipped express overnight. In my supermarket, I have occasionally come across something vaguely like it, called pork side meat, and that would be good to use, too.**

Chopped chili pepper, 1 tablespoon fresh jalapeño, OR 1 teaspoon dried red chili pepper, adjusting the quantities to taste and to the potency of the chili

Fine sea salt

½ cup dry white wine

1 cup tomatoes, cut up with their juice, either ripe, firm, fresh plum tomatoes, peeled and seeded, OR canned imported San Marzano Italian tomatoes

A warm serving platter

For 4 to 6 persons

1 Cut each pepper lengthwise along the creases, remove the stem, seeds, and pithy core, then skin with a swivel-blade vegetable peeler. (For more details, see Peppers on page 79 of The Why and How of Prepping Vegetables.) Cut into 1- to 1½-inch pieces.

2 Wash the chicken pieces under cold running water and pat thoroughly dry with kitchen towels.

3 Pour the olive oil into a 12-inch sauté pan, add the garlic cloves, the pancetta or other cured pork you may be using, and the chili pepper and turn on the heat to high. Cook the garlic, stirring it two or three times, until it becomes colored a very pale gold. Add the chicken pieces and brown them on both sides.

4 Remove the 4 breast pieces from the pan, and transfer them to a plate. Pour in the white wine, and let it bubble away for about 1 minute. Add the green pepper pieces and cook them for 4 to 5 minutes, turning them over once or twice.

5 Add the tomatoes with their juice, reduce the heat down to very low, and cover the pan. Cook for about 40 minutes, turning the chicken pieces over from time to time. Return the breast pieces to the pan and turn them over once or twice to coat them well. Cover the pan and cook for about 15 minutes. The chicken is done when the meat come easily off the bone, not any sooner. Transfer the fricassee to the warm serving platter and serve at once.

AHEAD-OF-TIME NOTE: If you intend to have the chicken for dinner, you can cook it through to the end as early as the morning of the same day. Reheat it gently in the pan just before serving. You may also refrigerate it in a tightly sealed container for 2 or 3 days. Bring it back to room temperature before reheating.

FRICASSEED CHICKEN ASTI STYLE WITH PANCETTA, SWEET BELL PEPPERS, HERBS, AND ANCHOVIES

Pollo in Fricassea all'Astigiana con la Pancetta, i Peperoni, gli Odori, e l'Acciuga

A 3- to 3½-pound chicken

1 tablespoon vegetable oil

2 tablespoons butter

A single slice of pancetta ⅓ inch thick, about 3 ounces, cut into narrow strips

2 long sprigs of Italian flat-leaf parsley and 2 sprigs of fresh rosemary, stems tied together with white cotton twine or thread

Fine sea salt

Black pepper ground fresh from the mill

1 cup dry white wine

4 meaty bell peppers, 2 red and 2 yellow

3 or 4 garlic cloves, peeled and chopped very fine

4 flat anchovy fillets, chopped very fine

¼ cup red wine vinegar

A warm deep serving platter

For 4 to 6 persons

1   Wash the chicken, pat it dry with paper towels, and pare away the fat you find around both the front and rear cavities. Cut the bird into 12 pieces: 2 drumsticks, 2 thighs, 2 wings, 2 pieces from the back, and 4 from the breast.

2   Pour the oil into a 12-inch sauté pan or skillet, add the butter, the pancetta, and the rosemary and parsley bouquet, and turn on the heat to high. When the fat gets hot, sauté the ingredients for a few seconds, stirring, then add all the chicken pieces, skin side down. Brown the chicken deeply on one side, then turn and brown the other side, about 20 minutes in all.

3   Remove the breast pieces to a deep dish or small bowl, and reserve.

> *Marcella Says:* **The breast meat must not cook for as long as the other parts of the chicken because it will dry out. When the other parts of the chicken are nearly done, you will return the breast meat to the pan for a few last minutes of cooking, all it needs.**

4   Sprinkle salt and pepper on the chicken pieces in the pan. Add the white wine, turn the heat down to medium, and continue to cook at least another 40 minutes, turning the chicken over from time to time.

5   Turn on the broiler.

6   While the chicken is cooking, wash the bell peppers, put them on a baking sheet, and place it under the preheated broiler. Turn the peppers from time until the skin is charred all over.

> *Marcella Says:* **Don't keep them under the broiler too long because they will steam in their own vapors and become soggy. You are not cooking them, you are only charring the skin so that you can lift it off. If you have gas burners, you can char the peppers right on top of the stove, and, of course, on a grill, whether it is an outdoor or indoor one.**

7   When their skins are blackened all over, put them in a plastic bag, a supermarket bag is just fine, and close the bag tightly. Wait about 10 to 12 minutes, until the peppers have cooled enough to handle, then take them out of the bag and pull off all the skins. Split each pepper lengthwise, remove the stem, seeds, and pithy core, and cut into 1-inch squares.

8   Put the chopped garlic and anchovies into a saucer or very small bowl, and mash them together, using the back of a spoon. Pour the vinegar over them, blending it in with the spoon.

9 When the chicken meat in the skillet has become tender enough to come easily away from the bone, after about 40 minutes, return the breast pieces to the pan along with any juice that has accumulated in the dish, add the cut-up peppers, the garlic and anchovy mixture, some salt and pepper, and turn all the ingredients over once or twice. Cook over medium heat for about 15 minutes. If the pan juices should become too runny, remove the chicken pieces only, using a slotted spoon or tongs, turn up the heat to high, scrape loose any cooking residues on the bottom of the pan, and when the juices have cooked down some, put the chicken back in the pan. Turn the pieces over once or twice, then transfer the fricassee to the warm serving platter and serve promptly.

AHEAD-OF-TIME NOTE: You can make the dish all the way through to the end up to a day in advance of serving. Reheat the fricassee over medium heat on top of the stove until thoroughly warmed through.

FRICASSEED CHICKEN WITH ALMONDS
⌖ *Pollo in Fricassea con le Mandorle*

A 3½-to 4-pound chicken, cut into 8 pieces

2 ounces, about ⅓ cup, whole almonds, shelled but not peeled

> *Marcella Says:* **I don't buy peeled almonds because I never know how long they have been on the shelf and blanched almonds turn rancid more quickly than unpeeled ones.**

2 tablespoons butter

1 tablespoon vegetable oil

3 garlic cloves, peeled and lightly smashed with the flat part of a heavy knife blade

1 cup flour, spread on a plate

1 cup dry Marsala wine

Fine sea salt

Chopped dried hot red chili pepper, 1 teaspoon or more, adjusting the quantity to taste and to the potency of the chili

A warm serving platter

For 4 to 6 persons

1 Wash the chicken pieces under cold running water, then set in a footed colander to drain.

2 Drop the almonds in to a small saucepan of boiling water. Two minutes after the water returns to a boil, drain through a sieve. Wrap the almonds in a dampened dish towel. Rub the almonds briskly in the towel, unwrap the towel, and remove those almonds with loosened peels. Remove the peels. Wrap up the remaining almonds and repeat the rubbing procedure until all the almonds are peeled. Put the almonds in a food processor fitted with the steel blade and chop until pulverized.

3 Put the butter and oil in a 12-inch sauté pan together with the garlic and turn on the heat to high. Stir the garlic from time to time. When the butter melts completely and its foam begins to subside, dredge one chicken piece at a time in the flour and slip it into the pan to brown. When all the chicken pieces have been browned on one side, turn them and brown the other side. When they have all been thoroughly browned, remove the breast pieces, and set them aside in a bowl.

4 Add the chopped almonds to the pan, stirring them with a wooden spoon for about a minute to brown. Add the Marsala, salt, and the chili pepper, turning mixture over with the wooden spoon. When the Marsala has bubbled for about 1 minute, turn the heat down to the lowest setting and cover the pan. Cook for 1 hour, or as long as necessary for the meat to come easily off the bone, then return the breast pieces to the pan. Cook for another 15 minutes. Transfer the fricassee to the warm platter and serve at once.

AHEAD-OF-TIME NOTE: If you are serving the chicken for dinner, you can cook it through to the end that morning. Refrigerate and reheat gently in the same pan.

FRICASSEED CHICKEN WITH FRESH HERBS AND SUN-DRIED TOMATOES

Pollo in Fricassea con gli Odori e i Pomodori Secchi

Contrary to popularly held notions about the use of herbs in Italian cooking, it is rare to find more than one herb in a dish, and it is used rather sparingly at that. Here is one of the exceptions that uses both sage and rosemary. It's not a formula to be applied with abandon, but it works quite well with the sun-dried tomatoes and the garlic, endowing this chicken fricassee with exceptionally rich fragrance.

A 3-pound chicken, cut into 10 pieces: 2 drumsticks, 2 thighs, 2 wings, and 4 pieces the breast. If keeping the meat from the back, add 2 more pieces.

2 tablespoons extra virgin olive oil

3 garlic cloves, peeled and chopped fine

6 fresh sage leaves, chopped

The leaves from 2 sprigs of fresh rosemary, chopped fine, about ½ tablespoon

3 slices choice-quality thick-cut bacon, cut into 1-inch pieces, about ½ cup

6 to 8 halves sun-dried tomatoes, cut into 1-inch pieces

Fine sea salt

Chopped dried red chili pepper, ¼ teaspoon or more, adjusting the quantity to taste and to the potency of the chili

1 cup dry white wine

4 large or 6 medium potatoes, peeled and cut into pieces no larger than a walnut

A warm serving platter

For 4 to 6 persons

1   Wash the chicken under cold running water and pat dry with kitchen towels.

2   Pour the oil into a 12-inch sauté pan or skillet and turn on the heat to high. When the oil is hot, add the chicken pieces, skin side down. Cook until browned to a nice deep gold, turn, and brown the other side. Transfer the pieces to a medium bowl, using a slotted spoon or spatula.

3   Add the garlic to the pan, turn the heat down to medium, and as soon as the garlic aroma begins to rise, add the sage, rosemary, and bacon. Cook the bacon, turning it over once or twice, until it is lightly browned, but not crisp. Add the sun-dried tomatoes, turn all the ingredients over once or twice, then return the chicken pieces to the pan, leaving the breast pieces in the bowl. Sprinkle the chicken in the pan with salt and the chili pepper, and turn the pieces over to coat them well.

4   Add the wine, increase the heat to high, and let it bubble for a few seconds. Turn the heat down to low and cover the pan. Cook the chicken, turning it from time to time, until the meat comes easily off the bone, about 45 minutes. If, during this time, the pan juices should become insufficient to keep the chicken from sticking to the pan, add up to ¼ cup of water.

5   When the chicken is done, transfer the pieces to the bowl with the breast pieces. Put the potatoes in the pan, turning them over to coat them well. Sprinkle them with salt, turn the heat down to medium, and cover the pan. When the potatoes are almost done but still not quite tender, return all the chicken pieces to the pan, including the breasts. Cook, turning the chicken over once or twice, until the potatoes are done.

6   Transfer the fricassee to the warm platter and serve at once.

AHEAD-OF-TIME NOTE: You can prepare the fricassee to the end several hours in advance of serving. Reheat gently just before serving, adding a tablespoon or two of water if needed.

Veal

Ground Veal Patties Done Two Ways

Veal is delicate, but not tasteless. No other meat has such finesse, but it is a fragile finesse that may vanish into blandness or, worse, dryness if you don't apply a suitable cooking method. The juiciest way to cook ground veal patties would be to fry them. It's how I do them, but if you wish you can grill them. You need a very hot grill, whether electric or natural charcoal doesn't matter, but I don't recommend the broiler of a standard home oven because it rarely gets hot enough. You need strong heat because you mustn't keep the patties too long on the grill or the meat will dry out.

The recipes that follow demonstrate two quite distinct approaches, each capitalizing on one of veal's singular attributes, its adaptability to different flavors. The first recipe has a vivacious southern Italian accent contributed by capers. The second is in the Bolognese style, reminiscent of homemade pasta fillings that use greens, Parmesan cheese, and nutmeg.

SAVORY LITTLE BRACIOLE OF CHOPPED VEAL
⌘ Bracioline Appetitose di Vitello Macinato

2 tablespoons capers, drained and rinsed in cold water if packed in vinegar,
OR if packed in salt, rinsed, soaked in cold water for 10 minutes, then rinsed again

1 pound ground veal

½ teaspoon garlic, chopped very fine

2 tablespoons chopped Italian flat-leaf parsley

1 egg

Fine sea salt

Black pepper ground fresh from the mill

2 cups fine, dry, unflavored bread crumbs, spread on a plate or on a sheet of wax paper or aluminum foil

⅓ cup vegetable oil

A steel-mesh drying rack, placed over a sheet of aluminum foil

A warm serving platter

For 4 to 6 persons

1 Chop the capers fine, then put them in a bowl. Add the veal, garlic, parsley, egg, salt, and a few grindings of black pepper and mix. Knead the mixture gently with your hands and shape it into flat patties, each about 1 inch thick and 3 inches wide. Dredge each patty as you form it in the bread crumbs, turning it over and pressing it gently into the crumbs with the palm of your hand to make the crumbs adhere.

2 Pour the oil into a 12-inch skillet—there should be enough to come at least ½ inch up the sides of the pan—and turn on the heat to high. When the oil is quite hot, slip in the veal patties. When the sides facing the bottom of the pan have formed a lovely dark crust, turn the patties over and brown the other sides. As soon as both sides are nicely crusted, use a slotted spoon or spatula to transfer the patties to the drying rack to drain. When they are all drained, transfer the bracioline to a warm platter and serve promptly.

VEAL AND SPINACH PATTIES

Polpette di Vitello e Spinaci

¾ pound fresh young spinach (you may need an additional ounce or two if it is older spinach with thick stems) OR a 10-ounce bag of prewashed spinach

Fine sea salt

1 pound ground veal

1 egg

1 garlic clove, chopped fine, about 1 teaspoon

⅓ cup freshly grated Parmigiano-Reggiano cheese

⅛ teaspoon freshly grated nutmeg

Black pepper ground fresh from the mill

Fine, dry, unflavored bread crumbs, spread on a plate or on a sheet of wax paper or aluminum foil

Vegetable oil

A steel-mesh drying rack, placed over a sheet of aluminum foil

A warm serving platter

For 4 to 6 persons

1   If the spinach is mature with large leaves and thick stems, detach and discard the stems. Soak the spinach in a clean basin or sink full of cold water for a few minutes, then lift it out of the water with your hands, drop it into a bowl, and empty the basin or sink, rinsing away any soil that has settled on the bottom. Repeat the procedure until the water is clear of any soil. Follow this step at least one time even with prewashed spinach.

2   Bring a large saucepan of water to a boil, add 2 tablespoons of salt, and drop in the spinach. Cook until very soft, then drain and set aside to cool. When cool enough to handle, squeeze it in your hands to force out as much water as possible, then chop very fine with a knife.

Marcella Says: **Do not be tempted to use the food processor to chop the spinach because it would cause more liquid to be released, making the spinach too soggy.**

3 Put the veal and the chopped spinach in a bowl and add the egg, garlic, grated cheese, nutmeg, salt, and several grindings of black pepper. Mix very thoroughly to integrate all the ingredients into a uniform mass.

AHEAD-OF-TIME NOTE: You can complete the recipe up to this point several hours in advance. Cover the bowl tightly with plastic film and refrigerate. Bring it to room temperature before resuming the preparation of the dish.

4 Scoop up enough of the veal and spinach mixture to make a ball the size of a small lemon, then flatten it with your hands, shaping it into a patty no thicker than 1 inch. Proceed thus until you have used all the mixture, then dredge each patty on both sides in the bread crumbs, pressing it gently into the crumbs with the palm of your hand to make the crumb coating adhere.

Marcella Says: **Do not execute this step until you are ready to cook the patties because if you let them stand for any length of time the bread coating becomes too soggy to form a crisp crust when fried.**

5 Pour enough vegetable oil into a 12-inch skillet to come at least ½ inch up the sides of the pan and turn on the heat to medium high. When the oil is hot, slip only enough patties into the pan that can fit in a single uncrowded layer. If they don't all fit at the same time, you can cook them in batches. Cook the patties until the sides facing down have deeply browned, then turn and cook the other sides. As each patty is done crisply on both sides, use a slotted spoon or spatula to transfer it to the drying rack to drain. Transfer the patties to the warm platter and serve.

AHEAD-OF-TIME NOTE: These patties are at their best when just done and still piping hot, but they are also very tasty even at room temperature. If that is how you might want to serve them or as part of a buffet, say, you can make them several hours in advance on the day you will serve them. They don't keep too well overnight because the spinach picks up off flavors after a night in the refrigerator.

Veal Shanks with Lemon

⌖ Ossobuco al Limone

Veal and lemon juice get on famously with each other. Is there anyone who has never had and enjoyed one of those veal and lemon classics, *scallopine al limone*? It occurred to me that the simple, direct fragrance of lemon would work well with ossobuco, a cut naturally so well endowed that it can dispense with the piling up of other flavors to which it is often subjected. Ossobuco has to cook slowly for a long time for its tissues to relax and achieve a delectably creamy consistency. It will reach that goal better if it is not cut too thick, not more than 1½ inches. The shanks are cooked in the traditional Italian home kitchen style, on top of the stove, which coaxes so much more flavor from them than oven cooking would.

¼ pound pancetta, sliced very thin

4 veal shank slices, each 1 to 1½ inches thick

Kitchen twine or all-cotton white twine

2 tablespoons butter

1 tablespoon vegetable oil

All-purpose flour, spread on a plate

Fine sea salt

Black pepper ground fresh from the mill

⅓ cup freshly squeezed lemon juice

Optional: homemade meat broth (page 48)

A warm serving platter

For 4 persons

1 Wrap 3 to 4 pancetta slices around each of the shanks and fasten them on with the twine.

2 Chop the leftover pancetta.

3 Choose a saucepan in which the shanks will fit snugly without overlapping. Put in the butter and oil and turn on the heat to high.

4 While the butter is getting hot, dredge the shanks in the flour, coating them on all sides. When the butter's foam begins to subside, slip in the shanks and the chopped pancetta. Brown the shanks thoroughly on one side, then on the other.

5 Add salt, pepper, and lemon juice, turn the heat down to very low, and put a lid on the pan. Cook the shanks for at least 1½ hours, until the meat feels very tender when poked with a fork. Turn the shanks over two or three times while they cook. If at any time you find that the juices in the pan are insufficient to keep the meat from sticking to the bottom, add 2 to 3 tablespoons of water, or better, homemade meat broth if you have some in the freezer.

6 When done, transfer the ossobuco to the warm platter, pour all the pan juices over the pieces, and serve at once.

AHEAD-OF-TIME NOTE: You can cook the ossobuco all the way through in advance, but to preserve the freshness of its fragrance, preferably not earlier than the morning of the day when you will have it for dinner. Reheat it gently in a covered saucepan, adding a tablespoon or two of water. Again, homemade meat broth would be preferable, if the juices appear to be too skimpy to keep the meat from drying out. You may also reheat the dish covered in a preheated 350° oven for about 30 minutes.

Braised Veal Chops with Milk and Capers

‹❧ Costate di Vitello in Tegame Brasate al Latte e ai Capperi

This is another of Lele Rivolta's dishes (if you want to know more about Lele turn to Leek Sauce on page 172). She mentioned this veal recipe one day at lunch when we were having my pork with milk. In fact, this does resemble that preparation, but the capers give it a much tangier accent. Like the pork, this slow top-of-the-stove braising takes a long while and it requires a cut of meat that can come through that kind of cooking with moistness and natural flavors uncompromised. The one that has worked the best for me is the chop, cut very thick. I find, too, that the bone of the chop adds something of its own to the rich flavors of the braise.

2 tablespoons capers, drained and rinsed in cold water if packed in vinegar,
OR if packed in salt, rinsed, soaked in cold water for 10 minutes, then rinsed again

1 cup whole milk

2 tablespoons butter

1 tablespoon vegetable oil

2 veal rib chops, each at least 1½ inches thick

Fine sea salt

Black pepper ground fresh from the mill

A warm serving platter

For 4 persons

1 Put all the capers and ¼ cup of the milk in a food processor and blend thoroughly to a runny, creamy consistency.

2 Put the butter and oil in a 12-inch sauté pan and turn on the heat to high. When the fat is very hot, slip in the chops. Brown them deeply on one side and then on the other.

3 Sprinkle the chops lightly with salt, pour the caper mixture over them, turning them over a couple of times, and put a lid on the pan. As soon as the liquid begins to simmer, turn the heat down to very low.

4 Braise the chops for about 1½ hours, turning them from time to time, until the meat feels tender when poked with a fork. Keep an eye on the milk in the pan and when it cooks off add ⅓ of a cup. It will cook off again, at which time you must add all the remaining milk.

5 When the meat is tender, take the pan off the heat, lift out the chops, and place them on a cutting board. Use a sharp knife to detach the meat from the bones and cut it into angled slices ½ inch thick, or less. Put the pan back on the burner, turn the heat on to medium, put in the sliced meat, and turn the slices in the warming sauce for about a minute. Transfer the meat and all the sauce to the warm platter and serve at once.

AHEAD-OF-TIME NOTE: You can cook the veal all the way through a few hours in advance of serving, keeping the slices covered in the sauce. Reheat gently in a covered saucepan, adding a tablespoon or two of water if the liquid appears to be too scanty to keep the meat from drying out.

Beef

COLD BOILED BEEF SALAD

⟨ᴇ⟩ *Insalata di Manzo Lesso*

When you make your own meat broth, which is so critically important to the flavor of your cooking, you are likely to end up with more boiled beef than you can use immediately. That might be, in fact, a result strongly to be wished for because then you have the makings of this extraordinarily good beef salad. A neighbor to whom I sent some of it wrote back, "You can keep the broth, I'll take all the beef salad that you have no use for." Unfortunately for her, I can never make enough of it to satisfy the men in my family, and my dinner guests to whom I serve it as an appetizer. It's also the perfect cold meat dish for summer lunches al fresco.

1½ to 2 pounds boiled beef chuck or brisket, cooked as described in Making the Broth on page 50 of Aᴛ Mᴀsᴛᴇʀ Cʟᴀss

1¼ tablespoons Dijon mustard

1 tablespoon red wine vinegar

Fine sea salt

½ cup extra virgin olive oil

2 tablespoons chopped Italian flat-leaf parsley

2 tablespoons chopped fresh basil leaves

½ cup chopped onion of any sweet variety, such as Vidalia, Maui, or fresh Florida Sweet

2 tablespoons chopped cornichons (small pickles)

3 or 4 flat anchovy fillets, chopped fine

1 medium garlic clove, peeled and chopped fine

2 tablespoons capers, drained and rinsed in cold water if packed in vinegar,
ᴏʀ if packed in salt, rinsed, soaked in cold water for 10 minutes, then rinsed again;
whole, if of nonpareils size; chopped, if larger

Black pepper ground fresh from the mill

For 4 to 6 persons

1   Retrieve the meat from the broth in which it has cooked and let it cool down completely. Cut away and discard as much of the fat as possible. Cut the remaining meat into 1½- to 2-inch pieces.

> *Marcella Says:* **If, after you have removed the fat, you find you are left with noticeably less meat, reduce the seasoning ingredient measurements accordingly.**

AHEAD-OF-TIME NOTE: Unless you plan to prepare the salad at this point, put the beef in a tightly lidded container and refrigerate. You can keep it this way for 2 days. If you don't expect to use the meat until much after that, freeze it. Remember to thaw it and bring it back to room temperature before composing the salad.

2   Put the mustard, vinegar, and a few pinches of salt in a small bowl and mix with a fork. Add the olive oil, beating it in with the fork to emulsify the mixture.

3   Put the boiled meat in a larger bowl, and add all the remaining ingredients. Turn all the ingredients over several times to coat the meat well, then cover tightly with plastic film and refrigerate overnight. When you take the bowl out of the refrigerator, toss the contents thoroughly, and let them come to room temperature before serving the salad.

Three Juicy Beef Roasts and a Tasty Stew

My idea of what a roast, or braise, or beef stew should be is tender, the muscle fibers relaxed by slow cooking but still saturated with their own natural moisture, and savory. I am tempted to put savory first because what is the point of eating just another piece of cooked meat? But not one thing is more important than the other, and if one is missing the appeal of the others vanishes. In the four examples that follow the triple objective of tenderness, juiciness, and savoriness is pursued in different ways.

The first recipe in this special collection is a braised beef from the beautiful city of Macerata in the Marches region of central Italy. This piece of meat is studded, as is the following pot roast, but here there is a trio of ingredients, salt pork, garlic, and lemon peel. From there on, the procedure takes a different direction. The meat is browned first over very high heat and

is removed from the pan. Over lowered heat a flavor base of vegetables—onion, celery, and carrots, together with more garlic—is sautéed and made ready for the return of the meat, which will braise slowly with the addition of wine, tomatoes, and thyme.

In the recipe for old-style pot roast from the Brianza Hills north of Milan, pork has two taste-enhancing roles to play: Pancetta is inserted into the meat, and the rind from a piece of salt pork cooks alongside it. The pancetta bastes the meat from the inside, the rind from the outside. From that point on, grappa, wine, a few herbs, but most of all, long, slow, controlled cooking on top of the stove—much longer than you might be accustomed to—assume most of the responsibility for producing a memorable roast to which tiny onions and cut-up carrots provide the mellow finishing touches.

The flavor of my other pot roast, a Piedmontese one from Novara, is one of those rare examples of meat dishes that Italian cooks call *a crudo*. It skips the classic *insaporire* sequence in which the flavors are built one upon the other by the ingredients being sautéed one at a time. Here, they all go in at once in their raw—*a crudo*—state. With slow cooking, that method can produce wonderfully expansive flavor. (If you have my *Essentials of Classic Italian Cooking*, look up another example of an *a crudo*, the Lamb with Juniper Berries.) The garlic, anchovies, mustard, and vinegar with which the beef is simmered give this pot roast a sprightly flavor profile, and it is slow, watchful cooking on top of the stove that makes it all come together.

The last recipe is a stew of my own devising. I first brown the cubes of chuck in very hot butter and oil, then I remove them. I cook chopped onion and sage over lowered heat to prepare a flavor base for the meat, which then goes back into the pan. I finish cooking the meat with mushrooms and potatoes. And, once again, it is the slowly paced, patiently monitored top-of-the-stove cooking that preserves the juiciness of the meat and gives all the accompanying ingredients the opportunity to evolve.

Braised Beef with Vegetables, Red Wine, and Thyme

✎ *Umido di Manzo alla Maceratese*

2 garlic cloves, chopped very fine

⅓ cup salt pork, chopped very fine

The peel of ½ a lemon, only the outer yellow layer, not the inner white pith, chopped very fine

Fine sea salt

Black pepper ground fresh from the mill

A 1-pound piece of beef brisket, boneless flat cut

3 tablespoons butter

1 tablespoon vegetable oil

1 cup onion, sliced very thin

½ cup celery, stripped of its strings using a vegetable peeler and sliced crosswise very thin

½ cup small, young—but not baby—carrots, peeled and cut into thin disks

1 garlic clove, peeled and sliced very thin

Thyme leaves, ½ teaspoon if fresh, ¼ teaspoon if dried

1 cup dry red wine, preferably a Montepulciano, a Chianti, or any central Italian red made from the Sangiovese grape

1 cup tomatoes, cut up with their juice, either ripe, firm, fresh plum tomatoes peeled and seeds scooped away OR canned imported San Marzano Italian tomatoes

A warm serving platter

For 4 persons

1 In a small bowl mix the chopped garlic, salt pork, and lemon peel together with some salt and several grindings of black pepper.

2 Poke several holes into both sides of the brisket, using any pointed tool—the thick end of a Chinese chopstick, a zucchini corer, a larding needle, a very thin knife—and pack the garlic, pork, and lemon peel mixture into the holes, forcing it in with your fingertip.

AHEAD-OF-TIME NOTE: The step may be completed a day in advance. Refrigerate the meat until ready to proceed with the cooking.

3 Put the butter and oil in a 12-inch sauté pan and turn on the heat to high. When the fat is hot and the butter foam begins to subside, slip in the brisket. Brown it quickly on both sides, then take it out of the pan.

4 Turn the heat down to medium, add the sliced onion, and cook it, stirring occasionally, until it becomes colored a light nut-brown. Add the celery, turn it over, and cook for about 1 minute. Add the carrots, turn them, and cook another minute. Add the sliced garlic, turn all ingredients over once or twice to coat them well, and cook for a minute or two, stirring once or twice.

5 Return the brisket to the pan, sprinkle it with salt and ground pepper, and add the thyme and red wine. When the wine begins to bubble, turn the heat down to medium low and put a lid on the pan. Check the wine level every once in a while and when it has nearly bubbled away, add the tomatoes with their juices. Turn the heat down to low, and put the lid back on.

6 Cook the meat, turning it from time to time, for about 2 hours if its thickest part is about 2 inches. If it is thicker, cook it a while longer. When the meat feels quite tender at the prodding of a fork, remove the brisket from the pan and let it cool down completely. When cool, slice the meat against the grain into thin slices, then slip the slices into the pan, turning them in the pan juices.

AHEAD-OF-TIME NOTE: You can cook the brisket up to this point several hours in advance of serving.

7 When ready to serve, turn on the heat under the pan to medium and gently reheat the sliced brisket, turning the slices once or twice. When fully reheated, lay the meat slices on the warm serving platter, pour all the vegetables and pan juices over them, and bring promptly to the table.

OLD-STYLE POT ROAST FROM THE BRIANZA HILLS
↬ *Stracotto Vecchia Brianza*

A larding needle or a stout round Chinese chopstick

2 ounces pancetta, cut into thin strips ¼ inch wide or less, about ½ cup

A 2½- to 3-pound piece rib roast of beef, bone in

2 tablespoons butter

1 tablespoon vegetable oil

Fine sea salt

Black pepper ground fresh from the mill

¼ cup good-quality grappa

2 cups dry white wine

The rind from a 12-ounce package of salt pork, cut into strips about ¼ inch wide or less, at least ½ cup (but more won't hurt)

1 bay leaf

4 stems—no leaves—Italian flat-leaf parsley

The leaves from 2 or 3 sprigs of fresh thyme, about 1 teaspoon

18 to 20 tiny pearl onions

4 medium carrots

A warm serving platter

For 6 persons

1 Use the larding needle or Chinese chopstick to insert strips of pancetta into the roast. Try to distribute the strips of pancetta so that the ones with the most fat reach the central, leanest part of the roast.

2 Choose a lidded saucepan with a heavy, heat-retaining bottom, such as enameled cast iron. It should be just large enough to hold the roast snugly. Put in the butter and oil and turn on the heat to high. As soon as the fat is hot, put in the meat and brown it well on all sides. Add salt and several grindings of black pepper, turning the roast to season it evenly.

3 Turn the heat down to medium and add the grappa. When it has bubbled away, add the wine, pork rind, bay leaf, parsley stems, and thyme leaves. When the pot comes to a lively simmer, turn the heat down to low and cover with a tight-fitting lid. Cook at a very gentle, steady simmer for at least 3 hours, turning the meat over from time to time.

4 While the meat is cooking, bring water to a boil in a small saucepan. Drop in the pearl onions with their peels on. Retrieve them with a slotted spoon before the water comes back to a boil. Let them cool completely, then peel them and cut a cross in the root end of each one.

5 Peel the carrots and cut them into pieces 2 inches long where the carrot is thickest and into longer pieces where the carrot is thin and tapered.

6 When the meat has simmered for 3 hours, add the blanched onions and cut-up carrots, turning them in the pan juices. Cover the pot and cook at a gentle, steady simmer for about 20 minutes, until the carrots and onions are tender, turning them over from time to time.

AHEAD-OF-TIME NOTE: You can cook the meat up to this point several hours in advance of serving. Refrigerate it in the pan with the juices and let it come to full room temperature before proceeding with the dish.

7 Remove the roast from the pan, and let it settle for a few minutes. Tip the pan and spoon off much, but not all, of the fat. (See Marcella Says below for a good use for it.) Leave all the tasty pan juices in the pan.

8 Turn on the heat under the pan to low, and let the contents come to a slow, intermittent simmer. Detach the bones and cut the roast into slices. Lay each slice flat in the pan, turning it to moisten it on both sides with the pan juices. When all the slices are sauced, retrieve them and arrange them on the warm serving platter. Pour all the contents of the pan over them and serve promptly.

Marcella Says: Use the fat that you have drawn off to make delicious sautéed potatoes. Peel 4 or 5 medium potatoes and cut them into 1-inch pieces. Heat the fat you've skimmed off in a large skillet. When hot, add the potatoes and cook them over medium heat, turning them from time to time, until tender. Season with salt and pepper, and serve piping hot as an accompaniment to the sliced pot roast.

Pot Roast of Beef with Garlic, Anchovies, Vinegar, and Pancetta
᚛ *Arrosto di Manzo alla Novarese*

A 2½-pound boneless piece of beef chuck

4 tablespoons extra virgin olive oil

2 whole garlic cloves, unpeeled

4 flat anchovy fillets, packed in olive oil

2 tablespoons good-quality Dijon-style mustard

¼ cup good-quality red wine vinegar

2 tablespoons water

A ½-inch-thick slice of pancetta, cut into 4 to 6 pieces

Fine sea salt

Black pepper ground fresh from the mill

A warm serving platter

For 4 to 6 persons

1 Choose a sturdy, heavy-bottomed saucepan—enameled cast iron would be my choice—just large enough to hold the beef. Pour in the olive oil and add the garlic, anchovies, mustard, vinegar, water, pancetta, and beef. Turn on the heat to low and cook for about 15 minutes, turning the meat over with all the other ingredients every 3 minutes or so. Season with salt and pepper, turn the meat over once or twice, and cover the pot. Reduce the heat to the lowest setting, and cook the roast for 2 hours or more, until the beef feels tender when prodded with a fork. Turn the meat over from time to time while it cooks. If during this time the liquid in the pan should prove insufficient to prevent the meat from sticking, add 2 tablespoons of water.

2 Remove the pan from the heat and let it settle for a few minutes. Remove the meat from the pan to a cutting board. Turn the heat on again to very low, slice the beef, and put it back in the pan, turning each slice in the juices over very gentle heat. Transfer the slices of pot roast and juices to the warm serving platter and serve at once. If you like garlic a lot, squeeze the cloves out of their skins and mash them into the cooking juices.

AHEAD-OF-TIME NOTE: You can complete the dish a full day in advance, refrigerating the meat unsliced with all its juices. When ready to serve, slice the beef and reheat it in its juices as described above in step 2.

STEWED BEEF WITH MUSHROOMS AND POTATOES

ᘓ *Stufato di Manzo alla Salvia con Funghi e Patate*

2 tablespoons butter

1 tablespoon vegetable oil

1 pound boneless, not-too-lean beef, preferably chuck, cut into 1-inch cubes

½ cup chopped onion

8 to 10 whole fresh sage leaves OR 1 tablespoon chopped dried sage leaves

½ cup dry white wine

Fine sea salt

Black pepper ground fresh from the mill

¼ pound or slightly more fresh shiitake mushrooms

2 large boiling potatoes

A warm serving platter

For 4 persons

1 Put the butter and olive oil in a heavy-bottomed saucepan, turn the heat on to high and when the butter foam begins to subside, slip in as many of the beef cubes as will fit without overlapping. Brown the meat on all its sides. Use a slotted spoon or spatula to transfer the cubes to a bowl or deep dish, and add to the pan any pieces that remain to be browned. When the last batch is done, add it to the other already browned pieces.

2 Turn the heat down to medium, add the chopped onion and sage leaves, and cook, stirring frequently, until the onion becomes colored a deep blond.

3 Return the browned cubes to the pan, add the wine, salt, and pepper and scrape the bottom of the pan with a wooden spoon or spatula to loosen any cooked-on residue. When the wine has bubbled for a moment or two, turn the heat down to the lowest setting and put a lid on the pan.

4   While the meat cooks, detach and discard the stems of the shiitake mushrooms, wash the caps rapidly under cold running water, and cut them into strips about ½ inch wide. Add the sliced mushrooms to the pan ½ hour after the meat started cooking, turning the mushrooms and the beef cubes over two or three times. Cook at a slow, steady pace, checking to make sure there is sufficient liquid in the pan. If not, add ⅓ cup water.

5   Peel the potatoes, cut them into medium-size dice, rinse the dice in two changes of cold water, and add them to the stew with a little more salt. Turn all the ingredients over two or three times.

6   Cook the stew for a minimum of 2 hours total, but longer if necessary for the potatoes to become completely tender. Check from time to time to make sure that the stew is not drying out. Should it become necessary, add 2 tablespoons of water. When both the meat and the potatoes feel tender when tested with a fork, empty the pan onto the warm serving platter and serve.

AHEAD-OF-TIME NOTE: You can make the stew a day or two in advance of serving. Refrigerate it in a tightly covered container. Bring to full room temperature before reheating it, which you can do either on top of the stove over gentle heat or in a preheated 375° oven.

SPICY BEEF MEATBALLS WITH BELL PEPPERS

Polpettine di Manzo Piccanti con i Peperoni

The role that tomatoes have always played in the making of Italian meatballs is filled here by red bell peppers. You have, moreover, a say in the direction of that role. If you want the peppers to star—that is, if you would like them to maintain enough of their shape to show on the plate—cook them just until a fork slips easily into them, about 10 minutes. If you think that you may enjoy them more as sauce, and a very tasty sauce it would be, just continue to cook them until they begin to dissolve.

4 meaty red bell peppers

2 tablespoons chopped Italian flat-leaf parsley

½ cup chopped onion

Chopped fresh jalapeño pepper, 2 to 3 tablespoons, or to taste

> *Marcella Says:* **Jalapeño pepper is not commonly available to cooks in Italy, but it has attributes that make it worth introducing into Italian cooking: its fine fragrance and mellow style of spiciness. I don't see why one should be too dogmatic about authenticity because what matters is whether the taste of an ingredient is compatible with Italian flavors. Not all exotic ingredients pass that test. Cilantro, for example, does not. Jalapeño pepper does. If you prefer to use an ingredient more indigenous to the Italian repertoire substitute one of the dried small hot chili peppers, the kind Italians call *diavoletti*.**

⅔ cup torn fresh bread crumb—the soft, crustless part of a slice of bread

⅔ cup whole milk

1 pound ground beef chuck

1 egg

Fine sea salt

1½ cups fine, dry, unflavored bread crumbs, spread on a plate or a sheet of wax paper or aluminum foil

4 tablespoons extra virgin olive oil

A warm serving platter

YIELD: *30 to 35 meatballs, serving 4 persons*

1   Cut the bell pepper lengthwise along the creases, remove the stem, seeds, and pithy core, and skin them with a swivelblade vegetable peeler. (For more details, look up Peppers on page 79 of The Why and How of Prepping Vegetables.) Cut the peppers into strips about ½ inch wide.

2   Put the parsley, onion, and jalapeño pepper in a bowl and mix together well. In a small bowl soak the bread crumb in the milk. As soon as the bread is saturated with the milk, squeeze it out gently in your hand and add it to the onion mixture, working it in until combined. Add the ground chuck, egg, and salt, kneading the mixture very gently with your hands.

3   Pull off a piece of the meatball mixture about the size of a very small egg and shape it in your hands into a ball, being careful not to squeeze it hard. Roll the meatball in the bread crumbs. Pull off another piece of the meat mixture and repeat the procedure until you have used all of it and the balls have all been rolled in bread crumbs.

4   Pour the oil into a 12-inch skillet and turn the heat on to high. When the oil is hot, slip in the meatballs. Brown them to a dark color on one side, then turn them and do the other side. Do not turn them more than once. If the meatballs do not fit into the pan in a single uncrowded layer, do a batch at a time. When you have browned them all, put all the meatballs into the pan before continuing.

5   Add the peppers with a little bit of salt, turn the contents of the pan over using a wooden spoon and a light touch, lower the heat, and cover the pan. You have a choice of how long to continue cooking. Please refer to the introductory note at the top of the recipe. When the peppers are done to taste, transfer the contents of the pan to a warm platter and serve at once.

AHEAD-OF-TIME NOTE: You can complete the cooking several hours or even 2 or 3 days in advance of serving. In the latter event, refrigerate the meatballs with the peppers in a tightly closed container. Return to room temperature before reheating over medium-low heat.

BEEF AND PORK MEAT LOAF WITH MUSHROOMS
↶ *Polpettone di Manzo e Maiale con i Funghi*

Someone riffling through these pages might think that I have been having a lot of fun with mushrooms. And they'd be right. You'll find them in various guises in soups, in pasta sauces, in meat dishes, with seafood, and simply as a vegetable. Italians, and I am one, have a special affection for mushrooms. During the season of foraged mushrooms, a country trattoria may announce their arrival with outdoor signs reading "Funghi." I have never seen that done for any other ingredient. But it isn't only a native predilection that has so often drawn me to mushrooms. The more I cook, and the more I am exposed to other people's cooking, the more I look for flavor that issues out of the ingredients themselves, rather than from herbs, spices, and other culinary contrivances. And there is nothing else I can find in the produce bins that is such a potent and dependable source of flavor as a mushroom. It not only manifests its own flavor, but it stimulates full-throated expressions of flavor from any other ingredient that it accompanies. The important point to remember if you want to benefit from a mushroom's gifts is that it releases them only after long, slow cooking, and preferably when they cook in olive oil rather than in butter. There may be no better example of what those gifts can bring to a dish than the taste of this meat loaf—deep, rich, and immensely comforting—because its flavors come from within. No fancy sauce is needed, we allow the ingredients to speak for themselves.

For the mushrooms

¼ pound fresh shiitake mushrooms

1 pound fresh cremini mushrooms, also known as baby bella

1 pound fresh white button mushrooms

3 tablespoons extra virgin olive oil

½ cup onion chopped very fine

Fine sea salt

Black pepper ground fresh from the mill

For the meat

1 cup torn fresh bread crumb—the soft, crustless part of a slice of bread

¾ cup whole milk

1 pound ground beef, preferably chuck

½ pound ground pork

2 tablespoons chopped Italian flat-leaf parsley

2 eggs

½ cup freshly grated Parmigiano-Reggiano cheese

¼ heaping teaspoon freshly grated nutmeg

Fine sea salt

Black pepper ground fresh from the mill

⅔ cup fine, dry, unflavored bread crumbs, spread on a plate or a sheet of aluminum foil or wax paper

2 tablespoons vegetable oil

3 tablespoons butter

⅔ cup dry white wine

½ cup heavy whipping cream

A warm serving platter

For 6 to 8 persons

AHEAD-OF-TIME NOTE: The meat loaves can be cooked completely through to the end as much as 2 days in advance. Store the loaves with all the contents of the pan in a sealed container in the refrigerator. Return to room temperature before proceeding.

1 For the mushrooms: Detach and discard the shiitake stems.

2 Briskly wash all the fresh mushrooms in running cold water, then cut them into thin slices. For speed, you can do this in a food processor fitted with the slicing disk.

3 Pour the olive oil into a 12-inch skillet or sauté pan, add the ½ cup chopped onion, turn on the heat to high, and cook, stirring from time to time, until it becomes colored a light gold.

4 Add all the mushrooms, salt, and pepper, and turn the heat down to medium low. Turn the mushrooms over every once in a while. When all the liquid they release has evaporated, continue to cook them for 30 to 45 minutes more, until they are very soft.

5 In a small bowl soak the bread crumb in the milk. Squeeze all the milk out of the soaked softened bread.

6 For the meat: Put the two ground meats, the parsley, eggs, Parmesan, softened bread, nutmeg, salt, and pepper in a large bowl. Knead the meat and other ingredients by hand to form a well-integrated mixture. (The bread should be so thoroughly distributed that you no longer see bits of it.) Divide the meat mixture in two parts and shape each part by hand into a salami shape about 3½ to 4 inches thick.

7 Gently turn each meat roll in the dry bread crumbs until coated all over.

8 Choose a saucepan in which the two meat rolls can fit snugly. Add the vegetable oil and butter and turn the heat on to high. When the butter foam begins to subside, slip in the meat rolls, one at a time. Brown them on one side, then keep rolling them over until they are browned on all sides.

9   Pour the wine into the pan. When the wine has bubbled away, cover the pan, and turn the heat down to the lowest setting. Cook the rolls for about 1½ hours, carefully turning them over from time to time. Add the cooked mushrooms, and cook for another 15 minutes. Add the heavy cream, turn all ingredients over to combine, and cook for another 10 to 15 minutes.

> *Marcella Says:* **When you shape the meat rolls, apply just enough pressure with the palms of your hands to force out any air, but do not press too hard or you will make holes.**

10   Lift the meat rolls out of the pan and cut them into portion-size slices. (If you have made the loaves ahead of time and refrigerated them, separate them from the mushrooms and gently reheat the mushrooms and all the cooking juices over medium heat.) Add the slices to the pan and cover them with the mushrooms. Reheat briefly over low heat. Transfer the slices to the warm serving platter, top with the mushrooms and any cooking juices, and serve at once.

Lamb

FRICASSEED LAMB SHOULDER MARCHES STYLE

ᏟᏩ Agnello in Fricassea alla Marchigiana

A fricassee can be made with chicken or lamb, cut into pieces, and sautéed. In Italy, lamb is butchered when it is very small, and a fricassee can include different parts of the animal, just as a chicken fricassee does. When using the larger lamb that comes to market in America, I limit myself to using the shoulder, which is very tasty and easy to cut into stewing-size pieces.

Lamb is a specialty of the Marches, a region in central Italy on the slopes of whose hills flocks of sheep are a common sight. The recipe given here, in which the cooked lamb pieces are tossed with egg yolks beaten with lemon juice, is the classic version practiced by generations of Marches cooks.

A 2-pound piece of lamb shoulder

¼ cup extra virgin olive oil

4 to 5 large whole garlic cloves, peeled

Fine sea salt

Black pepper ground fresh from the mill

⅔ cup dry white wine

2 egg yolks

2 tablespoons freshly squeezed lemon juice

A warm serving platter

For 4 persons

1 Cut the lamb shoulder into 1½- to 2-inch pieces. They don't all need to be identical in size or shape as long as they are not too large. Pick out and remove any small bones.

2 Choose a lidded sauté pan or saucepan that can comfortably accommodate the lamb. Put in the olive oil and garlic cloves and turn on the heat to medium high. Cook the garlic to a light nut-brown color, but no darker, then add the lamb. Brown the meat well on all sides. If all the pieces cannot fit into the pan in a single level layer, put in as many as do fit, brown those, remove them to a plate or bowl, and replace them with more lamb pieces until you have browned them all. Once they have all been browned, return them to the pan.

> *Marcella Says:* **You won't normally see me putting garlic in a pan to sauté before I brown the meat, and I wouldn't do it if I were using chopped or sliced garlic. But here the cloves are whole and large and should withstand the heat, but if they become very dark, remove them.**

3 Sprinkle the pieces with salt and liberal grindings of black pepper, turning the meat over once or twice to season it evenly, then add the wine. Use a wooden spoon or spatula to loosen any cooking residue stuck to the pan bottom. When the wine has bubbled away, cover the pan and turn the heat down to low. Cook for 1 hour or more, until the meat feels tender when tested with a fork. Turn the pieces over from time to time. If you find the cooking juices drying up, add 2 tablespoons of water.

AHEAD-OF-TIME NOTE: You may cook the lamb to this point several hours or as much as 1 day in advance of serving. Let cool, then refrigerate, covered.

4 The fricassee must be served hot. If you have prepared it in advance and refrigerated it, bring it to room temperature, then reheat it gently but thoroughly. While it is reheating, in a small bowl lightly beat the egg yolks with the lemon juice. Pour the yolks over the lamb. Turn the pieces over two or three times, empty the contents of the pan onto the warm platter, and serve at once.

LAMB CHOPS CALABRIA STYLE WITH TOMATOES, PEPPERS, AND OLIVES

☞ Costolette d'Agnello alla Calabrese

This is a recipe that starts out as two before becoming one. The chops and the sauce of tomatoes, peppers, and olives are cooked separately. Small rib chops should be cooked very briefly to a moist, flaming pink. Cook them too long and they will turn gray and lose all their juice. When the very nice sauce is done, the chops are turned over into it and the dish is done.

1 large or 2 small red bell peppers

8 rib lamb chops, each about 1 inch thick

> *Marcella Says:* **Small frenched rib chops are closer in both sweetness and tenderness to the chops used in Italy, where lambs are butchered at a much younger age. While rib chops are recommended, if it is more convenient to use loin lamb chops, do so.**

Fine sea salt

2 tablespoons extra virgin olive oil

½ cup chopped onion

2 cups peeled, ripe, fresh plum tomatoes, cut up with their juice OR canned imported Italian San Marzano tomatoes

3 tablespoons chopped Italian flat-leaf parsley

¼ cup green olives in brine, pitted and coarsely cut up

Black pepper ground fresh from the mill

A warm serving platter

For 4 persons

1   Cut each pepper lengthwise along the creases, remove the stem, seeds, and pithy core, and skin with a swivel-blade vegetable peeler. (For more details, see Peppers on page 78 of The Why and How of Prepping Vegetables. Cut into approximately 1½-inch squares.

2   Sprinkle the chops on both sides with a little salt.

3   Put the olive oil in a 12-inch skillet and turn on the heat to high. When hot, slide in the lamb chops. Brown them thoroughly on one side, turn them, and brown them thoroughly on the other side. Remove them from the pan to a plate.

4   Put the chopped onion in the pan and cook it over lively heat, stirring frequently, until it becomes colored a rich gold. Add the tomatoes with their juice, turning them over in the pan once or twice, and cook for 5 minutes. Add the cut-up peppers, parsley, olives, salt, and generous grindings of black pepper. Turn the heat down to medium. Cook, stirring occasionally, for about 8 minutes, until the peppers are tender, but firm.

5   Sprinkle the chops with pepper and put them in the pan with the sauce. Turn the chops over several times to coat them well and after a minute or so empty the full contents of the skillet onto the warm serving platter and promptly bring to the table.

Lamb Shanks

When I had a cooking school in Bologna and Venice, Victor and I used to walk our students by the stalls and shops of the food markets and when we stopped at the butcher's one of the things we'd draw their attention to would be the whole small lambs on display. Skinned, but with head, tail, and even hooves on, they might weigh no more than fifteen or sixteen pounds. We'd explain that although we had many lamb dishes to share there was not enough meat on our lambs to divide into all the different cuts that are available in an American supermarket. We'd never be able to use the front shank alone, for example. To put enough food on the plate, we'd have to cook it along with the shoulder and possibly even some of the chops.

The little foreshanks that my Florida market carries have a pound or more of tender, savory meat on them. They are very easy to prepare pan-roasted in the Italian manner as in the two recipes that follow. They are, moreover, as economical as they are tasty, which makes them one of the meat counter's most attractive values.

PAN-ROASTED LAMB SHANKS WITH SUN-DRIED TOMATOES AND SAVOY CABBAGE
✒ *Stinco d'Agnello in Tegame con Pomodori Secchi e Verza*

---

4 to 5 tablespoons extra virgin olive oil

Three 1½-pound lamb foreshanks, or 4 if they are smaller

4 garlic cloves, peeled and sliced very thin

8 to 10 sun-dried tomatoes—not the ones packed in olive oil—coarsely chopped

Fine sea salt

Black pepper ground fresh from the mill

5 cups Savoy cabbage, the root end removed and the leaves shredded very fine

Marcella Says: **If you have a large head of cabbage, shred just enough of it to make the 5 cups you need. The remainder of the head, if in one piece, will keep quite well in the refrigerator for a week or more, and you can use it in one of the salad or soup recipes in this book. (See the Index.)**

¾ cup dry white wine

A warm serving platter

For 6 persons, allowing ½ shank per person

1   Choose a saucepan large enough to accommodate all the shanks without overlapping. Pour the olive oil into the pan and turn the heat on to high. When the oil is hot, slip in the lamb shanks, brown them on one side, then turn them and brown them on the other side.

2   Add the sliced garlic, turn the heat down to medium, stir the garlic for a few seconds just until it becomes colored a deep gold, then add the chopped dried tomatoes. Stir for a few seconds, add salt, several grindings of pepper, and the shredded cabbage. Turn the cabbage over a few times to coat it well, and cook until it has wilted down.

3   Pour in the wine, turn over the contents of the pan, put the lid on, and turn the heat down to low. Cook for 1 hour or more, until the meat falls easily off the bone. Remove any bone to which no meat is attached, transfer to the warm platter, and serve at once.

AHEAD-OF-TIME NOTE: The shanks taste sweetest if they are served when just done, but if you must, you may finish cooking them several hours or a day in advance. After refrigerating them, bring them back to room temperature before reheating them thoroughly over gentle heat.

A SERVING SUGGESTION: I particularly like to accompany these shanks with Mashed Potatoes and Baked Onions, on page 332.

Pan-Roasted Lamb Shanks
with Mushrooms and Potatoes

✒ Stinco d'Agnello in Tegame con Funghi e Patate

A 1½- to 2-pound assortment of fresh mushrooms, preferably including some shiitake

> *Marcella Says:* **As I have related elsewhere in this book, there is more flavor to a combination of different mushrooms than any single variety can deliver on its own. The proportions will certainly vary depending on what you find and what you want to make of it. In this dish I would make liberal use of fresh shiitake because its deep woodsy accent fits the rich taste of lamb so well.**

4 tablespoons extra virgin olive oil

2 tablespoons garlic, chopped fine

2 tablespoons Italian flat-leaf parsley, chopped very fine

Fine sea salt

Black pepper ground fresh from the mill

2 lamb foreshanks

> *Marcella Says:* **Shanks may vary in weight. There is enough meat on a shank weighing 1½ pounds with the bone to satisfy the normal appetite of two persons. If the shanks are any smaller, buy an extra one.**

1 medium onion, sliced very thin, about 1½ cups

⅔ cup dry white wine

5 medium potatoes, peeled, rinsed in cold water, and cut into 1-inch pieces

A warm deep serving platter

For 4 persons

1 If using shiitake, detach the stems and discard them. Wash all the mushrooms rapidly in cold running water and slice them very thin, using a knife or the slicing disk of a food processor, as you prefer.

2 Pour 2 tablespoons of the olive oil in a 10-inch skillet, add the garlic, turn on the heat to medium high, and cook the garlic, stirring it from time to time, until it becomes colored a pale gold.

3 Add the chopped parsley, stir two or three times, then put in the mushrooms, sprinkling them with salt and pepper. Turn them over once or twice to coat them well, turn the heat down to medium, and cook them until all the liquid they shed has evaporated. Take the pan off the heat.

4 Choose a heavy-bottomed saucepan just roomy enough for the lamb shanks and all the mushrooms. Pour the remaining 2 tablespoons of olive oil into the pan and turn the heat on to high. When the oil is hot, put in the lamb shanks, brown them well on one side, then turn them and brown the other side.

5 Add salt and pepper and the sliced onion, and turn the heat down to medium. Cook until the color of the onion turns to gold, then add the wine, letting it bubble gently until it has evaporated. Put in the mushrooms, cover the pan, and turn the heat down to very low. Cook for 1 hour, turning the shanks over several times.

6 Put in the potatoes, and sprinkle them with salt. Turn all the contents of the pan over once or twice, put the lid back on, and cook over very gentle heat until the potatoes feel very tender when tested with a fork. Should you find, as you well may, during the course of the cooking, that the liquid in the pan has become insufficient to keep the food from sticking, add ¼ cup of water.

7 Remove any bone to which no meat is attached, transfer the contents of the pan and all the cooking juices to the serving platter, and serve promptly.

AHEAD-OF-TIME NOTE: You can cook the dish completely either several hours or even 1 day in advance. When ready to serve, bring to room temperature, then reheat gently but thoroughly, adding a tablespoon or two of water if it appears necessary.

Pork

Pork as Comfort Food

The affinity that cooking has with language has always intrigued me. They both have vocabulary and syntax, they both serve to transmit sensations and revelations from the sender to the receiver. I was intrigued, in this context, to read an article about the linguist Noam Chomsky wherein he proposes a theory that explains the existence of languages as the ability to express ourselves within certain syntactical forms hard-wired into us by birth. I have a theory of my own about food and it is that, notwithstanding the multifarious ways of preparing it, there are some foods whose sensual message finds a ready response in the taste buds of many—hard-wired—as it were. These are the foods we have placed in the category called "comfort." Prominent among them is pork in guises that may be beyond counting—in hams, sausages, salami, lard, cracklings, bacon—to which we can add the immense repertory of cooked dishes.

There are four examples of Italian pork cookery that follow. Two of the dishes unite pork with one of its most congenial companions (and one of mine), Savoy cabbage. In one of them, the cabbage leaves serve as wrappers for ground pork filling, and in the other, ground pork and chopped cabbage combine to produce a loaf. There is also a pork stew with black-eyed peas, and there is a dish of pork ribs with caramelized onions. One or the other is reminiscent of dishes from other cultures, from Central and Eastern Europe, from the American South, from Asia. Yet every one of them is distinctly Italian. All of them, it seems to me, should engage gustatory emotions wherever the savory comfort of pork is welcomed.

Savoy Cabbage Rolls Stuffed with Pork

cβ Rollatini di Verza e Maiale

A 1½-pound head of Savoy cabbage

A footed colander or a large strainer set in or over a bowl

1 cup white bread, trimmed of its crust and cut up

1 cup whole milk

1½ pounds ground pork

1 whole egg plus 1 yolk

½ cup freshly grated Parmigiano-Reggiano cheese

½ teaspoon freshly grated nutmeg

Fine sea salt

Black pepper ground fresh from the mill

⅓ cup extra virgin olive oil

⅔ cup chopped onion

⅔ cup dry white wine

3 cups tomatoes cut up with their juice, either peeled, ripe, firm, fresh plum tomatoes, their seeds scooped away OR canned imported San Marzano Italian tomatoes

For 4 persons

1 Bring 4 quarts of water to a boil in a large saucepan.

2 While the water is coming to a boil, trim the cabbage: Cut off about 1 inch from the root end. Carefully pull off the leaves, loosening them first from the base of the head, then working your way toward the tip. Try not to tear the leaves, but do not worry if a few do. Detach 12 leaves in all.

3 When the water boils, drop in some of the leaves, up to half of them depending on their size and the capacity of the pan. You do not want to do them all at one time because they might tear in an overcrowded pan. Cook until they have become tender enough to be pliant. Retrieve them with a skimmer or a large colander spoon and lay them gently in the colander or strainer that you have set in or over a bowl to drain. Cook the remaining leaves, in one or more batches as necessary.

4 Put the bread in a small bowl and pour the milk over it. Turn the bread over once or twice to help it sop up the milk.

5 Put the ground pork, the whole egg and egg yolk, Parmesan, and nutmeg in a large bowl. Sprinkle with salt and several grindings of black pepper. When the bread has become fully saturated, retrieve it with your hand, gently squeeze out the excess milk, and crumble it into the bowl. Knead the contents of the bowl with your hands until they are a homogeneous mixture.

6 Retrieve the cabbage leaves, one at a time, and gently lay each flat on the work surface. With the point of a knife, slice away the tough central rib from each leaf but do not cut the leaf in two. Trim the base of the leaf to 6 or 7 inches in width. If some of the leaves are not that wide, overlap two smaller ones.

7 Pinch off large, nut-size portions of pork mixture. Roll each into a sausage shape about 2 to 3 inches long and 1 inch thick. Place the roll in the center of the leaf at the edge and roll up the leaf, folding in its sides if possible. Squeeze the finished roll in your hand to make a tight seal that will not open up when cooked. Form rolls with the remaining cabbage leaves and pork mixture in the same manner.

8 Put the olive oil and chopped onion in a 12-inch skillet, preferably nonstick, and turn on the heat to medium high. Cook the onion, stirring from time to time, until it becomes colored a light gold. Lay the cabbage rolls with the overlapping edge of each roll down in the skillet. Cook, without touching them, letting one side brown, for 6 to 7 minutes. Turn the rolls over gently and brown the other side, sprinkling them with two or three pinches of salt. When the second side is browned, pour in the wine.

9 Let the wine bubble for 5 or 6 minutes, then add the tomatoes. Turn down the heat and cover the pan. Cook at a gentle simmer for 30 to 40 minutes, turning the cabbage rolls over once or twice. If you find that during the cooking the liquid in the pan becomes insufficient, add 1 or 2 tablespoons of water. Transfer the cabbage rolls to a serving platter with all the pan juices and allow them to settle for a few minutes before serving.

AHEAD-OF-TIME NOTE: You can complete the dish several hours in advance, but preferably not the night before. Reheat gently, adding a tablespoon or two of water, if necessary.

Pork and Savoy Cabbage Loaf

Polpettone di Maiale e Verza

½ pound Savoy cabbage

Fine sea salt

1 pound ground pork

½ cup chopped onion

1 garlic clove, peeled and chopped fine

1 tablespoon extra virgin olive oil

1 egg

Black pepper ground fresh from the mill

½ cup freshly grated Parmigiano-Reggiano cheese

1½ cups fine, dry, unflavored bread crumbs, spread on a sheet of wax paper or heavy-duty aluminum foil

2 tablespoons vegetable oil

2 tablespoons butter

½ cup dry white wine

Optional: homemade meat broth (page 48)

A warm serving platter

For 4 to 6 persons

1 Detach and discard the thick outer leaves on the cabbage and cut away the solid core. Wash the cabbage in cold water. Bring a large saucepan of water to a boil, add 1 to 2 teaspoons salt, and slip in the cabbage. Cook until it feels very, very tender when prodded with a fork. It will take at least 40 minutes after it begins to boil. Drain and set aside to cool.

2   When the cabbage is cool enough to handle comfortably, squeeze it in your hands, forcing out as much water as you can. Chop it very fine.

3   Choose a bowl large enough to hold all the ingredients. Put in the chopped Savoy cabbage, ground pork, onion, garlic, olive oil, egg, salt, a liberal grinding of black pepper, and the Parmesan. With your hands knead all the ingredients into a homogeneous mass, then mold it into a thick cylindrical shape, about 3 to 3½ inches thick, squeezing out any air that may have been trapped inside.

4   Roll the loaf in the bread crumbs, pressing gently on the loaf to make the crumbs adhere.

5   Choose a lidded saucepan with a heavy, heat-retaining bottom, just large enough to hold the loaf comfortably. Add the vegetable oil and butter, and turn on the heat to medium high. When the butter foam has subsided and the fat is hot, slip in the pork and cabbage loaf. Brown it well on one side, letting it form a firm, crisp crust so that it won't break apart when you turn it to brown it. Turn the loaf to brown it on all sides, always waiting for that crisp crust to form before you turn it again. When you have browned it evenly all over, add the white wine.

6   When you can no longer smell the wine's alcohol, turn the heat down to very low and cover the pan. Cook for 1 to 1¼ hours, turning the loaf from time to time. If you find that the pan juices are insufficient to keep the loaf from sticking, add 2 to 3 tablespoons of water or, if you have some in the freezer, homemade meat broth.

AHEAD-OF-TIME NOTE: You may cook the pork and cabbage loaf a full day in advance of serving. It is as good cold as it is when piping hot.

7   Carefully lift the loaf out of the pan and place it on a cutting board. Cut it into slices, lay the slices on a warm platter, and pour all the pan juices over them. Serve promptly if having it hot.

PORK SHOULDER STEW WITH ONIONS AND BLACK-EYED PEAS

Spezzatino di Maiale con le Cipolle e i Fagioli dall'Occhio

1½ cups dried black-eyed peas

3 tablespoons extra virgin olive oil for the stew, 2 teaspoons for cooking
the peas

2 pounds pork shoulder, cut into 2-inch pieces, with the bone in

2½ cups onion, sliced very thin

Fine sea salt

Chopped dried Italian red chili pepper to taste

⅔ cup dry white wine

2 garlic cloves, peeled and sliced very thin

1 cup tomatoes, cut up with their juice, either peeled, ripe, firm, fresh plum tomatoes,
their seeds scooped away, OR canned imported San Marzano Italian tomatoes

A warm serving platter

For 4 persons

1 Drop the black-eyed peas into a bowl, cover amply with warm water, and let soak for
2 to 3 hours.

2 Pour the 3 tablespoons olive oil into a low-sided saucepan and turn on the heat to high.
When the oil is hot, slip in as many pieces of pork shoulder as will fit without overlapping.
Brown the pieces on one side, turn them over, and brown the other side. Transfer the pieces
to a bowl, using a slotted spoon. Slip in the remaining pieces of pork, repeat the browning
procedure, and add them to the bowl.

3 Add the onions to the pan, add salt, lower the heat, and cook the onions, turning them over occasionally, until they are very soft, about 30 minutes.

4 Return all the meat to the pan with any juices that may have collected in the bowl. Add salt, the chili pepper, wine, sliced garlic, and the chopped tomatoes, stir to combine, and cover the pot. Cook over very low heat for at least 2 hours. Turn the meat over from time to time and, if it should prove necessary, replenish the juices in the pan by adding 2 to 3 tablespoons of water.

5 While the meat is cooking, drain and rinse the black-eyed peas. Put the peas in a saucepan with enough water to cover by about 2 inches. Add 1 teaspoon salt and the remaining 2 teaspoons olive oil. Bring to a boil over high heat, then lower the heat to cook at the gentlest of simmers and cover the pan. Simmer until the peas are tender through and through, about 45 minutes.

6 When the peas are done, drain them and add them to the stew. Turn the meat, peas, and onions over once or twice and cook over low heat for at least 15 minutes, or until the meat feels very tender when tested with a fork.

7 Transfer the stew to the warm serving platter and bring at once to the table.

Pan-Roasted Pork Ribs with Caramelized Onions, White Wine, and Chili Pepper

Costicine d Maiale in Tegame con Cipolla e Peperoncino

3 tablespoons extra virgin olive oil

4 pounds baby back ribs, split into pairs

½ cup dry white wine

2 very large onions, sliced very thin, about 6 cups

Fine sea salt

Chopped chili pepper, 2 tablespoons fresh jalapeño, OR ¾ tablespoon dried red chili pepper, adjusting the quantities to taste and to the potency of the chili

For 4 persons

1 Pour the olive oil into a 12-inch sauté pan, turn the heat on to high, and when the oil is hot, slip in the meat. Turn the ribs two or three times to brown them well. If all the ribs crowd the pan too much for efficient browning, do a batch at a time, then return them all to the pan. Pour in the wine and turn the ribs once or twice while the wine bubbles completely away.

2 Add the sliced onions, salt, and the chili pepper, cover the pan, and turn the heat down to low. Cook for 2 to 3 hours, turning the ribs over occasionally, until the meaty part of the ribs feels very tender when tested with a fork and the onions have cooked down to a light-brown, creamy consistency. Serve at once.

AHEAD-OF-TIME NOTE: The dish never tastes quite so luscious as when it is freshly made but, if obliged to, you can make it a few hours in advance. Reheat it gently in the sauté pan over low heat, adding a tablespoon or two of water, if needed, to keep the ribs from sticking.

Vegetables

Béchamel Sauce on Vegetables

It's time, I hope, to put aside the wrangling over whether *béchamel* or *balsamella* came first, whether it's a French or Italian sauce. For generations it has been an essential component of a host of indisputably native dishes such as Bolognese lasagne and, regardless of where it may have originated, it is a legitimate part of Italian cooking. It is a marvelous part of the cooking of vegetables to which it bestows a luxurious succulence. The three recipes that follow demonstrate the use of béchamel in vegetable dishes that range from rustic to sophisticated: There is baked Savoy cabbage, an uncommon lentil custard, and leeks with herbs and cheese.

MY BASIC BÉCHAMEL SAUCE

NOTE: The quantities will vary depending on the amount of sauce a recipe requires, but neither the proportions nor the method vary.

> 2 cups whole milk
>
> 4 tablespoons butter
>
> 3 tablespoons all-purpose flour
>
> ¼ teaspoon fine sea salt

YIELD: *about 1⅔ cups medium-thick béchamel*

✦ Pour the milk into a saucepan, turn the heat on to medium low, and bring the milk just to the verge of boiling, when it begins to form a ring of pearly bubbles.

✦ While the milk heats, put the butter in a heavy-bottomed 4- to 6-cup saucepan, and turn the heat on to low. When the butter has melted completely, add all the flour, stirring it in with a wooden spoon. Cook, stirring constantly, for about 2 minutes. Do not allow the flour to become colored or the béchamel will taste bitter. Remove from the heat.

Marcella Says: **I take the pan off heat because I shall begin adding milk only 2 tablespoons at a time to avoid lumps, and such a small amount of milk would cook too fast over heat. When the sauce acquires a smooth, liquid consistency, I stir in the rest of the milk at a more rapid pace and when it is all in I can safely return the sauce to low heat to cook it down without lumps forming.**

◆ Add the hot milk to the flour-and-butter mixture, no more than 2 tablespoons at a time. Stir steadily and thoroughly. As soon you have incorporated the first 2 tablespoons of milk into the mixture, add 2 more, continuing to stir. Repeat this procedure until you put in ½ cup milk; thereafter you can add the rest of the milk ½ cup at a time, stirring steadfastly, until you have smoothly amalgamated all the milk with the flour and butter.

◆ Place the pan over low heat, add the salt, and cook, stirring without interruption, until the sauce is as dense as thick cream. To make it even thicker, should a recipe require it, cook and stir a little longer. For a thinner sauce, cook it a little less. If you find any lumps, dissolve them by beating the sauce rapidly with a whisk.

AHEAD-OF-TIME NOTE: Because béchamel takes so little time to prepare, try to make it only when you need it, so that it is soft and easily spread. If you must make it in advance, reheat it slowly in the upper half of a double boiler, stirring constantly as it warms up, until it is once again supple and spreadable. If you are making béchamel one day in advance, store it in the refrigerator in a tightly sealed container.

Increasing the Recipe

You can double or triple the quantities given above, but no more than that for any single batch. Choose a pan that is wider than it is high so that the sauce cooks more quickly and evenly.

Baked Savoy Cabbage with Parmesan Cheese

Ⓡ *Verza Gratinata al Parmigiano*

1 medium head of Savoy cabbage, about 2 pounds

Sea salt

1⅔ cups medium-thick béchamel sauce, made as described on page 300

Freshly grated nutmeg, slightly less than ¼ teaspoon

⅔ cup freshly grated Parmigiano-Reggiano cheese

An oven-to-table baking dish, about 8 by 12 inches or its approximate equivalent in another shape

½ cup fine, dry, unflavored bread crumbs

2 tablespoons butter

YIELD: *8 servings*

1 Pull off and discard the outer, looser leaves on the cabbage. Split the cabbage in half lengthwise.

2 Choose a saucepan large enough to accommodate the cabbage and fill it with sufficient water to cover the cabbage amply. Bring the water to a boil, add 3 tablespoons of salt, and as the water returns to a boil put in the cabbage. Cook until quite tender, then drain and set aside to cool.

3 Make the béchamel, then stir in the grated nutmeg and half the grated Parmesan.

4 When the cabbage is cool enough to handle, squeeze it with your hands to force out as much water as you can. Remove the core. Chop the leaves coarsely and mix them with the béchamel. Taste and correct for salt.

5 Turn on the oven to 400°.

6 Choose a baking dish that can accommodate the cabbage and béchamel mixture in a layer about 1 to 1½ inches thick. Smear the dish lightly with some of the butter, then spread half the bread crumbs evenly over the bottom. Pour in the cabbage mixture, leveling off the top.

7 Mix the remaining grated Parmesan with the remaining bread crumbs and sprinkle over the top of the cabbage mixture.

8 Cut the remaining butter up into small pieces. Dot the top of the cabbage with the butter.

AHEAD-OF-TIME NOTE: The dish may be prepared several hours in advance up to this point.

9 Bake in the preheated oven until a golden crust forms on top, about 20 minutes. Let settle out of the oven for about 5 minutes before serving.

SAVORY LENTIL CUSTARD

❧ Sformato di Lenticchie

1 tablespoon butter plus additional for smearing the baking dish

½ cup chopped onion

3 tablespoons celery, chopped fine

2 tablespoons carrot, chopped fine

⅔ cup lentils

Fine sea salt

Black pepper ground fresh from the mill

Béchamel sauce, made as described on page 300, using 1 cup milk,
2 tablespoons butter, and 1½ tablespoons flour

¼ teaspoon freshly grated nutmeg

A 4- to 5-cup oven-to-table baking dish

For 4 persons

1 Put the 1 tablespoon of butter and the chopped onion in a saucepan and turn on the heat to medium high. Cook the onion, stirring occasionally, until it becomes colored light gold. Add the celery and carrot, turn them over a few times to coat them well, and sauté for 3 to 4 minutes .

2 Rinse the lentils in cold water, drain them well, and add them to the saucepan along with some salt and grindings of black pepper. Turn the lentils for a few seconds, coating them well, then add 2½ cups of water. Turn the heat down to low, and cover the pan. Cook for 45 to 50 minutes, or until the lentils are very tender. If during the cooking it should prove necessary to replenish the liquid in the pan, add 2 to 3 tablespoons of water. Bear in mind that there should be no liquid left when the lentils are done. If, when they are done, there still is some liquid left, uncover the pan, raise the heat, and boil away the liquid while you stir the lentils.

AHEAD-OF-TIME NOTE: You may cook the lentils hours or even 2 or 3 days in advance. In the latter case, refrigerate in a tightly covered container. Reheat before proceeding with the recipe, adding a tablespoon or two of water that you will make sure evaporates by the time the lentils are warm.

3   While the lentils cook, make the béchamel sauce with the proportions given in the ingredients list above. Stir in the grated nutmeg.

4   Turn on the oven to 400°.

5   When the lentils are done, mix the béchamel sauce into them, turning them over several times to distribute the sauce evenly. Taste and correct for salt.

6   Grease the baking dish with butter, pour the lentil and béchamel mixture into it, and level off the top. Bake in the preheated oven until a little bit of golden-brown crust has formed on top. Let settle out of the oven for a few minutes before serving.

BAKED LEEKS WITH HERBS AND CHEESE

⟋ Teglia di Porri con gli Odori e i Formaggi

6 or 7 leeks, their bulbs no thicker than 1 inch

Fine sea salt

Béchamel Sauce, made as described on page 300, using 1 cup milk, 2 tablespoons butter, and 1½ tablespoons flour

2 tablespoons chopped Italian flat-leaf parsley

1 tablespoon chopped fresh basil

1 tablespoon chopped fresh marjoram or ½ tablespoon dried

1 tablespoon chopped fresh rosemary leaves or ½ tablespoon dried

2 eggs

¼ teaspoon freshly grated nutmeg

⅓ cup freshly grated Parmigiano-Reggiano cheese

Black pepper ground fresh from the mill

2 tablespoons butter plus additional for greasing the baking dish

An 11 by 7-inch rectangular oven-to-table baking dish or other shape with equivalent capacity, about 6 cups

1 heaping cup of at least 3 cheeses, cut into pieces about the size of a raspberry (see Suggested Cheeses below)

2 tablespoons fine, dry, unflavored bread crumbs

SUGGESTED CHEESES: A combination of any 3 of the following will work: Fontina, Gruyère, a young, soft Pecorino, a mature Taleggio, Brie, Montasio, or a mild, soft goat cheese

For 4 to 6 persons

1 Cut off the leek roots. If an outside leaf of any of the leeks is bruised or discolored, discard that as well. Cut the leeks lengthwise in half, then cut them crosswise into 2-inch pieces, starting with the white bulb end. When you reach the green tops, discard the tough outer leaves before slicing the tender inner ones, as described on page 76 of The Why and How of Prepping Vegetables. Wash the cut-up leeks in cold water.

2 Pour 3 to 4 quarts of water into a 6-quart saucepan and bring to a boil. Add 2 to 3 tablespoons of salt, drop in the leek pieces, and cover the pan. When the water begins boiling again count off 2 minutes, then drain the leeks and set them aside to cool.

3 Make the béchamel sauce, with the proportions given in the ingredients list above.

4 Turn on the oven to 400°.

5 Put all of the chopped herbs in a good-sized bowl. Break both eggs into the bowl and beat them lightly to incorporate the herbs. Add the nutmeg, Parmesan, and béchamel sauce and mix with a fork to distribute the ingredients uniformly.

6 Squeeze the leeks with your hands to remove any water they may still retain. Put 1½ tablespoons of the butter in a 10-inch skillet, turn the heat on to medium, and when the butter foam begins to subside, put in the leeks. Cook them for 2 or 3 minutes, turning them from time to time. Add them to the bowl with the béchamel and herb mixture, sprinkle with liberal grindings of black pepper, and turn the leeks over a few times to coat them well.

7 Smear the baking dish with butter, then cover the bottom with half of the leek and béchamel mixture, spreading it evenly. Over it distribute the assorted cheeses, making sure that pieces of each cheese are distributed across the entire surface. Cover with the remaining leek and béchamel mixture, leveling it off. Sprinkle with the bread crumbs and use the remaining ½ tablespoon of butter to dot the top.

AHEAD-OF-TIME NOTE: You can complete the dish up to this point several hours ahead of time. Cover tightly with plastic film before refrigerating it, and bring it to full room temperature before baking.

8 Bake in the preheated oven until the top becomes colored a light mottled gold, about 30 minutes. Let settle out of the oven for about 10 minutes before serving.

SAUTÉED RAPINI WITH CHICKPEAS

🐇 *Cime di Rapa Saltate con i Ceci*

In good home cooking, ingredients are combined for no other reason than how they will act upon each other to produce a lively and harmonious conjunction of flavors. Rapini is somewhat bitter and vegetal, chickpeas are sweetly nutty, and the taste of the two together will not tire from the first to the last forkful.

1 bunch rapini, about 1 pound

Sea salt, fine or coarse

¼ cup extra virgin olive oil

2 tablespoons garlic, chopped very fine

A 15.5-ounce can chickpeas (Goya brand is recommended), drained

Chopped dried red chili pepper, *peperoncino,* ½ teaspoon, or to taste

For 4 persons

1   Detach the thicker stems of the rapini from their tops and peel away their tough outer rind. Soak both stems and tops in a large bowl of cold water.

2   Bring 4 cups of water to a boil in a saucepan, then add 1 tablespoon of salt. Drain the rapini and drop it into the boiling water. Cook at a moderate boil until tender, about 15 minutes, or slightly longer. Poke the stems with a sharp fork; it should enter easily.

3   Drain the rapini and cut it up into coarse pieces.

4   Pour the olive oil into a 12-inch skillet, add the garlic, and turn the heat on to high. Cook the garlic, stirring it from time to time, until it becomes colored a light gold.

5   Slip in the rapini. The oil will spatter at first, so be ready to stand back from the pan for a moment or two.

> *Marcella Says:* **You can avoid having the oil spatter by lowering the heat, but then the rapini would not brown quickly and would absorb a lot of oil, becoming greasy. Just don't throw the vegetable into the pan; slip it in quickly but gently, and stand back.**

6   Cook the rapini for about 5 minutes, turning it over and over the whole time to coat well. Add the drained chickpeas and the chili pepper, and cook for 5 minutes more, turning the contents of the pan over from time to time. Serve hot.

PURÉED FAVA BEANS WITH RAPINI
☞ *La Purea di Fave con le Cime di Rapa*

There are many reasons for traveling to Apulia, the spur of the boot-shaped Italian peninsula. There is the landscape, with its twisted centenarian olive trees, the hill towns gleaming white like mounds of bones bleached by the sun, the *trulli*—the cone-shaped white stone ancient granaries on the plains still in use as farmhouses and sheds. And then there is the food, some of Italy's best fish and probably its tastiest vegetables. Among its vegetable masterworks there is this puréed dried fava bean with rapini union that you can reproduce quite accurately and simply at home.

1 pound dried fava beans, sea salt, and 1 to 2 tablespoons olive oil

Salt

¼ cup whole milk

A slice or two of crustless white bread, torn up into pieces and placed in a small bowl

A food mill or potato ricer

Up to 1 cup fruity extra virgin olive oil

A double boiler

A few garlic cloves, peeled and lightly smashed with the flat part of a heavy knife blade

1 bunch rapini, about 1 pound, trimmed and blanched as described in steps 1 and 2 on page 309 of the preceding recipe

A warm serving platter

YIELD: *enough for a side dish or appetizer serving 6 persons*

1   Soak the fava beans in water to cover for at least 6 hours or overnight. Drain the beans, rinse them, and cook them in water to cover with a tablespoon or two of olive oil and a pinch of salt, as described on page 60, until they are tender, approximately 40 minutes after they have begun to simmer.

2   Heat the milk in a small saucepan without letting it come to a simmer.

3   Pour the warm milk over the bread. Let soak for at least 5 minutes, then gently squeeze the bread in your hand to force out the excess milk.

4   Purée the cooked fava beans through the food mill or potato ricer into a bowl, passing them through the disk with the smallest holes, if one is available.

5   Add ½ cup of the olive oil and the bread, and blend, beating the mixture with a whisk, to a smooth consistency.

6   Put the fava mixture in the upper half of a double boiler. Make sure that there is water in the lower half of the pan, and turn the heat on to medium high. When the water comes to a simmer, begin stirring the fava mixture with a wooden spoon or whisk, and continue doing so vigorously for about 5 to 6 minutes, adding a tablespoon or more of olive oil.

7   Pour 3 tablespoons of olive oil into a 10-inch skillet, add the garlic cloves, and turn the heat on to medium. When the garlic becomes colored a pale gold, remove it from the skillet and add the blanched rapini. Sauté the greens for 5 to 6 minutes, stirring frequently.

8   Taste and correct both the fava mixture and the rapini for salt. Spread the puréed favas on the warm platter and distribute the sautéed rapini over the top. Drizzle olive oil over everything and serve at once.

Sautéed Artichokes Baked with Mozzarella
ᦆ *Carciofi Saltati e Fusi al Forno con la Mozzarella*

I have derived this dish from one that I had in Rome and that I included in my last cookbook, *Marcella Cucina*. The original dish also had shrimp, which I dropped for this version. It is a dish produced in two stages because the artichokes must first be deeply browned in a skillet and only then are they baked in the oven with mozzarella. For those who love to have bread with their food, the tasty juices of this preparation beg to be sopped up.

A 2-pound bag of baby artichokes, usually containing about 20 pieces, OR 8 full-size artichokes

½ lemon

2 tablespoons extra virgin olive oil

4 whole garlic cloves, peeled

Fine sea salt

Black pepper ground fresh from the mill

An oven-to-table baking dish, about 11 by 7 inches if rectangular, or its equivalent in another shape

2 tablespoons butter

⅓ cup freshly grated Parmigiano-Reggiano cheese

8 ounces mozzarella, sliced thin, no thicker than ¼ inch

For 4 to 6 persons

1   Trim the artichokes, stripping them of all the tough inedible portions of their leaves, as described on pages 72 to 73 of The Why and How of Prepping Vegetables. If you are working with baby artichokes, which I recommend, cut them lengthwise in half. If you are using the full-size ones, cut them into four pieces. As you trim each piece, drop it into a bowl of water acidulated with the juice of the lemon half.

AHEAD-OF-TIME NOTE: You can prepare the artichokes up to this point several hours in advance. When ready to proceed with the cooking, drain the artichokes and rinse them in cold water to wash off the lemon from their soak.

2 Choose a skillet wide enough to contain the artichokes in a single uncrowded layer. Put in the olive oil and garlic cloves and turn the heat on to medium high. Cook the garlic to a light brown color, stirring from time to time. Remove the garlic from the pan, discard it, and put in the artichokes.

3 Cook the artichokes for 25 minutes or more, always at lively heat, until they are completely tender. Turn them over frequently, letting them brown all over. If they stick to the pan, as it is likely and even desirable for them to do, add 2 to 3 tablespoons of water and loosen them from the bottom using a wooden spoon or spatula. When done, add salt and pepper, turn them over once or twice, and take them off the heat.

> *Marcella Says:* **Here is an excellent example of the principle of** *insaporire,* **"making tasty" (discussed at length on page 15 of** AT MASTER CLASS**) in action. Whenever I have demonstrated this dish, professional cooks in the audience were startled at how dark I allowed the artichokes to get. But it is only then, when they have deeply and confidently browned, that they develop flavor,** *sapore.*

4 Turn on the oven to 400°.

5 Use 1 tablespoon of the butter to smear the bottom of the baking dish. Spread the artichokes in the dish with any juices from the skillet. Sprinkle half the grated Parmesan over them. Cover with the sliced mozzarella. Top with the remaining grated cheese and dot with the remaining 1 tablespoon butter, cut into small pieces.

6 When ready to eat, put the dish in the preheated oven and bake just until the mozzarella melts and becomes partly colored a light brown. Serve at once with crusty bread to sop up the delicious juices. Do not let the dish sit after baking because as the mozzarella cools it contracts and becomes stiff.

BRAISED ARTICHOKE WEDGES
WITH BACON AND SUN-DRIED TOMATOES

Carciofi in Tegame con la Pancetta Affumicata e i Pomodori Secchi

The approach to building up flavor here is different from the one at work in the preceding recipe. For this dish, the flavor is in the base, the garlic, parsley, bacon, and sun-dried tomato sauté. The artichokes wedges are braised over the flavor base, cooking gently and long enough to reach complete tenderness.

4 large artichokes

½ lemon

¼ cup extra virgin olive oil

1 tablespoon garlic, chopped fine

3 tablespoons chopped Italian flat-leaf parsley

½ cup chopped good-quality thick-cut bacon (1-inch pieces)

½ cup strips of sun-dried tomatoes, ¼-inch wide

Fine sea salt

Black pepper ground fresh from the mill

¼ cup water or homemade meat broth (page 48)

For 4 to 6 persons

1   Trim the artichokes, stripping them of all the tough inedible portions of their leaves as described on page 72 of The Why and How of Prepping Vegetables. Cut each pared artichoke into quarters and as you do drop each piece into a bowl of water acidulated with the juice of the lemon half.

AHEAD-OF-TIME NOTE: You can prepare the artichokes up to this point several hours in advance. When ready to proceed with the cooking, drain the artichokes and rinse them in cold water to wash off the lemon from their soak.

2 Pour the olive oil into a 10- or 12-inch sauté pan or skillet, add the chopped garlic, and turn the heat on to medium high. Cook the garlic, stirring it occasionally, until it becomes colored a pale blond.

3 Add the parsley, stir two or three times, then add the bacon. Cook the bacon, turning it from time to time, for 3 or 4 minutes, but do not let it become crisp. Add the sun-dried tomatoes, turn them over to coat, and cook for another minute.

> *Marcella Says:* **Don't let the sauté become very dark. If you find that it is beginning to darken, slide the pan off the burner for a few seconds before continuing.**

4 Add the artichokes. Sprinkle with salt and generous grindings of black pepper and turn all the ingredients over two or three times to coat them well. After about 2 minutes, add ¼ cup of water (if you have it available, in the freezer perhaps, homemade broth would be better). Cover the pan, and turn the heat down to medium. Cook until the artichokes feel tender when tested with a fork. Should it become necessary during the cooking, add 2 to 3 tablespoons of water—or broth—to keep the artichokes from sticking to the pan.

BEANS MADE IN THE GAME-BIRD STYLE WITH OLIVE OIL, GARLIC, AND SAGE
✒ *Fagioli Borlotti all'Uccelletto*

There is always sage in the pan when Italians cook game birds, and it is the presence of sage that gives this dish its name, *all'uccelletto*, small game-bird style. The bean that tradition prescribes here is cannellini, which one associates instantly with Tuscan cooking. I am also very fond, however, of the bean that northerners favor, *borlotti*, which are closely related to cranberry beans.

Rare are the shell beans that are harvested to be sold fresh and of these the beautiful cranberry—whose pod and raw bean are splashed with bright red or purple in a marble-like pattern—has the richest and most versatile flavor. When cooked to full tenderness it can taste sweetly of puréed chestnut. It is the staple bean of the Veneto and an essential component of one of that region's happiest gastronomic accomplishments, *pasta e fagioli*. It is an excellent bean for mixed salads or as an accompaniment to good-quality tuna packed in olive oil or entirely on its own, as in this *uccelletto* recipe. I urge you to try this bean tossed with olive oil, cracked pepper, and some thinly sliced raw onion when freshly cooked and still lukewarm: sublime.

Although cranberry beans are grown in both the eastern and western United States, it isn't every market that offers them fresh. The dried are available at specialty food stores, by mail, and online, sometimes even by their Italian name, *borlotti*.

1½ to 2 pounds unshelled fresh cranberry beans OR 1 cup dried cranberry beans OR 1 cup dried or 2 cups canned cannellini beans

Fine sea salt

¼ cup extra virgin olive oil

4 whole garlic cloves, peeled

5 or more whole fresh sage leaves OR 1 tablespoon dried leaves, cut into fine shreds

Black pepper ground fresh from the mill

For 4 persons

1 If you are using fresh beans: Shell them, discard the pods, and rinse the beans under cold running water.

2 If you are using dried beans: Put the beans in a bowl, cover them amply with lukewarm water, add 2 or 3 pinches of salt and let them soak overnight or no less than 6 hours. Drain.

3 Put the reconstituted dried beans or the shelled fresh beans in a saucepan and pour in enough water to cover them by 1 to 1½ inches. Add salt, cover the pan, and turn on the heat to very low. Bring the water to a gentle simmer. Continue to simmer gently, but constantly, for another 45 minutes or more, until the beans are fully tender.

AHEAD-OF-TIME NOTE: Whether they are dried or fresh, you can prepare the beans up to this point a day or two in advance. When cooked, transfer them to a storage container or glass jar with all the cooking water. Cover tightly, and refrigerate until you are ready to proceed with the recipe.

4 Drain the beans, whether you have used dried, fresh, or canned ones.

5 Pour the olive oil into a saucepan, add the garlic and sage, and turn the heat on to medium high. Cook the garlic, stirring from time to time, until it becomes colored a light nut-brown. Remove and discard.

6 Add the drained beans to the pan with several grindings of black pepper. Turn them over to coat them well, taste and correct for salt, and lower the heat to cook at a gentle, but steady simmer for about 10 minutes, turning the beans over from time to time. Serve with all the juices from the pan.

Baked Radicchio with Pancetta and Fontina

❧ Radicchio al Forno con Pancetta e Fontina

When I am cooking I sometimes feel like the coach of a ball team, shuffling the players around to different positions to encourage new and vigorous expressions of their talents. In the recipe below, the radicchio is partly a holdover from the one simply baked with olive oil, salt, and pepper that appears in my previous cookbooks. It is also borrowed in part from the sauce of radicchio and pancetta for pasta that I have also previously published. The new entry, which I brought in to pull the dish together, is Fontina, the mellow cow's milk cheese from the Alpine meadows of the Val d'Aosta in northwestern Italy.

To read more about radicchio, refer to the Lasagne Treviso Style on page 184.

3 heads of radicchio, about ½ pound each and preferably the elongated Treviso variety

A 13 by 9-inch rectangular bake-and-serve dish or another of equivalent capacity

⅓ cup extra virgin olive oil

Fine sea salt

Black pepper ground fresh from the mill

12 thin slices of pancetta

½ pound Fontina cheese

For 4 to 6 persons

1 Turn on the oven to 400°.

2 Pull off and discard any bruised or discolored outer leaves on the radicchio. Cut each head lengthwise into four parts. Make 2 or 3 lengthwise incisions in the root, running from the base of the leaves to the butt end of the root.

Marcella Says: **The incisions will allow the heat to penetrate the root better so that it will cook apace with the more tender leaves.**

Rinse the radicchio in cold water and pat it dry with kitchen towels.

3   Lay all the radicchio sections flat, without overlapping, in the baking dish. Pour the oil over them, sprinkle with salt and pepper, and place the dish in the preheated oven. Turn the radicchio after 15 minutes, then continue baking for another 20 to 25 minutes, until they feel very soft when prodded with a fork.

4   While the radicchio is cooking, sauté the pancetta in a nonstick skillet, lightly browning the slices on one side, then on the other, without crisping them. Transfer them to a plate.

5   Cut the cheese into very thin slices, bearing in mind that you will need enough slices to cover all of the radicchio.

6   When the radicchio is tender, remove the dish from the oven. Over each radicchio quarter lay a slice of pancetta, then cover it with Fontina. Return the dish to the oven and bake until the cheese melts. Serve while still hot, before the cheese seizes and becomes stiff.

AHEAD-OF-TIME NOTE: You can cook the radicchio until tender up to a day in advance. Add the pancetta and cheese when you reheat it before serving.

YELLOW AND RED BELL PEPPERS
SAUTÉED WITH ANCHOVIES AND BLACK OLIVES
❧ *Peperoni Gialli e Rossi Saltati con le Acciughe e le Olive Nere*

You can call on these exceptionally savory peppers to be a vegetable dish, an appetizer—alone or as one of many on a party table—or a sauce for boiled meats. In this guise it is related to the warm red sauce with peppers, onions, and tomatoes that appears in *Essentials of Classic Italian Cooking.*

4 large, meaty bell peppers, 2 yellow and 2 red

3 tablespoons extra virgin olive oil

2 large garlic cloves, peeled and chopped very fine

5 flat anchovy fillets, packed in olive oil

3 tablespoons chopped Italian flat-leaf parsley

Fine sea salt

Black pepper ground fresh from the mill

30 small, cured, black olives, such as the niçoise or *picholine* variety, or about 15 larger Greek olives

YIELD: *enough for 4 servings as a vegetable dish, more if one of several small appetizers*

1 Cut each pepper lengthwise along the creases, remove the stem, seeds, and pithy core, then skin with a swivel-blade vegetable peeler. (For more details, see Peppers on page 78 of The Why and How of Prepping Vegetables.) Cut the peppers into very narrow strips about ¼ inch wide.

2 Pour the olive oil into a 10- or 12-inch skillet, add the garlic and anchovies, and turn the heat on to medium high. Cook, stirring and mashing the anchovies with a wooden spoon to help them dissolve. When the garlic becomes colored a pale blond, even if the anchovies have not yet dissolved, add the parsley.

3 Stir two or three times more, then add the peppers with a little bit of salt, and a few grindings of pepper. Turn the peppers over with the wooden spoon to coat them well and turn the heat down to medium low.

4 While the peppers are cooking, rap the olives with the flat blade of a heavy knife to expose the pits so you can pick them out. If you are using the large Greek olives, halve them after pitting.

5 When the peppers are partly done—not yet completely tender—add the pitted olives.

> *Marcella Says:* **I prefer to put the olives in when the cooking is nearly finished because long cooking draws out their latent bitterness.**

Cook, stirring from time to time, until the peppers are very soft. Serve warm or at room temperature.

AHEAD-OF-TIME NOTE: You can cook the peppers through to completion up to a day in advance. Refrigerate in a tightly sealed container.

GRATINÉED ASPARAGUS WITH BOILED HAM AND CREAM
⤳ *Asparagi Gratinati al Prosciutto Cotto*

The coupling of asparagus and ham, blessed by heavy cream, is one of the most elegant in Italian vegetable cooking. You will also come across it elsewhere as a pasta sauce, a rather distinguished one known as *alla Saffi*.

Fine sea salt

2½ pounds asparagus, trimmed and washed, as described on page 74 of The Why and How of Prepping Vegetables

2 tablespoons butter plus additional for greasing the baking dish

⅔ cup chopped onion

¼ pound plain boiled ham, cut into narrow julienne strips

> *Marcella Says:* **Please do not substitute smoked ham because its smoky accent would be too intrusive. Use the best-quality boiled ham you can get, possibly one of the imported Italian ones, such as Parmacotto, Gran Biscotto, or Beretta. Also see my comments on page 325.**

⅔ cup heavy cream

A 13 by 9-inch rectangular bake-and-serve dish or another dish of similar capacity

⅔ cup freshly grated Parmigiano-Reggiano cheese

YIELD: *enough for 4 servings as a vegetable dish, more if one of several small appetizers*

1 Bring water to a boil in a 12-inch sauté pan or skillet, add 2 tablespoons salt, and slide in the trimmed asparagus. Put a lid on the pan and cook at a steady simmer until an asparagus stalk bends easily when lifted with tongs or a fork. Using tongs or a slotted spoon or spatula, retrieve the asparagus and set it aside to cool.

2 Put the butter and chopped onion in a 7- to 10-inch skillet and turn the heat on to medium high. Cook the onion, stirring from time to time, until it becomes colored a deep gold. Add the ham strips, turn them over two or three times to coat them well, and cook for about 2 minutes, stirring from time to time. Pour in the cream and cook it down to half its original volume. Take the pan off the heat.

3 Turn on the oven to 400°.

4 Lightly smear the bottom of the baking dish with butter, lay half the asparagus lengthwise over the bottom, and spread half the cream and ham sauce over them. Sprinkle with 2 tablespoons of the grated Parmesan. Top with a second layer of asparagus, cover with the remaining sauce, and sprinkle with the remaining grated Parmesan.

AHEAD-OF-TIME NOTE: You can prepare the dish up to this point several hours in advance, in the morning if you are serving it that day at dinner. Cover with plastic film and refrigerate. Remove the plastic film and return the dish to room temperature before proceeding with the next step.

5 Bake in the preheated oven until the top becomes colored a light golden brown, about 15 minutes. Let settle for about 5 minutes before serving.

STUFFED ZUCCHINI WITH HAM AND PARMESAN

❧ *Zucchine Ripiene al Prosciutto Cotto*

The urge to fill a vegetable with some other thing or combination of things is a strong one in many cuisines. Peppers, tomatoes, mushroom caps, onions, potatoes, artichokes, eggplant, cabbage leaves, zucchini, and squash blossoms are the first that come mind when I think of which vegetables are likely to be called upon to play host to savory fillings. Not all are equally well cast for the part. Peppers enjoy and deserve wide popularity. Who has not had or at least

heard of stuffed peppers? Stuffing squash blossoms, on the other hand, seems to me an affectation and a waste of time. Nothing you can do with them tastes as good as opening them up flat and frying them crisp in flour-and-water batter. If there is one vegetable that seems to have been designed as an ideal wrapper it is zucchini. It is easily hollowed out into a seamless tube that acts as a perfect—and delicious—cooking vessel for virtually any tender and appetizing compound you want to pack into it. There has been a stuffed zucchini recipe in each of my previous books that used ground beef mixtures or tuna. The principal component in the filling here is boiled ham reinforced by pancetta. The zucchini is then cooked with a small amount of tomato. It is as tasty a combination as any of its predecessors but with a lightness and delicacy of flavor that is uniquely its own.

1½ to 2 pounds medium zucchini

A long-bladed coring tool OR a vegetable peeler OR any narrow-bladed knife

½ cup bread crumb—the soft part of bread—soaked in ⅓ cup milk

3 ounces plain boiled unsmoked ham, chopped very fine, about 1 cup

> *Marcella Says:* **If you can find it at your local source of Italian foods, the most desirable ham to use is** *prosciutto cotto,* **imported from Italy. It is made from pork shoulder and it is neither cured nor smoked, but steam-cooked. It is sweet-tasting and fragrant and a couple of slices of it on buttered bread make a wonderful sandwich. Some of the better-known brands are Parmacotto, Gran Biscotto, and Beretta.**

A ¼-inch-thick slice of pancetta, chopped very fine, about 2 tablespoons

2 tablespoons Italian flat-leaf parsley, chopped fine

1 egg

½ cup freshly grated Parmigiano-Reggiano cheese

2 tablespoons butter

1 tablespoon vegetable oil

Fine sea salt

Black pepper ground fresh from the mill

1 cup tomatoes cut up with their juice, preferably ripe, firm, fresh plum tomatoes, peeled and seeds scooped away, OR canned imported San Marzano Italian tomatoes

For 4 persons

1 Soak the zucchini in cold water to cover for about 20 minutes, then rub their skin clean under cold running water. Trim off the ends, then cut each zucchini crosswise in half. Use your corer or the blade of a peeler or a narrow-bladed knife to hollow out the zucchini. Be careful not to perforate the side wall.

AHEAD-OF-TIME NOTE: You can prepare the zucchini up to this point as much as 2 days in advance. Refrigerate, covered, until you are ready to finish making the dish.

> *Marcella Says:* **Do not discard the scooped-out zucchini flesh. Refrigerate it in a tightly closed container or a plastic bag with a zipper closure and sauté it later in the week, with chopped onion, for use either in a frittata or as the base of a risotto.**

2 Retrieve the milk-soaked bread, squeeze it gently in your hand to remove the excess milk, and put it in a bowl with the chopped ham, pancetta, parsley, egg, and Parmesan cheese. Mix the ingredients thoroughly with a fork.

3 Pull off some of the ham mixture with your fingers and cram it into one of the zucchini pieces. Pack the zucchini tightly, taking care not to let it split. Proceed thus until all the zucchini have been filled. If there should be any stuffing left over, shape it into small meatballs.

4 Put the butter and oil in a 12-inch skillet or sauté pan and turn the heat on to high. When the fat is hot, slip in the stuffed zucchini pieces and, if there are any, the meatballs. Brown the zucchini well on one side, about 6 minutes, turn, and brown the other side.

5 Sprinkle with salt and pepper, add the tomatoes with their juice, turn the ingredients over once or twice, lower the heat to medium low, and cover the pan. Cook until the fat floats free of the tomatoes, about 20 minutes. Turn the zucchini from time to time. Transfer to a serving platter and serve at once.

AHEAD-OF-TIME NOTE: You can cook the dish through to completion several hours in advance of serving. Reheat gently but thoroughly when ready to serve.

Braised Zucchini with Pork Jowl or Pancetta

✒ *Zucchine al Guanciale*

Except for pancetta and salt pork, it's very difficult to find such cuts of pork that have been cured without smoking. A great pity because they have a lot of flavor to give, but it is all filtered through heavy smoke. On a few occasions I did find both pork jowl and a kind of bacon called side meat that were simply salt- and air-cured, but there doesn't seem to be much demand for them in my market because once they disappeared they never came back. If you should come across them, they are what you need for this dish. If not, there is always pancetta.

In this vegetable braise the zucchini are exposed to the same treatment I would give a meat braise or stew. They are *insaporiti*, made tasty as explained on page 15, with the sautéed pork over high heat, then they are braised with fresh tomatoes. I do keep the heat high, which I would normally not do with meat, because I want the tomato juices to evaporate before the zucchini become too mushy.

2 pounds fresh young zucchini

2 tablespoons extra virgin olive oil

⅔ cup (about ¼ pound) cured but not smoked pork jowl or pork side meat OR pancetta, cut into 1-inch-long strips

Fine sea salt

4 or 5 ripe, firm, fresh plum tomatoes, peeled raw, and seeded, as described on page 80 of The Why and How of Prepping Vegetables, and cut into ¼-inch-wide strips, about 1½ cups

For 4 persons

1 Soak the zucchini in water to cover for about 20 minutes, then rub their skin clean under cold running water. Trim off the ends, then cut them into thin rounds.

2 Pour the olive oil into a 12-inch skillet, put in the pork, and turn the heat on to medium high. Cook the pork, turning it once or twice to color it on both sides, but do not let it become crisp.

3 Add the zucchini, sprinkle with salt, and turn up the heat. Cook at high heat, turning the zucchini frequently. When they are halfway done—they should still be quite firm—add the tomatoes. Continue to cook at high heat, turning the contents of the pan over from time to time, until the zucchini slices have become very soft and any liquid in the pan has completely evaporated. Serve promptly.

AHEAD-OF-TIME NOTE: You can complete the recipe several hours in advance of serving. Reheat the dish before serving.

Baked Cannellini Beans with Vegetables and Thyme

✑ *Teglia di Fagioli Cannellini al Forno*

Before Tuscans got on the pasta bandwagon, their first courses had more genuine regional character: the soups, for example, of which there are none better, and the bean dishes, of which this is a fine example. Substantial enough to be a full first course, it can also be divided into smaller portions for a vegetable side dish. It requires a certain commitment of time to put the dish together, but it can be done days in advance and baked shortly before serving.

1 cup dried cannellini beans

Fine sea salt

6 tablespoons extra virgin olive oil plus 1½ teaspoons for smearing the baking dish

½ cup chopped onion

½ cup chopped carrot

½ cup chopped celery

2 garlic cloves, peeled and lightly smashed with the flat part of a heavy knife blade

1 slice pancetta, ¼ inch thick, cut into strips

3 ripe, firm, fresh plum tomatoes, peeled raw and seeded, as described on page 80 of The Why and How of Prepping Vegetables, and chopped

Black pepper ground fresh from the mill

5 to 7 sprigs fresh thyme

1 beef bouillon cube

An 11 by 7-inch rectangular bake-and-serve dish or any another dish of similar capacity

⅓ cup fine, dry, unflavored bread crumbs plus 2 tablespoons for dusting the baking dish

⅓ cup freshly grated Parmigiano-Reggiano cheese

2 tablespoons chopped Italian flat-leaf parsley

YIELD: *4 to 6 servings as a first course, perhaps 8 as a side dish*

1 At least 6 hours before making this dish, or even the preceding night, put the beans in a bowl with enough lukewarm water to cover by at least 3 inches and a teaspoon of salt.

2 Pour 3 tablespoons of the olive oil into a medium saucepan, add the chopped onion, and turn the heat on to medium high. Cook the onion, stirring occasionally, until it becomes colored a pale gold. Add the carrot, celery, garlic, and pancetta. Turn all the ingredients over with a wooden spoon to coat them well and cook, stirring from time to time, for about 10 minutes.

3 Add the cut-up tomatoes, a little salt, liberal grindings of pepper, and the thyme sprigs. Turn all the ingredients over once or twice.

4 Drain the cannellini beans, rinse them in cold water, and add them to the saucepan. Turn them over once or twice, then pour enough water into the pan to cover the contents by about 1½ inches and add the bouillon cube. Cover the pan, turn the heat down, and bring to a slow, steady simmer. Maintain that simmer, adding a tablespoon or two of water if it becomes necessary, for about 1½ hours. The beans must be fully cooked, not al dente, but tender through and through. If they are not tender after 1½ hours, continue simmering until they become so, adding a little water from time to time if it becomes necessary.

5 Use a slotted spoon to retrieve the beans and put them in a bowl.

6 Turn on the oven to 375°.

7 Uncover the pan, turn the heat up to high, and cook down the pan juices (or runny contents) to the density of sauce. When dense, pour it over the beans. Thoroughly combine the contents of the bowl.

8 Smear the baking dish with 1½ teaspoonfuls of the olive oil and then dust it with 2 tablespoons of the bread crumbs. Pour the beans with all the bowl contents into the dish, and level it off.

9 Put ⅓ cup of the bread crumbs in a small bowl, add the grated Parmesan, chopped parsley, and the remaining 3 tablespoons of olive oil. With your hand, mix the ingredients to a crumbly consistency, and spread the mixture over the beans.

10 Bake in the preheated oven for 20 minutes, or until a thin crisp crust forms on the top.

AHEAD-OF-TIME NOTE: You can assemble, but not bake the dish 2 or 3 days in advance. Refrigerate it in the baking dish, covered tightly with plastic film. Bring to room temperature before baking it.

MASHED POTATOES WITH BAKED ONIONS

⌘ *Puré di Patate con Cipolle al Forno*

Mashed potatoes in the Italian style, which is to say mashed boiled potatoes into which you incorporate butter and Parmesan cheese, are fine on their own, but they are also hospitable to other ingredients when these expand the flavor and textural interest of the dish. I don't care for garlic in this context because it comes distractingly forward, stealing the show from its host, the potato. What I look for is an ingredient with a supporting player's temperament, such as the sautéed zucchini I added to the mashed potatoes in my last book. Now I use baked onions. I split the onions, bake them until they are very tender, then chop them in a food processor. When mixed into the potatoes, their characteristically piquant sweetness enlivens, but does not compete.

3 pounds large onions, preferably yellow onions on the flattish side

Fine sea salt

Black pepper ground fresh from the mill

3 tablespoons vegetable oil

3 or 4 medium-size boiling potatoes

> *Marcella Says:* **What I mean by boiling potatoes is a mature potato such as a Yukon Gold or Maine or Long Island white. I exclude new potatoes and Idaho baking potatoes because, when mashed, the former becomes too gummy and the latter too dry and mealy.**

A food mill or potato ricer

A double boiler OR 2 saucepans of unequal size, the smaller one set into the larger, resting on a trivet or other heatproof object

1½ tablespoons butter, cut into small pieces

½ cup freshly grated Parmigiano-Reggiano cheese

1 tablespoon chopped Italian flat-leaf parsley

A warm serving bowl

For 4 to 6 persons

AHEAD-OF-TIME NOTE: The onions may need to bake for as much as an hour, depending on their size, and then drain for about 2 hours. But you can do this a day or two in advance of boiling and mashing the potatoes. Although the cooking time is long, it requires next to no attention on your part, leaving you free in the interim to do other things.

1 Turn on the oven to 400°.

2 Peel the onions and cut them in half, not from top to bottom but across the middle.

3 Use the sharp point of a small knife to make ½-inch-deep crosshatch incisions over the whole cut surface of each onion half. Avoid cutting through to the edges.

4 Place the onions, cut side up, in a baking pan. (Lining the pan with aluminum foil will save you some cleaning up later.) Sprinkle on salt, add liberal grindings of pepper, and pour the oil over the onions.

5 Bake the onions in the preheated oven until they feel very soft when prodded with a fork. If they are as much as 5 inches in diameter, it may take up to 1 hour. Transfer the onions to a work surface, remove the charred outer layer, and cut them into pieces. Cut away and discard the root end. Set a strainer or colander over a bowl and place the cut-up onions in the colander. Let them drain for about 2 hours, or until they stop shedding liquid. If making them in advance, as suggested above, place them in a storage container and refrigerate. Bring to room temperature before proceeding with the recipe.

6 Bring a saucepan of water to a boil and drop in the potatoes with their skins on.

7 While the potatoes are boiling, chop the onions to a fine consistency in a food processor.

8 Shortly before the potatoes are done, put water in the lower half of the double boiler or in the larger of the two saucepans that you are using. Fit the upper part of the double boiler onto the lower, or place the smaller saucepan into the larger, resting it on the trivet, and bring the water to a simmer.

9 When the potatoes are done, drain them, and peel them while still hot.

> *Marcella Says:* **Depending on their size, the potatoes may take about 40 minutes to cook. They are done only when they are completely tender all the way through. To determine that, pierce them with a long-tined fork or a sharp skewer or trussing needle. If they offer no resistance, they are cooked.**

10 Fit the disk with the smallest holes into the food mill or into the ricer if it comes with interchangeable disks and mash the peeled potatoes into the top of the double boiler. Mix in the chopped onions, and add the butter, grated Parmesan, and chopped parsley. Mix vigorously with a fork or whisk, taste and correct for salt—it will need some—and grind in more pepper. Mix once again, transfer to the warm serving bowl, and serve at once.

MUSHROOM MEDLEY WITH ROSEMARY

⤷ *Misto di Funghi al Rosmarino*

In the introduction to the veal and mushroom pasta sauce on page 164, I explained how I came to learn something very useful about mushrooms: When you cook several kinds together you are rewarded with a levitation of flavor that surpasses what any single variety, even the most savory, can produce alone. Elsewhere I have applied that principle to sauces and fillings for stuffed pasta. Here it serves no other cause than that of enjoying the mushrooms on their own, as a dish unto themselves.

> 2 pounds assorted mushrooms
>
> > *Marcella Says:* **The more varied, the better. Start with at least two, the basic white button mushrooms and the cremini, or baby bellas. To these you can add shiitake and, if they are in your market, such wild fresh mushrooms as porcini, morels, and chanterelles. Oyster mushrooms and enoki contribute little more than texture. Their flavor is so feeble that I, at least, would not bother with them.**
>
> *Optional:* for heightened fragrance and flavor, 1 ounce imported dried Italian porcini
>
> ⅓ cup extra virgin olive oil
>
> 6 or 7 whole garlic cloves, peeled
>
> 3 or 4 sprigs fresh rosemary
>
> Fine sea salt
>
> Black pepper ground fresh from the mill

For 4 to 6 persons

1 If you are using shiitake, detach and discard the stems because they are very tough. Rinse all the fresh mushrooms under cold running water. Cut them into very thin slices, an operation for which you may use a food processor fitted with the slicing disk.

2 If you are adding dried porcini in the dish, let them steep in warm water to cover for at least 30 minutes, until they are fully reconstituted—they must become soft—then retrieve them without discarding the soaking liquid. Rinse them in several changes of cold water to rid them of grit. Fit a coffee filter or a paper towel into a strainer and strain the soaking liquid into any suitable container.

3 Put the olive oil, garlic, and rosemary sprigs in a 12-inch skillet and turn the heat on to high. Cook the garlic, stirring frequently, until it becomes colored a nut-brown. Remove from the pan and discard.

4 If you are using reconstituted porcini, add them to the pan now. Cook them over lively heat for about 1 minute, turning them over once or twice. Pour the reserved strained porcini soaking liquid into the pan, and let it bubble away completely, stirring once or twice.

5 Add all the sliced fresh mushrooms, sprinkle with salt and liberal grindings of pepper, turn them over once or twice to coat them well, then lower the heat and cover the pan. Continue cooking in the covered pan until when you check you see that the mushrooms have released a quantity of liquid. Then remove the lid and raise the heat to medium. Cook, stirring from time to time, until all the liquid shed by the mushrooms has evaporated. After this point, cook for another 10 minutes, turning the mushrooms over once or twice. Serve while still warm or at room temperature.

AHEAD-OF-TIME NOTE: You can cook the dish up to 3 days in advance of serving. Refrigerate the mushrooms with all the pan juices in a tightly closed container. Bring them to room temperature before serving or before reheating.

> *Marcella Says:* **These mushrooms provide a different and tasty way to serve a *tagliata di manzo,* the twice-cooked beefsteak: Grill a 1½-inch-thick steak on a charcoal grill or over the stove in a cast-iron pan. Cook it very, very rare, slice it on the diagonal into thin strips, and quickly transfer the slices to the hot pan containing the mushrooms. Turn the slices over twice, coating both sides, empty the full contents of the pan onto a warm platter, and serve at once. The mushrooms from the recipe above are enough for two thick rib-eye steaks, serving at least four persons.**

PORTOBELLO MUSHROOMS AND YELLOW BELL PEPPERS SAUTÉED IN OLIVE OIL

⇜ *Tegamino di Funghi e Peperoni Gialli*

This is one more instance of how two vegetables act upon each other. The portobello comes to this exchange with the dark accent of the woods and their underbrush. The accent of the peppers is sweet and sunny as their color. Together they evoke expressions of flavor that they would never have produced alone.

3 meaty yellow bell peppers

¼ cup extra virgin olive oil

3 large or 5 small garlic cloves, peeled and sliced very thin

Fine sea salt

1 pound portobello mushroom, sliced about ¼ inch thick

Black pepper ground fresh from the mill

For 4 to 6 persons

1   Cut each pepper lengthwise along the creases, remove the stem, seeds, and pithy core, then peel them, as described on page 79 of The Why and How of Prepping Vegetables. Cut the peppers into narrow strips about 2 inches long.

2   Pour the oil into a 12-inch sauté pan or skillet, drop in the sliced garlic, and turn the heat on to medium high. Cook the garlic for just a little while, stirring once or twice, and when its aroma begins to rise and it becomes colored a pale, pale gold, add the peppers. Sprinkle with salt and turn the peppers over to coat them well. Cook for 5 to 6 minutes to brown the peppers, stirring from time to time.

3   Add the sliced mushrooms, sprinkle them with salt and generous grindings of pepper, turn them over once or twice, put a lid on the pan, and turn the heat down to the lowest setting possible. As the mushrooms begin to cook down you will find that they release liquid. Continue

to cook, turning the mushrooms over occasionally, until all the vegetal liquid in the pan has completely evaporated and the mushrooms are very soft. At that point—a half hour or more will have elapsed, depending on the mushrooms themselves—uncover the pan, turn the heat up to high, and cook for 1 minute more, turning the mushrooms over frequently.

AHEAD-OF-TIME NOTE: You can cook the mushrooms through to the end 2 or 3 days in advance of serving. Reheat in a smaller skillet on top of the stove over medium heat.

Belgian Endive Fried in Pastella Batter
❧ *La Belga Fritta nella Pastella*

When my son was pitching for the position of executive chef at an Italian restaurant in Portland, Oregon, an appetizer of sliced zucchini fried in pastella batter that he included in his presentation was decisive in getting him the job. Zucchini is just one of many vegetables that, when fried in *pastella* batter, illustrate the merits of well-executed frying: The pristine, juicy flavor of the vegetable sealed by a deliciously crisp, firmly clinging, weightless crust. Other suitable vegetables are asparagus, sliced tomatoes, onion rings, and the one featured in this recipe, Belgian endive.

The endive, I find, works particularly well. It doesn't lose any of its moisture and so it tastes sweeter than it sometimes does with other cooking methods, and it offers a lot of surface area for the *pastella* crust to cling to. You can serve it before you sit down for dinner as an appetizing accompaniment to an aperitif, or you can serve it at table as an antipasto, or as a vegetable side dish. However you elect to present it, make it and serve it at once. Good fried food likes neither to be reheated nor to be kept waiting.

1 cup plus 2 tablespoons all-purpose flour

1 cup water

4 heads Belgian endive

Vegetable oil

Fine sea salt

A wire-mesh drying rack placed over aluminum foil

For 4 persons

1   Prepare the pastella batter, using either the hand method or the food processor as described on page 26 of At Master Class. If using the processor, transfer the batter to a bowl.

2   Wash the endive in cold water and discard any wilted or bruised outer leaves. Trim a very thin slice off from the root end. Cut each head lengthwise into three or four sections, making sure that each still has a part of the root end attached at its base to hold the leaves together.

3   Pour enough oil in a 10-inch skillet to come at least ½ inch up the sides. Turn the heat up to high.

4   When the oil is hot, pick up an endive section and, holding it by its root end, dip it into the batter, making sure it is coated all over. Let any excess batter flow back into the bowl, then slip the endive into the hot oil. Repeat, filling the pan with a single, nonoverlapping layer of endive. As soon as you see the edges of a piece becoming brown, turn the section. When you have browned both sides, transfer the endive to the drying rack to drain. Sprinkle immediately with salt. Proceed in this manner until all the endive is fried. Serve promptly.

Salads

Savoy Cabbage Salads

Raw, shredded Savoy cabbage is a classic element in those Italian salads that are intended to give one's teeth slightly more exercise than the usual greens are wont to do. Savoy's crunch is just firm enough to make the experience enjoyable, but not so intractable to make it laborious. The texture is juicy rather than stringy, and the flavor is of the sweet, uncabbagy kind that makes Savoy cabbage so delicious not just in salads, but in soups, in pasta sauces, in risotto, or as a sautéed vegetable.

Savoy cabbage can stand alone in a salad paired with its nearly inseparable companion, garlic, and dressed with a fruity olive oil. But it is also very good when coupled with a creamy and somewhat more reticent partner. The two salads that follow are an example. Cannellini beans are an almost compulsive choice. Nothing could work better, especially if you are working with very good beans, preferably not the mushy canned kind. The second example, with avocado, derives from the present circumstances of my life. I am now living in Florida and who, in Florida, can resist one of those glossy-skinned, tender-fleshed, sweet-tasting avocados that are grown here? I see no reason to resist them. It seems that avocados have become quite popular in Italy, too. I love them paired with Savoy cabbage; each component completes what is one-sided in the flavor profile of the other, bonding in a very satisfying manner.

SAVOY CABBAGE SALAD WITH WARM CANNELLINI BEANS
౭ౢ *Insalata di Verza Cruda con i Fagioli Cannellini Tiepidi*

1 small head Savoy cabbage

4 garlic cloves, peeled and lightly smashed with the flat part of a heavy knife blade

A deep salad bowl

¾ cup dried cannellini beans, presoaked and cooked with sea salt and 1 tablespoon extra virgin olive oil (See Knowing Beans on page 57 of AT MASTER CLASS.)

Marcella Says: **In this salad you really do need the superior texture and flavor of a good-quality dried bean, which explains why I am not listing canned beans as an option.**

Fine sea salt

1 tablespoon wine vinegar, preferably white

¼ cup extra virgin olive oil

Black pepper ground fresh from the mill

For 4 to 6 persons

1 Cut enough of the Savoy cabbage into very fine shreds until you have approximately 2 cups. Try not to include any portion of the root end or of the thick ribs. If there is much cabbage left over, save to use in a soup.

2 Put the shredded cabbage in the salad bowl with the smashed garlic cloves. Toss once or twice.

AHEAD-OF-TIME NOTE: The cabbage needs to steep with the garlic for at least 2 hours, but no longer than 6, before serving.

3 When ready to serve, warm up the cannellini beans in the water in which they cooked. They need to be very warm because then they will soften the cabbage, and the respective sweet and sharp flavors of the two ingredients will act vigorously each upon the other.

4 Remove the garlic cloves from the salad bowl. Drain the beans and add them to the bowl together with salt, the vinegar, the oil, and generous grindings of black pepper. Toss thoroughly and serve with good crusty bread.

Savoy Cabbage Salad with Avocado

⤚ *Insalata Cruda di Verza ed Avocado*

3 to 4 cups shredded Savoy cabbage (Use only the tenderer pale central leaves, discarding the ribbed dark-green outer leaves and the solid core.)

2 garlic cloves, peeled and lightly smashed with the flat part of a heavy knife blade

½ large ripe avocado or 1 small, peeled and cut into thin strips

Fine sea salt

1½ tablespoons wine vinegar

2 tablespoons extra virgin olive oil

Black pepper ground fresh from the mill

A deep salad bowl

For 4 persons

1 Put all of the ingredients in the salad bowl, toss thoroughly, and let stand at room temperature for 30 to 40 minutes.

2 Remove the garlic cloves and serve at room temperature.

Avocado and Red Bell Pepper Salad with Red Onion

Insalata di Avocado, Peperone Rosso, e Cipolla di Tropea

One of the things I admire about avocados is their gift for reconciling and binding into harmony the contrasting features of other salad ingredients. Try this combination of avocado, bell pepper, and red onion and you will see what I mean. The creamy juices that are produced yearn to be sopped up with good bread. The amount of avocado needed for this salad makes it an expensive dish, but also a nourishing and satisfying one. A small portion of it, as an appetizer, can go a long way, but it can easily be transformed into a refreshing condiment for grilled steaks or for a cut of boiled beef, such as brisket or short ribs. To use it thus, you must make it a little less "dense" by adding more olive oil, about two more tablespoons, and doubling the amount of vinegar.

1½ cups Bermuda red onion, cut into ¼-inch dice

1 red bell pepper

2 large or 4 small ripe avocados

The freshly squeezed juice of 1 medium lemon

Fine sea salt

1½ tablespoons good-quality red wine vinegar (not balsamic)

4 tablespoons extra virgin olive oil

Black pepper ground fresh from the mill

YIELD: *enough for 6 servings as an appetizer salad or up to 8 condiment servings for grilled or boiled meat*

1 Put the diced onion in a bowl of cold water. Squeeze it in your hands, then replace the water. Repeat two or three times, squeezing the onion each time. Then cover the onion with cold water and let it soak until you are ready to combine it with the pepper and avocados.

Marcella Says: If I were making this in Italy during late spring or summer, when the very sweet red onions from Tropea in Calabria are in season, I would skip this step, but the pungency of a Bermuda onion needs a little preparatory taming in water.

2 Cut the pepper lengthwise along the creases, remove the stem, seeds, and and white pithy core. Cut the flesh into ¼-inch dice to measure about 1½ cups. If the pepper is too small to yield that amount, cut up another. Any leftovers can be saved to use in another salad, a sauce, or a soup.

3 Cut each avocado in half, remove the pit and peel, and slice into very thin wedges. Put the avocado wedges in a salad bowl and drizzle them immediately with the lemon juice to keep them from discoloring.

4 Add the diced pepper to the bowl.

5 Drain the onion, wrap it in one or two sheets of paper towels, and squeeze out as much water from it as you can. Unwrap and add it to the bowl.

6 Sprinkle the salad liberally with salt, add the vinegar and olive oil, toss thoroughly, and season with several grindings of fresh pepper. Toss again, and serve.

CELERY, AVOCADO, AND BELL PEPPER SALAD WITH BLACK OLIVES
Insalata di Sedano, Avocado, e Peperone con Olive Nere

The avocados I occasionally used to buy at the Rialto market in Venice seldom met the expectations for flavor and texture that I had formed from eating really good avocados in America, so I was delighted to find that in my new home base in Florida the native avocado could be as good as any I had ever tasted. It has prompted me to use it more liberally than I've ever been able to before and I find it has added a luscious touch to some of my Italian salads. Avocados are most appealing when one capitalizes on their creaminess to balance the snap and crunch of other ingredients, as the fruit does here, where it is joined with celery and raw bell pepper. I find the flavors and texture of this salad to be particularly agreeable immediately following a seafood course.

2 or 3 medium celery stalks

1 small or ½ large ripe avocado

½ red bell pepper, washed, stemmed, seeded, and pithy core removed

⅓ cup black Greek olives, pitted and cut in two

Fine sea salt

1 tablespoon red wine vinegar

3 tablespoons extra virgin olive oil

Black pepper ground fresh from the mill

For 4 persons

1   Wash the celery stalks under cold running water, then peel the outer layer of the stalks with a swivel-blade vegetable peeler to remove as many of the strings as possible. Cut the celery into skinny strips 2 to 3 inches long and no more than ¼ inch wide. (I'd rather you did this by hand, but if you must use the food processor, insert the large shredding disk and cut the celery into pieces short enough to fit horizontally down the processor feed tube.) You want about 1½ cups of celery strips.

2   Cut the avocado in half, remove the pit and peel, then cut each half lengthwise into thin slices no more than ½ inch wide.

3   Cut the bell pepper half into ¼-inch dice to measure about ⅔ cup.

4   Combine the celery, avocado, bell pepper, and black olives in a ceramic or glass bowl. Sprinkle liberally with salt, and add the vinegar, olive oil, and several grindings of pepper. Toss thoroughly, being careful not to mash the avocado. Serve at once.

> *Marcella Says:* **The salad should be served promptly after tossing, but if you wish, you can prepare all the vegetables for it—but not the avocado—several hours in advance. Peel and slice the avocado when you are ready to toss the salad.**

FENNEL AND ORANGE SALAD

↬ *Insalata di Finocchio e Arance*

You can find fennel and oranges in the market all year long, but their best seasons coincide, from late fall through winter into early spring. The juiciest, sweetest fennels for salad are the fat, round ones that Italian cooks call the males. The flatter, elongated ones are stringier and have a sharper licorice aroma that is not as appealing when eaten raw. Look for glossy, pearly-white bulbs and pass up any that are badly bruised, cracked, or discolored.

In Sicily I have had this salad with *tarocchi*, the native, intensely aromatic, dark red blood oranges. Blood oranges from California are overpriced, and they are short on both juice and aroma. Florida has a marvelous navel blood orange, but its season is despairingly brief. The salad works well with any juicy orange, but if you want to look for something special I'd recommend a navel, a tangelo, or a temple orange.

1 medium fennel

Optional: a mandoline

2 oranges (see introductory note above for suggested types)

Fine sea salt

2 tablespoons extra virgin olive oil

Optional: black pepper ground fresh from the mill

For 4 to 6 persons

1 Trim off the fennel tops, all the way down to where the stalks rise from the bulb. Cut the bulb in half lengthwise. If the first outside leaf is blemished, discard it. Pare away a thin slice from the root end. Slice the fennel crosswise as thin as you are able. If you have a mandoline, this would be a good time to use it.

2 Cut away enough of the top and bottom of the oranges to expose the tips of the orange sections. Use a very sharp paring knife to cut off the peel, all the pulpy white pith beneath it, and the thin membrane covering the orange sections. Loosen and detach the sections one by one by slipping the blade of the sharp knife between the flesh and the membrane to which each section is still attached.

3 Put the fennel slices and the orange sections in a deep dish, not in a salad bowl.

AHEAD-OF-TIME NOTE: You can prepare both the fennel and the oranges up to this point several hours in advance. Cover the dish tightly with plastic film before refrigerating.

4 When ready to bring the salad to the table, toss with salt, pour the olive oil over it, and toss once more. Grind black pepper over it, if desired, and serve at once.

Fennel and Goat Cheese Salad

✥ Insalata di Finocchio e Caprino

I had this salad years and years ago in Friuli, at Josko Sirk's marvelous restaurant, Al Cacciatore, and my memory of it is as fresh as though I had just had a taste of it. Josko's chastely white-on-white salad is a refreshing juxtaposition of the flavors and textures of its two components, the fennel's whispery anise fragrance merging with the sharp, astringent tang of the goat cheese, the yielding softness of the cheese playing off the crispness of the vegetable. A fresh, creamy goat cheese is a better choice than a dry, crumbly kind.

> 1 large, round fennel
>
> Fine sea salt
>
> ¼ pound goat cheese (see introductory note above for type)
>
> Black pepper ground fresh from the mill
>
> 3 tablespoons extra virgin olive oil

For 4 to 6 persons

1   Trim off the fennel tops and a thin slice off the butt end. Cut off and discard any blemished part of the bulb's outer leaves. With a sharp chef's knife, cut the bulb horizontally into very thin slices. You may use a mandoline if you have one, or the slicing disk of a food processor. If using the food processor, first cut the fennel into vertical sections that will fit down the feed tube. Soak the slices briefly in cold water, drain, and pat them dry with a cloth towel or shake the water off in a salad spinner.

2   Put the slices in a deep serving dish and sprinkle lightly with salt.

3   Cut the cheese into ¼-inch rounds and place them over the fennel.

4   Set the pepper mill to medium coarse and grind a liberal amount of pepper over the salad.

5   Drizzle the olive oil over the salad, distributing it evenly. Taste and correct for salt. Serve.

SERVING NOTE: The salad in an Italian meal is customarily served after the entrée, but this one also makes an excellent appetizer.

Baked Desserts

APPLE CAKE WITH RAISINS AND RUM

☙ *Torta di Mele con Uva Passa e Rum*

As I review the dessert and ice-cream recipes I have put into this book, I am not astonished to find that there is so much fruit in them. It was always a struggle to persuade my American and British students that, to an Italian, ripe, sweet fruit is more tempting than the most luscious dessert. If you try some of the suggestions for marinating fresh fruit that you'll find on page 67 of AT MASTER CLASS, you will see what I mean. We also like baked desserts, if there is fruit in them, but they must be light and unspiced, such as this apple cake from the Trentino region in northeastern Italy.

About 2 pounds Red Delicious apples

The freshly squeezed juice of 2 lemons, approximately ⅓ cup

1⅓ cups all-purpose flour plus additional for dusting the baking pan

1½ teaspoons baking powder

1 heaping cup sugar

9 tablespoons butter, melted, plus additional for greasing the pan

3 extra-large eggs

1 tablespoon dark rum

1 cup whole milk

A pinch of fine sea salt

½ cup (2 ounces) golden raisins, steeped in water for 30 minutes

A 9½-inch springform pan

YIELD: *8 servings*

1 Turn on the oven to 350°.

2 Peel the apples, cut them in half, core them, then slice them the very thinnest that you can. Put the slices in a bowl and pour the lemon juice over them, turning them over two or three times.

3 Put the flour and the baking powder in another bowl, and mix well. Add the sugar, melted butter, eggs, rum, milk, and salt and mix well.

4 Drain the raisins, squeeze them dry in a kitchen towel, and add them to the batter, stirring until they have been evenly distributed.

5 Pour the batter into the bowl over the sliced apples, turning them over several times to coat them well. Separate any slices that stick together.

6 Grease the bottom and sides of the springform pan with butter. Dust with flour, then turn the pan over and rap it against the counter to shake out the excess flour. Pour the cake batter into the pan and level it off with a spatula. Bake in the preheated oven for 1 hour.

SERVING SUGGESTION: You can serve the cake when it is still slightly warm, if you like desserts at that temperature. I prefer this one when it has cooled down completely because it is firmer then.

AHEAD-OF-TIME NOTE: When the cake has cooled completely, wrap it in heavy-duty aluminum foil and refrigerate. It will keep perfectly for several days. Serve it slightly chilled or fully restored to room temperature.

HALF-MOON PASTRIES FILLED WITH CHOCOLATE AND APRICOT JAM

✑ *Mezzelune Farcite di Cioccolato e Marmellata di Albicocche*

I have never worked up too much enthusiasm for making pastries. They aren't something the two of us eat. We breakfast solely on coffee, and we hardly ever snack. At a wedding we had been invited to I had these homemade filled half-moon pastries and I must have liked them because I asked if I could have the recipe. When it surfaced among my papers, I remembered the taste, and, I knew that if I could succeed in making them they'd go over well. I love apricot jam, and Victor is hooked on dark chocolate. We still don't have pastries very often, but when we do it is these over every other kind.

4 cups all-purpose flour for the dough plus additional for rolling it out and for dusting the baking pan

4 extra-large eggs

Fine sea salt

8 tablespoons (1 stick) butter, softened at room temperature, plus additional for greasing the baking pan

3½ teaspoons baking powder

The grated peel of 1 large lemon (the outer yellow layer, only with none of the bitter white pith beneath)

1 cup sugar

¼ cup whole milk

A 3½-inch diameter cookie cutter or a drinking glass of equal size

7 tablespoons good-quality apricot jam

7 tablespoons chopped semisweet chocolate or chocolate chips

> *Marcella Says:* **In making these pastries I found it very practical to use miniature semisweet chocolate drops. If you want a better quality and darker chocolate, try the nuggets that Scharffen Berger makes.**

1 or more jelly-roll pans, preferably nonstick

1 or more cooling racks

YIELD: *50 half-moon pastries*

1 Mix together the flour, 3 of the eggs, a pinch of salt, the butter, baking powder, lemon peel, sugar, and milk, then knead just until it becomes a homogeneous mass, no longer. You can do this in a food processor, hitting the pulse button on and off until the ingredients mass together.

AHEAD-OF-TIME NOTE: You can prepare the dough a few hours in advance and refrigerate it, tightly wrapped in plastic film, until you are ready to proceed.

2 Pull off a piece of dough the size of a small apple and roll it out on a lightly floured pastry board to a thickness of ⅛ inch. If the dough begins to stick as you roll it, sprinkle both sides very lightly with flour.

3 Cut the sheet into 3½-inch disks using the cookie cutter or a drinking glass. Remove the disks from the sheet of dough and lay them out on a floured work surface. Knead the dough scraps with another piece of dough from the mass and repeat the full operation of rolling out the dough and cutting it into disks until you have used up all the dough. You should end up with approximately 50 disks.

4 Turn on the oven to 375°.

5 Combine the chocolate drops and apricot jam in a small bowl and mix them thoroughly with a small spatula or other suitable tool.

6 Dot the center of each dough disk with slightly less than a teaspoon of the chocolate and jam mixture.

7 Separate the remaining egg, pouring the white into one small bowl and the yolk into another. Beat each lightly with a fork.

8 Dip your finger or a pastry brush into the beaten egg white and smear the rim of each of the dough disks, moistening it about a third of the way in. As soon as you have moistened one disk,

fold it over into a half-moon shape and firmly press the edge all around to make a tight seal.

9 Thinly smear the jelly-roll pan (or pans) with butter, dust with flour, then turn the pan over and tap it on the counter to shake out any excess flour. Arrange the pastries in the pan placing them about 1½ inches apart. (If you only have one pan, you can do a batch at a time, reusing the pan as soon as it has cooled down after each batch is baked.)

10 Lightly beat the egg yolk again. With a clean pastry brush, brush egg yolk over the top of each pastry.

11 Bake for 15 minutes in the preheated oven. Remove the pastries from the pan with a spatula to the cooling rack. Some pastries that didn't have a very tight seal may leak a little of their filling, which will have caramelized on the pan. It's nice to nibble on while you are working.

AHEAD-OF-TIME NOTE: When the pastries have cooled completely, they will keep for 2 to 3 weeks stored in a tin box.

BREAD PUDDING WITH CHOCOLATE AND APPLES
◄ *Budino di Pane, Cioccolato, e Mele*

The only bread pudding I had been making for most of my life was my mother's, a basic and comforting pudding indeed, the recipe for which I put into my first book (*The Classic Italian Cook Book*), back in 1973. I don't discriminate among sources of ideas for dishes to try out, they may come from gossipy weeklies on a hairdresser's table or scholarly tomes, and I am not embarrassed to admit that some of the best ones have come from the former. And so it was with this new bread pudding of mine. The combination of dark chocolate and apples intrigued me. I worked with the recipe a few times, adjusting the proportions and looking for ways to simplify it. I omitted the caramel glazing that often attends bread puddings, I baked it in a springform pan rather than in a loaf pan, and, on an occasion, when I didn't have any stale bread on hand I picked up a loaf of thinly sliced white bread at the supermarket that, when lightly toasted, was so easy to work with and produced such a satisfying, compact consistency that I continued to use it. I have been sampling the results rather broadly and, among people who are as fond of bread pudding as they are of chocolate, the rate of approval has been encouraging.

12 ounces 2- or 3-day-old good-quality plain white bread, trimmed of all crust, OR a fresh 1-pound loaf white bread, very thinly sliced and trimmed of its crust

2 cups whole milk

½ cup plus 2 tablespoons sugar

A pinch of salt

8 tablespoons (1 stick) butter plus additional for greasing the baking pan

4 ounces good-quality bittersweet chocolate, cut into small pieces, about ½ cup

2 Golden Delicious apples, peeled, cored, and sliced very thin

1⅓ cups golden raisins, steeped in lukewarm water for at least 30 minutes

2 eggs

A 9½-inch springform pan

Flour for dusting the pan

YIELD: *8 servings*

1 Cut up the day-old bread coarsely. If you are using the fresh loaf, discard the end slices, toast the others to a dry consistency, and cut up coarsely. Put the bread in a large bowl.

2 Put the milk and the ½ cup of sugar in a small saucepan and warm the milk over medium heat without letting it boil. When the milk approaches a simmer, forming pearly bubbles around its circumference, pour it over the bread, and let the bread soak it all up. Add a pinch of salt.

3 Mash the bread with a fork, or knead it with you hands if it is not too hot to handle, or even simpler, put it in a food processor and process it briefly to uniform consistency. After processing, return it to the bowl.

4 Turn on the oven to 350°.

5 Cut the 8 tablespoons of butter into small pieces, and put the butter and chocolate in the upper half of a double boiler. Pour water into the lower half of the double boiler, fit the two pans together, and turn on the heat to medium. Stir from time to time while the chocolate melts.

Marcella Says: **If you do not have a double boiler, you can easily improvise one. A stainless steel bowl set over a saucepan is one way of doing it. Another is to place a metal trivet or other heatproof support in a saucepan in which you will heat the water, then rest a smaller pan containing the butter and chocolate on it.**

6 Put the apple slices in a bowl and toss them with the 2 tablespoons of sugar.

7 When the chocolate and butter are completely melted, pour the mixture over the bread, stirring to incorporate it evenly.

8 Retrieve the raisins with your hand, squeeze them as dry as you can, add them to the bread and chocolate mixture, and stir thoroughly to distribute them evenly.

9 Add the eggs to the batter and stir very, very thoroughly.

10 Grease the bottom and sides of the springform pan with butter, dust the pan with flour, then turn the pan over and tap it once on the counter to shake out any excess flour. Pour the batter into the pan and level it off. Distribute the apple slices on top. Bake in the preheated oven for 1 hour. Remove the pan from the oven and let cool slightly.

11 As soon as you are able to handle the pan comfortably, release the spring latch and remove the sides. When the pudding has cooled down 10 minutes more, loosen it from the bottom by sliding a long, thin knife carefully underneath. Working carefully with one or two broad metal spatulas, transfer the pudding to a flat plate. Cover with heavy-duty aluminum foil, tucking the foil under the plate, and refrigerate. Let the pudding mature in the refrigerator overnight. The next day serve it cold. It will keep well under foil for at least 3 or 4 days in the refrigerator.

PEACH OR NECTARINE TART

▸ *Torta di Pesche o di Pesche Liscie*

The towns that Victor and I are from—his is called Cesena, mine Cesenatico, just eight miles apart—are celebrated throughout Italy for their peaches. The variety is called *Bella di Cesena*, The Beauty from Cesena, a huge yellow ball of juice-saturated fruit. As children, we used to sneak into the orchards and eat the super-ripe ones that had fallen to the ground, dribbling juice over our clothes. I have always been mad about peaches and hoped to discover a peach dessert I could be happy with. When I came across this recipe, I knew I had found it.

> 4 large peaches or nectarines, firm and not too ripe, about 2 pounds (but not over 2½)
>
> 3 extra-large eggs
>
> 1 heaping cup sugar
>
> 8 tablespoons (1 stick) butter, softened at room temperature, plus additional for greasing the baking pan
>
> 1⅓ cups unbleached all-purpose flour plus additional for dusting the baking pan
>
> 3½ teaspoons baking powder
>
> A pinch of fine sea salt
>
> A 10-inch springform pan

YIELD: *8 to 10 servings*

1 Turn on the oven to 375°.

2 Wash, peel, and pit the fruit. Cut them into thin slices no more than ¼ inch thick.

3 Put the eggs and sugar in a food processor and process until the eggs become colored a pale gold. Transfer the mixture to a large bowl. (If you don't have a food processor, you can whip the eggs and sugar with an electric hand mixer or a whisk in a bowl large enough to contain the remaining ingredients of the batter.)

4 Add the butter and mix until the batter is homogeneous.

5 In a separate bowl combine the flour, baking powder, and salt. Add the dry ingredients to the egg-and-butter base, mixing well until the batter is smooth and all the ingredients are integrated.

6 Lightly smear the bottom and sides of the springform pan with butter, dust the pan with flour, then turn the pan over and tap it once on the counter to shake out any excess flour.

7 Pour two-thirds and no more of the batter into the pan. Level it, then cover with the sliced fruit.

> *Marcella Says:* **I kept making this tart, mixing the peaches into the batter, and it tasted wonderful except that the peaches always came to rest on the bottom, saturating it. I had almost given up on it when I thought to pour most of the batter into the pan and only then to put in the fruit. It solved the problem.**

8 Level again and top it with the remaining batter, making sure all the fruit is covered. Level the top once more and place the pan in the preheated oven. Bake for 1 hour. Let it cool down about 15 minutes before removing from pan.

KEEPING NOTE: You can keep the tart, covered with aluminum foil, for up to 1 week in the refrigerator.

Neapolitan Squash Pudding with Golden Raisins and Pine Nuts

⤙ *Dolce di Zucca con Uva Passa e Pinoli*

If you are looking for opulent, imaginative desserts in Italy, you need not look any farther than the Neapolitan table. This luscious squash pudding is a good example. Usually, I forgo adapting Italian squash dishes for the American kitchen because trying to find American equivalents for Italian squashes is generally fruitless. Although botanists and growers have given us many varieties, they have evidently concentrated their efforts on appearance, for nearly all of them are better seen than eaten. I have not yet come across any squash comparable to *zucca barucca*, whose orange flesh is so sweet and silken that you don't really have to do much with it, just bake it and you have a ready-made dessert. The one American squash that for me has the most appealing taste and texture is butternut squash. Happily, both in appearance and flavor it resembles a *zucca napoletana*, the very same that Neapolitans use for this wonderful pudding.

1 butternut squash, about 1½ pounds

½ cup water

½ cup whole milk

½ teaspoon salt

3 tablespoons butter

⅓ cup honey

1 cup sugar and 3 tablespoons water for making caramel

A 9½ by 5½ by 3-inch loaf pan

1 cup all-purpose flour plus additional for dusting the raisins

⅓ cup golden raisins, steeped in lukewarm water for 30 minutes

3 extra-large eggs

⅓ cup pine nuts, chopped coarse

Marcella Says: **If I were not concerned about their settling at the bottom of the pudding I would leave the pine nuts whole and, in fact, some I do leave whole, but most of them should be cut into smaller pieces. If you have the choice, use imported Italian pignoli because their flavor is finer and nuttier than the stubby Southwestern *piñones* that most markets carry.**

The grated peel of 1 lemon, the outer yellow layer only with none of the bitter white pith beneath

YIELD: *about 12 servings*

1 Peel the squash with a swivel-blade vegetable peeler or paring knife. Take a chef's knife (or similar stout-bladed knife) and split the squash in two lengthwise. Scoop out all the seeds and strings. A grapefruit spoon or melon baller is helpful, but a soup spoon will do the job, too. Cut the flesh into rough cubes no larger than ½ inch each.

2 Put the cut-up squash in a saucepan with the water, milk, and salt. Cover the pan and turn the heat on to medium. When the liquid boils, cook the squash for 15 to 20 minutes, then remove the lid and cook for another 10 minutes, until it is very soft when tested with a fork.

3 Purée the cooked squash through a food mill or potato ricer into a bowl, or mash it with a wooden spoon. Set aside to cool.

4 Turn on the oven to 350°.

5 Put the butter and honey in a small saucepan and turn the heat on to low. When the butter has melted completely, pour the mixture into the bowl with the squash, mix thoroughly, and allow it to cool.

6 Make the caramel by putting the sugar and the 3 tablespoons of water in a small saucepan and turning the heat on to high. Resist the temptation to stir, otherwise the sugar will form large crystals. Cook the caramel until it becomes colored a golden brown, then pour it into the loaf pan. Tilt the pan this way and that to coat the bottom and sides with the caramel, leaving only about ¼ inch of the sides uncoated. Repeat the operation for as long as the caramel is runny enough to permit it. Coat the pan two or three times at least in order to achieve as thick and even a layer as possible.

7 With either with a sifter or a strainer, sift the 1 cup of flour, a very little bit at a time, over the cooled mashed squash.

8 Drain the raisins, squeeze out the water with your hand, then finish drying them in a paper towel. Put them in a small strainer, dust them with a little flour, then shake the strainer to prevent too much flour from collecting on them.

9 Separate the eggs, reserving the whites in a bowl and adding just the yolks to the squash. Mix well. Add the raisins, the pine nuts, and the grated lemon peel. Stir thoroughly to distribute all of the ingredients evenly in the batter.

10 With an electric mixer or by hand, whip the egg whites until they form stiff peaks. Spoon off a large dollop and mix it into the squash batter. Turn the remaining whites onto the batter and fold them in very gently and evenly.

11 Pour the batter into the caramel-lined loaf pan. Bake in the preheated oven for 35 minutes. Remove the pan to a cooling rack to cool completely.

12 When the pan is completely cool, cover it with plastic film and refrigerate it for at least 6 hours, or even better, overnight.

13 Fill a 12-inch skillet or sauté pan halfway up with water. Put a metal trivet, a clean shallow empty tuna or salmon can, or other flat metal support about 1 inch or so high, in the bottom of the pan. Rest the loaf pan on the trivet and turn the heat on to medium high. When the water has boiled for 30 seconds or so, tilt the pan to see whether the squash pudding shifts in the pan. When it does, turn off the heat and remove the pan from the skillet. Put a shallow level serving platter upside down over the loaf pan. Grasp the pan and the platter together using pot holders or a thick dish towel and invert them. Give a little shake and you should hear the pudding plop down. Lift off the loaf pan. If you wish to retrieve more of the caramel in the loaf pan, put it back on the trivet, and bring the water back to a boil. When some or most of the caramel dissolves, pour it over the pudding.

AHEAD-OF-TIME NOTE: If you are not serving the pudding promptly, refrigerate it. It will keep well for 4 or 5 days. Keep in mind, however, that squash is a vegetable and that, like other cooked vegetables, it does not improve with long refrigeration.

Gelati, Semifreddo, and Mascarpone

WHITE PEACH GELATO WITH LEMON ZEST

ᗡ Gelato di Pesca Bianca Profumato al Limone

The most refreshing aroma of peach comes from white peaches, which is why that white-peach-and-Prosecco drink, the Bellini, has become the favorite poolside beverage at the Cipriani Hotel in Venice. The charm of white-peach aroma, however, is directly proportionate to the fruit's ripeness. This ice cream can be the purest expression of that beguiling fragrance, but it works best with peaches that are really ripe. I suggest you taste one and then take note of the sugar suggestion in the ingredients list.

> 1¼ pounds fresh ripe white peaches
>
> 1 cup water
>
> ⅔ cup granulated sugar; increase to 1 cup if the peaches are just short of perfection
>
> The grated peel of ½ large lemon OR of 1 whole small lemon, the outer yellow layer only with none of the bitter white pith beneath
>
> ½ cup heavy whipping cream, chilled
>
> An ice-cream maker
>
> A lidded container already in the freezer for storing the finished gelato

YIELD: *8 to 10 servings*

1 Peel and pit the peaches, and cut them into pieces. Put the peaches in a food processor, add the water, sugar, and grated lemon peel, and purée until liquefied.

2 Using a whisk or an electric mixer, as you feel most comfortable, lightly whip the cream to a buttermilk-like consistency.

3 Pour the peach purée into the cream and stir to blend the ingredients thoroughly.

4 Transfer the mixture to the ice-cream maker and freeze, following the directions in the maker's manual. When done—the gelato should be compact, but creamy—take the storage container out of the freezer, scoop the gelato into it, cover, and place in the freezer.

TASTING NOTE: The gelato will taste its freshest and be at its best within 3 to 4 hours after it's made. That said, it keeps well in the freezer for up to 1 month.

FROZEN ORANGE DESSERT
Spumone all'Arancio

I have grown very fond of this spumoni since I have come to Florida. It is just perfect for a place whose orange season is also a warm one. This is ideal summer refreshment, both in appearance and taste. And there are oranges enough now anywhere, even in summer, that it can be made anytime anywhere.

> 3 extra-large eggs
>
> The grated peel of 2 large oranges, the outer orange layer only with none of the bitter white pith beneath
>
> ⅓ cup sugar
>
> ½ cup freshly squeezed orange juice
>
> A ¼-ounce envelope unflavored gelatin
>
> ⅔ cup heavy whipping cream, chilled
>
> Fine sea salt
>
> 8 5-ounce ramekins
>
> 3 teaspoons bitter orange marmalade

YIELD: *8 servings*

1   Separate the eggs, dropping the yolks into one mixing bowl, the whites into another. Set the whites aside. Add the grated orange peel and the sugar to the yolks. Whip, using either an electric mixer or a whisk, until the yolks drop from the beater back into the bowl in creamy ribbons.

2   Put the orange juice in a small saucepan and turn on the heat to medium. When the juice is hot, add the gelatin. Take the pan off the heat, and stir vigorously until the gelatin has completely dissolved in the juice. Set aside to cool slightly.

3   When the juice mixture is lukewarm, pour it into the bowl with the egg yolks. Swirl it in, incorporating it smoothly.

4   Using a whisk or mixer, whip the cream until fairly stiff. Fold it thoroughly into the yolk and juice mixture.

5   Add a pinch of salt to the egg whites, then whip them with the mixer until they form stiff peaks. Fold them gently into the yolk-and-juice mixture, then divide the mixture evenly among the ramekins. Refrigerate overnight.

6   To unmold the ramekins: When ready to serve, pour 2 inches of water into a small skillet or sauté pan and bring to a simmer. Slide the blade of a thin knife along the inside wall of the ramekin to begin loosening the spumone. Holding the ramekin, briefly submerge the bottom in the simmering water. Remove from the water, place a saucer over the ramekin, and turn the ramekin upside down. Shake sharply once or twice until you feel the dessert slip out onto the saucer. Lift away the ramekin. Unmold the remaining desserts in the same manner.

7   Dissolve the marmalade in 2 tablespoons of water. With the tip of a spoon, dab a small amount of the dissolved marmalade in the center of each dessert. Serve at once.

Lemon Spumone

The procedure for making this frozen lemon dessert is identical to that of the preceding recipe for Orange Spumone. Except for the garnish, which is different, you can retrace every step of that recipe, replacing the ½ cup of orange juice with ½ cup of freshly squeezed lemon juice and the grated rind of 2 oranges with that of 3 lemons.

For the garnish

⅓ lemon

1 tablespoon freshly squeezed lemon juice

1 tablespoon sugar

1   Remove the outer yellow layer of peel with none of the bitter white pith beneath. Cut the peel into short, wispy thin strips.

2   Bring 1½ cups of water to a boil in a small saucepan. Add the strips of lemon peel, and boil for 2 or 3 minutes. Drain.

3   In the same saucepan combine the lemon juice, sugar, 2 tablespoons of water, and the blanched lemon peel and simmer briskly until the sugar has dissolved. Take off the heat and let cool completely.

4   After unmolding the ramekins as described in the master recipe, top each dessert with a few strips of the candied lemon peel and about ½ teaspoon of the sugar syrup from the pan.

Frozen Nougat and Chocolate Dessert

Semifreddo al Torrone e Cioccolato

Until recent years there were no ice-cream machines made for the home cook in Italy so that gelato was—and mostly still is—one of those good things, like cappuccino or cream puffs, that you went out for. What people did and continue to make at home is the frozen dessert we call *semifreddo*, which translates literally as half-cold. It comes by its name because a *semifreddo* always contains some ingredient such as biscuits, candied fruits, nuts, or ricotta that does not freeze solid and hence does not require the freezing power of an ice-cream machine. All it needs is an overnight stay in the freezer.

This particular *semifreddo* was a favorite of a Piedmontese woman—her name was Graziella—whom I used to know a very long time ago. In the notes Graziella left me she wrote, "This is the dessert I always make when I want to bring an important dinner to a triumphant close." Triumph or not, it is irresistibly delicious. The key ingredient is *torrone*, the hard Piedmontese nougat bar that in northern Italy is an inseparable part of any well-stuffed Christmas basket. Classic hard white *torrone* is made from egg whites and almonds, but there are versions with hazelnuts and chocolate. The one with almonds, used for this *semifreddo*, is the most common, and you should be able to find it in grocery stores that carry Italian specialties, or in some Italian bakeries, or see the Appendix for online sources.

6 ounces Italian nougat, *torrone,* with almonds

6 eggs

6 tablespoons sugar

2 cups heavy whipping cream

½ cup small pieces of bittersweet or semisweet chocolate

> *Marcella Says:* **You must not pulverize the chocolate, otherwise the dessert will become dark. To avoid this problem, I use semisweet miniature chocolate chips that I use whole.**

1 tablespoon dark rum

A 2-quart or slightly larger bowl

A pinch salt

YIELD: *about 8 servings*

1 Use a sturdy chopping knife to cut the nougat into small pieces, then grind it to a granular consistency in a food processor fitted with the steel blade.

2 Separate the eggs; you will need only 4 of the whites. Refrigerate the remaining 2 for another use.

3 Put the yolks in a large mixing bowl, and add the sugar. With an electric mixer whip the mixture until it becomes pale yellow and creamy.

4 In another bowl, preferably a chilled metal one, whip the cream until it is quite stiff.

5 Add the whipped cream, the chocolate bits, the rum, and 1¼ cups of the ground nougat to the beaten egg yolks, stirring well to distribute all the ingredients uniformly.

6 In a clean bowl, with the mixer whip the 4 egg whites with a pinch of salt until they form stiff peaks. Fold them gently into the nougat batter.

7 Sprinkle the remaining ground nougat over the bottom and sides of the 2-quart bowl. Pour the nougat batter over it. Pull a sheet of plastic film tightly over the bowl and place it in the freezer. The *semifreddo* will be ready to serve the following day, but keeps, as I have kept it myself, a full week.

8 When ready to serve the *semifreddo*, remove the bowl from the freezer and take off the plastic film. Choose a serving plate with a lip and a diameter that accommodates the width of the bowl. Soak a dish towel in very hot water, wring it out, and wrap it around the chilled bowl. Slide the blade of a long thin knife around the inside edge of the bowl to loosen the dessert from the sides. Set the plate upside down over the bowl, hold the bowl and plate firmly together, invert the bowl, and give it a good shake. You will feel the *semifreddo* release from the sides of the bowl and drop onto the serving plate. Lift off the bowl and serve the dessert at once, cut into wedges.

Fresh Dates Stuffed with Mascarpone
❧ *Datteri Freschi Farciti di Mascarpone*

Mascarpone is a cheese made entirely from heavy cream. Its production originated near Milan, but there are imitations of it made in America now. I have never known it to be served as a cheese, but rather as a dessert. My favorite use for mascarpone is with a quince mustard that I used to buy in Venice and that I have imitated with acceptable results at home in Florida. (See Impromptu Mustard Fruit with Mascarpone on page 108.) When Victor came home from the supermarket on Longboat Key one day with a package of magnificent fresh dates, it reminded me of how much I loved them as a child, when my mother used to stuff them with mascarpone for *merenda*, the midafternoon snack.

    12 fresh dates, pitted or unpitted

    3 tablespoons mascarpone

1 Split open each date lengthwise on just one side, leaving the other hinged. If the dates have pits, use the tip of a paring knife to pry them out.

2 Stuff each date with a tiny scoop of mascarpone, about the size of a grape, then partially close the date over the cheese. Stuff the remaining dates in the same manner. Place the stuffed dates on a rimmed serving plate and refrigerate until you are ready to serve them.

SERVING SUGGESTION: You can snack on these stuffed dates at any time, but we like to serve them with espresso at the end of a meal. They are succulent and less banal than the usual after-dinner mints, petits fours, or chocolate truffles.

Appendix

❧∾❧

My Online Sources for Food Products

It was not easy to overcome my aversion to buying food voicelessly from a computer screen rather than from a person, food that I could not see, or touch, or smell. But I have learned to be thankful for well-stocked electronic food halls because they fill large gaps in the markets to which I have physical access. The list that you will find here does not want to be a definitive index to food suppliers on the Internet. These are simply the ones that I have used most often, that I have found most reliable, and that have best suited my needs as an Italian cook. I have supplied telephone numbers, in case you are not connected to the Internet.

General Food Emporiums

www.chefshop.com For the breadth and quality of its offerings, nothing equals this site founded many years ago by two Seattle friends of mine. In addition to well-chosen examples of an Italian kitchen's staples—factory-made pasta, rice, beans, olive oil, vinegar, canned tuna—there are excellent products from other parts of the world and, in season, fresh wild salmon from the Northwest, plus an item that has all but disappeared from neighborhood markets, genuinely tree-ripened, sugary fruits. If only some day they would expand into vegetables! Telephone: (877) 337-2491.

www.zingermans.com This Ann Arbor, Michigan, grocer offers a discriminating assortment of foods from Italy and other nations, accompanied by entertaining and instructive essays by its owner, Ari Weinzweig. Telephone: (888) 636-8162.

Italian Specialties

www.gustiamo.com The American offshoot of a celebrated Italian site, this is the preeminent online source for exceptional Italian products by cannily selected artisan producers in Italy who work to very high standards. It is expensive, but I have never been disappointed in a single shipment from it. Telephone: (877) 907-2525.

www.buonitalia.com I turn to Buon Italia for some of the things I don't find at Gustiamo, Sardinian sheet music bread, Apulia's irresistible *burrata* cheese, cured but not smoked pork jowl, which I prefer to pancetta in Amatriciana and other sauces, and fresh *cotechino*. If you don't see what you are looking for online, e-mail them at *info@buonitalia.com*. Telephone: (212) 633-9090. (Do not be startled if you hear from a woman named Marcella. It isn't me; I have no connection with the company.)

Cheese Mainly

www.idealcheese.com When, decades ago, I was teaching cooking in my New York apartment and living on the Upper East Side of Manhattan, the nearby Ideal Cheese shop was precisely that. They have added many superb Italian cheeses to the mainly French repertory that they had always concentrated on, and they also offer a few unexpected items, such as mustard fruit and other Italian preserves of artisanal quality. Telephone: (800) 382-0709.

Dried Beans

www.purcellmountainfarms.com They sell a huge variety of excellent dried beans from their Idaho farm. I sometimes yield to curiosity and try out the exotic-sounding ones, but I am happiest staying with those insuperable Italian classics, *borlotti* and cannellini. Telephone: (866) 440-2326.

Fish

www.freerangefish.com Very fresh imported *branzino, rombo* (turbot), *orata* (dourade), and sardines, as well as monkfish, diver scallops, and sweet mussels from Maine are now available to anyone willing to pay for overnight express shipment. Mark Drobman at the above address is my fishmonger. Telephone: (866) 700-8469.

www.Browne-Trading.com Rod Mitchell's company supplies many restaurants and private customers with imported and domestic seafood and caviar of unimpeachable quality. Telephone: (800) 944-7848.

Pasta Necessities

www.bakerscatalogue.com I got the board on which I roll out pasta from this site, as well as many useful tools. Their King Arthur Unbleached All-Purpose Flour is excellent for homemade egg pasta dough, better than anything else in fact, short of imported Italian 00 flour. My supermarket carries it, but if yours doesn't you can order it online. Telephone: (800) 827-6836.

Index

᠊᠊ᢒᡒᢗᢖ᠊᠊

Asti-Style Fricasseed Chicken
with Pancetta, Sweet Bell
Peppers, Herbs, and
Anchovies, 242–44
Avocado:
Celery, and Bell Pepper Salad
with Black Olives,
346–47
and Parmesan Crostini, 93
and Red Bell Pepper Salad
with Red Onion, 345–46
Savoy Cabbage Salad with,
344

Bacon:
Artichoke Wedges with Sun-
Dried Tomatoes and,
Braised, 314–15
Spaghetti "Rotolo" with
Zucchini and, 178–80
Balsamic vinegar, in marinades
for fresh fruit, 68, 69, 71
Bananas, 70, 71
Basil, 54
and Zucchini Frittata, No-
Butter, No-Cheese,
106–7
Batters for fried foods, 24–26
Pastella, 25–26
Beans, 57–61
Black-Eyed Peas, Pork
Shoulder Stew with
Onions and, 296–97
buying and storing, 57
canned, 57
cooked, storing, 61

cooking, 60–61
doneness of, 20, 61
fava, Pecorino and, 84
Fava, Puréed, with Rapini,
310–11
in Game-Bird Style with
Olive Oil, Garlic, and
Sage, 316–17
online source for, 375
soaking and salting, 59–60
varieties of, 58–59
see also Cannellini bean(s)
Béchamel Sauce, 300–301
Beef, 259–77
broth, 48–53. *See also* Broth
Cold Boiled, Salad, 260–61
Meatballs with Bell Peppers,
Spicy, 272–73
and Pork Meat Loaf with
Mushrooms, 274–77
Pot Roast, Old-Style, from the
Brianza Hills, 262, 266–68
Pot Roast of, with Garlic,
Anchovies, Vinegar, and
Pancetta, 263, 268–69
Stewed, with Mushrooms and
Potatoes, 263, 270–71
with Vegetables, Red Wine,
and Thyme, Braised, 262,
264–65
Beets, doneness of, 20
Belga Fritta nella Pastella,
339–40
Belgian endive:
Fried in *Pastella* Batter,
339–40

Lasagne Treviso Style with
Radicchio and, 184–86
Berries, 69, 70, 71
Black-Eyed Peas, Pork Shoulder
Stew with Onions and,
296–97
Black pepper, 55
in marinades for fresh fruit,
69, 70
Blanching, 16–17
Borlotti beans, 57, 58–59
Bottarga. See Mullet roe
Braciole of Chopped Veal,
Savory Little, 250–51
*Bracioline Appetitose di Vitello
Macinato,* 250–51
Bread crumbs, 64–65
as coating for fried foods, 25
Bread Pudding with Chocolate
and Apples, 357–59
Brianza Hills, Old-Style Pot
Roast from, 262, 266–68
Broccoletti, doneness of, 19
Broccoli:
and Cannellini Bean Soup, 116
doneness of, 19
prepping, 74–75
Broccolini and Cannellini Bean
Soup, 114–16
Broth, 48–53
defined, 49
ingredients for, 49
recipe for, 50–51
serving boiled meats from, 52
storing, 52–53
uses for, 53